SWANN'S WAY

SWANN'S WAY

A life in Song

DONALD SWANN

recorded and edited by
LYN SMITH

Illustrations by ALISON SMITH

HEINEMANN : LONDON

William Heinemann Ltd
Michelin House, 81 Fulham Road, London SW3 6RB
LONDON   MELBOURNE   AUCKLAND

First published in 1991
Copyright © Donald Swann and Lyn Smith 1991
Illustrations copyright © Alison Smith 1991

A CIP catalogue record for this title
is available from the British Library

ISBN 0 434 75292 4

Typeset by Hewer Text Composition Services, Edinburgh
Printed in Great Britain
by St Edmundsbury Press, Bury St Edmunds, Suffolk

Contents

For Alison

Preface

This book had its inception in the summer of 1988. The idea was Margot Richardson's who later saw from reading a transcript of an interview I had recorded with Donald Swann for the Imperial War Museum that there was much more to him than his partnership with Michael Flanders in the 'Hat' shows. Prior to this, Donald had shied away from autobiography, his genre being the spontaneous rhapsodic outpourings of *The Space Between the Bars* or *Swann's Way Out*. Donald and I were receptive to the idea: we had enjoyed collaborating on the Imperial War Museum's project which covered his experience as a pacifist in World War II, and Donald felt comfortable with the oral history approach. I certainly welcomed the opportunity to explore in greater depth topics tantalisingly touched upon our IWM interview but which, given the constraints of the World War II framework of the project, necessarily remained undeveloped.

The interview sessions were of an informal and spontaneous nature within a chronological order covering the different phases of his life. When each section was complete, I would transcribe, restructure and shape the material. Donald would then check and correct it, adding anecdotes, songs and other relevant material that had seeped up from his subconscious in the interim. Further edits followed to eliminate repetition and tighten the language, taking care not to lose Donald's voice, as we were concerned that the book should be in a spoken idiom, with readers hearing Donald reminisce on his life and music. Often there would be penetrating probings of the script: 'Was that really the way it was? Do I mean that? Is that a word I use . . .?' Such deliberations pointed to the differences between the spoken and the written word. As we progressed through the book it struck me that this was an exercise in revelation not just to myself on behalf of the readers, but of Donald to himself.

Only about a third of the transcribed material was used. Although Donald was not shown the full transcript, from the first rough draft stage he had full control over the content and language. If ghosts rustle through the leaves of Donald's story, they certainly did not materialise in the form of a writer! It was a full and equal partnership. The intuitive rapport which developed between us during the early IWM interviews allowed for an evolving relationship based on mutual trust; as the book progressed the fusion between his work and mine got ever closer until, in the end, we were playing a duet at the Amstrad in perfect harmony.

Formative influences, developing pacifism, musical development and career before and after Michael Flanders, as well as his ambivalent attitude towards the celebrity life the 'Hat' shows brought him – all are covered in the book with Donald's unique blend of merriment, lyricism and earnest questing. What I hope emerges is not just the picture of a gifted composer-performer but of the whole man: his complex personality and moods, his impish humour, his spirituality, values and philosophy as well as the deep springs of his creativity.

Lyn Smith, March 1991

Introduction

I believe there is a 'poem' in everybody's life whether they write it down or not. This book entitled *Swann's Way* is my fourth attempt to capture the 'poem', the inner meaning in words as opposed to music, and I know it will again only be a shaft of the truth. Can it be otherwise? An autobiography is, of course, a landscape with figures; in my case the landscape is as much one of ideas as of places, though both rival each other for space. Ideas and travel and time all seem one to me, as do music and words. In *Swann's Way* I have worked in a new way and with a new collaborator: telling my story on tape to Lyn Smith, an oral historian who became a good friend. This book therefore is qualitatively different because Lyn has sifted and edited and revised and probed, and she possesses a steadying historical mind. My mind works in a serpentine way. I think in assonances, in bursts, whereas Lyn has found a line, a 'story-line'. The book remains in a spoken style. This is the idiom that I am most familiar with from my concert and stage work, where soliloquy has always been my hallmark, that is 'talking songs in'.

Two observations occur to me as suitable for the foreword. One is to point to an underlying theme that comes to pervade, but also in a way to give unity to this book: the survival of artistic vision beyond war. In the first chapters I describe how my father escaped from the violence of the civil war in Russia to reach the Elephant and Castle in London, to play his beloved four-hand piano music. In my own war story among Quakers and Greek refugees, the Greek songs emerged and led me towards composing. From the same war Michael Flanders's wonderful sense of humour arose triumphant after he had suffered partial disablement from polio and two years in hospital; and in the last section, at the last bend of the river, I describe how poetry, music and ideas led me through conflict into tune; both inner conflicts, and outer ones such as my feelings about South Africa and the Middle East.

My second observation is about 'deeply personal' life. This is not revealed, as I respect my friends too much. Furthermore I have found a language for my deepest and most secret loves. It is in music, in sound, in songs. Music is my tongue. Yet . . . yet, with the help of Lyn, and with the encouragement of my publisher, this chance – this book – has appeared to speak and to correlate and to define, and I am grateful for it. In fact I welcome it with open arms. Have I not said that for me music and words are one?

A few have read this book in early stages, and the people I spoke to about permissions to quote lyrics have in almost every case been friends or collaborators who have wished me well. I thank them. But most of all I owe thanks to Alison Smith for discussing the variables and conundrums of this book with me, as well as contributing evocative illustrations.

Often in my concerts, as in *At the Drop of a Hat*, the show I devised jointly with Michael Flanders, there was a Russian song, or many Russian songs, as I am half Russian. So that is where I plunge my pen, or shall I say utter my first word to my interlocutor Lyn; I will go straight into Llanelli in south Wales, where a very new Anglo-Russian marriage is finding itself. Cue for song? No, cue for book.

Donald Swann

1 Russian Roots:
Lincolnshire to Kaloméa

I was born in Llanelli, which changed its spelling from a 'y' to an 'i' during my lifetime. I lived there for only two years but once you're born in Wales they take you on board as a Welshman, so I feel very warmly about Llanelli and go back there occasionally. But how did I come to be born in an Anglo-Russian family in Coleshill Terrace on 30th September 1923? And why was there a strange uncle doing a sword dance outside in the street, which a few people in Llanelli still recall?

I think my story really has to be pushed back into history to show how my great grandfather, Alfred Trout Swan – only one 'n' then – was drawn to Russia from Lincolnshire in 1840. I once went back to Morton in Lincolnshire with my father, Herbert, and we looked through the parish records to find him. Evidently he was a draper, and it's strange to think: why should a draper from the middle of Lincolnshire go off to Russia? One has to imagine these engineers and drapers thinking there are jobs around in Russia. Peter the Great opened the window into Europe and left it open. My great grandfather Alfred Trout, climbed through it.

It was in Russia that the Swans, living in St Petersburg, linked up with the Hynams through the marriage of Alfred Trout with Sarah, one of the Hynam daughters. Robert Hynam, her father, had gone to Russia earlier than Alfred Trout, in 1776 – attracted also by the opening up of the Russian Empire begun by Peter the Great, and continued by Empress Catherine whose 'Anglomanie' attracted a motley of British craftsmen to Russia. Robert Hynam, a clock-maker, built a reputation for himself and became revered by all the family by becoming the Court Horologer. Now we've got to imagine that Queen Catherine's Court was the place to be: rather like if you were winding up clocks for Queen Elizabeth in Britain, you'd be quite important. I've got a Hynam clock in my home now. I can never discover if it's ticking or not because it's so quiet, and it doesn't chime. It's a Grandfather clock. That's the *mot juste*, isn't it?

Some of the clocks he made are beautiful pieces, including an exquisite jewelled watch commissioned by Catherine the Great which is now in the Hermitage. Occasional relatives go to Leningrad today and ask to see this watch. They are immediately treated as VIPs because of the connection with old Hynam.

The Hynams were business people, part of the small Russian bourgeois class and doing reasonably well. But the story goes that the Hynam fortunes suddenly collapsed, and two of my great aunts, Sophie and Ellen, decided to throw themselves in front of Emperor Alexander's carriage at Tsárskoe Seló and present a petition to him. Shades of Sylvia Pankhurst. It's interesting that the personal touch was considered so important: if only you could get to the Tsar and touch the hem of his garment and say 'Please help me', then help would be forthcoming – rather like MPs deal with their constituents. Apparently they did stop the carriage and the Tsar intervened in their fortunes, ordering that a house on Vassilievsky Ostrov should be made available for them. (Do you think we could stop Prince Charles in the middle of an event and say 'I need a new loo'? I suppose we could actually, because he's very interested in architecture and that sort of thing.)

So that's the family the Swans married into. There were other Hynams, of course, but what I'm relating here are the family anecdotes told as we were sitting around at home with my father and his three brothers.

The name Swan changed in Russia. It seems that Alfred Trout added the second 'n' out of deference to the German-speaking business community with which he mixed, as they found it easier to pronounce the name as 'Schwann'. At various times some of the family dropped the double 'n' although others, like my father, kept it. I guess when you live in a foreign capital, you have to absorb the different parts of it. You can imagine how, after a while, this family became tri-lingual speaking Russian, German and English. In the home they spoke Russian, ate Russian food, and imbibed the culture. Although they leaned towards the Russian, none of them became Orthodox except, much later, uncle Alfred who became mad about Russian Orthodox music and wrote books about it. The children went to German schools because that happened to be the best education to be found, and the family mixed with Germans who formed the biggest foreign community there; yet all this didn't prevent them from feeling very British and going to the Anglican church in St Petersburg which, of all things, was in the diocese of London. So the Swanns were confirmed by the Bishop of London on tour at some point. I don't think any of them took very strongly to the Church of England: it was more a sort of formal religion linking them to the 'home' country.

I often try to imagine my grandfather's family in Russia at the turn of the century. I see them as being very business-like but with an artistic side. Grandfather, (also called Alfred) was a departmental manager of the Russo-American India Rubber Company known as 'The Triangle'. Every morning he must have gone off to the office with his piroshkí, and the story is told that he spent his evenings working out his domestic accounts. A peculiar thing, isn't it? You'd think he'd relax and enjoy the exotic life. He seems to have been a sort of clerical, meticulous man; possibly a bit pedantic, but self-effacing and very caring and generous, bringing up his four boys with a great love of England and working hard to give them the best possible education.

I don't think they were too involved with contemporary Russian politics although my father spoke of his awareness of the strikes and demonstrations in 1905. He vividly recalled seeing on his way home from school one afternoon a troop of Cossacks dispersing a hostile crowd: the drawn sabres, the breakneck speed of the Cossacks on their ponies and the fear on people's faces as they dashed for safety. He also spoke of an illuminating moment when he and his brothers clubbed together to treat their father to one of Repin's pictures. Repin was a wonderful Russian portrait painter. Around this time – 1905 – he painted a celebrated picture of a prisoner returning from prison or exile, surrounded by his family who are horrified to see him come back looking so emaciated and ghastly. When Alfred unwrapped his present and saw this vivid protest picture, he was horrified and thought: 'Good heavens! What's coming? Tolstoy! Revolutionary ideas! Secret Police!' He couldn't bring himself to hang such subversive stuff, but hid it. Interesting, isn't it? It illustrates the reaction of an English businessman to the cataclysmic events creeping up on him.

In such ways the rumblings of pre-Revolutionary Russia impinged on them; but, essentially, they considered themselves British and were proud of their British passports which allowed them to maintain contact with England. This was to prove very important later when the events of 1917 broke over them.

Can I jump quickly to Penelope Fitzgerald's book *The Beginning of Spring*? It is a most extraordinary novel about an English family living in Moscow. When I read it I thought: 'This is exactly my father's life!' and felt she must have lived there. But I'm told by Richard Davies of the Russian Archive at Leeds University that she used only a few facts, and virtually invented the rest. I'm almost inventing this part of my story too. I've no idea whether these things I'm telling you about my family are completely accurate as the facts and anecdotes get merged together. What I do remember is how the story came through to me as a son and nephew.

My father and his brothers would reminisce about their flat on Vassilievsky Island and how my grandmother played vint, or screw, which is a game like bridge without its conundrums; and how the floor polishers used to come and polish the wooden floors by gliding over them with great slippered feet; and when

Stilton cheese was sent to them from England, they cut out the green bits as being suspect; and how the piano was the pivot of the flat. I worry about that because whenever I've had a piano in a flat, I've been obsessed about noise and neighbours, but the brothers seem to have been playing all the time. I also imagine my father and his brothers going on the most rhapsodic long summer holidays on the Finnish lakes, Finland being just a short train ride across the frontier.

My uncles excite my imagination. Alfred was the eldest, then Edgar, then Herbert my father, and uncle Freddie the youngest. Like the old fairy tales, it's always the uncles who become legendary whereas your immediate family remains real. All my uncles had the most peculiar and amazing attributes (which will be revealed in time), but let's leave them for the moment in this flat in St Petersburg, an atmosphere full of music and learning. They were musically clever, all playing 'four-hands'. Records were barely known then, so all classical music was played in the 'four-hand' way as duets. I still have many copies of this music. Rachmaninov, Scriabin and Medtner were very popular with the family. Glazunov was then principal of the Academy and my uncle Alfred certainly took lessons from him. Alfred became enormously enamoured of Russian composers and wrote a book called *Russian Music* which is considered one of the authoritative works on the subject. He was interested in the old chants of the Russian Orthodox Church as well as Russian folk-music and linked them in an original way. But I'm jumping ahead . . .

I can picture these young chaps in the time just before the Revolution. They go to dances with partners from the celebrated Geltzer ballet school, which is thrilling for them. Music buffs, they're divided between the 'Rachmanists' and the 'Scriabinists' and ask each other which side are they on. Scriabin was like an early Pop Star: he had a huge Machine out of which streamed all sorts of colours and flashing lights while his *Poem of Fire* was playing; everybody would get terribly worked up and would scream and clap for him, so he became a cult figure. Rachmaninov was slightly more orthodox, but just as brilliant.

When they had divided into 'Scriabinists' and 'Rachmanists' they would solemnly ask the girls they danced with: 'Do you believe in God?' This is the intellectual part of the brothers coming out, their kinship with the Russian Intelligentsia (with whom I got involved and studied when I went to Oxford University). Their ultimate experience was to talk about life over tea – feeble, without milk. This mood is in Chekhov, whom my father adored, and Turgenev too; it's strange how ubiquitous are these Russian writers. I've said the brothers were more than a bit English; but what were they reading? Dostoevsky, Pushkin, Turgenev, Chekhov, and they're thinking: 'Oh yes, there's some new and exciting ideas here, something's going to happen soon in Russia.' Yet they're still thinking about music. I've just picked up my uncle's book on Russian music and read an extraordinary story. He's listening to a concert. Suddenly news comes: Rasputin has been assassinated. He says: 'We were all very disturbed, but it did not prevent us from enjoying the second part of the concert.'

Outside their door the Revolution was beginning to happen. My father used to say: 'Well, we were a bit far off, and we didn't hear much really.' But when it came to November 1917, it was a very different story. Outside a cataclysm was going on and they were going to have to live through a gigantic historical drama. How did they cope, I am now thinking? How was the family connected with Russian agony? I remember my father both spoke and wrote about skating in Prince Yussúpov's estate. Skating was a tremendous passion for him, as great as piano playing. Now Yussúpov was the one who finally got rid of Rasputin by giving him all those poisoned cakes. I've got a record at home:

> No disputin, he's Rasputin
> That highfalutin lovin man.

I think that's a wonderful song, but we'll get to the song-writing later. At the moment I'm picturing this family, and my father in particular, with the overtones of a Russian sea-change coming up.

When my father was a young medical student in 1912, and short of money, he took a vacation job as tutor on the estate of Konovalov – a famous Russian name; several Konovalovs were leading members of the Duma (a pseudo-parliament) and, would you believe it, my Professor of Russian at Oxford belonged to this family. One day as my father was travelling in Konovalov's car, with Konovalov driving, a peasant who'd been crouching in the hedge, tried to get his own back and hurled a huge stone at Konovalov, smashing the windscreen – yet another example of the troubles brewing. In this particular incident the ruffian was disarmed and there was some sort of happy ending. Herbert spent an idyllic summer on the grand estate. There were lots of important visitors and he dined with prominent Duma members, and listened enthralled to their political talk which in the main appeared to be highly critical of the Tsar's government.

But it's the piano playing that interests me so much and it seems to have been going on all the time. Father talks about Vera von Bodungen, a young graduate of St Petersburg Conservatoire, who used to put a kopek on his knuckles as he was playing – the idea being to keep a steady hand. When I started learning the piano my father tried this on me with a florin, but soon gave up because by then piano playing had developed in an essentially free way.

I think this is the moment to say that my grandfather sent all four boys to England. He was determined they should spend some time there to get acclimatised to the world they might have been in, and it was thanks to his foresight that they all managed to escape from Russia. When the time came, they could all look back on their holidays and think of England as a sort of haven. The expense of the trips must have been tremendous – no wonder my grandfather was always worried about his accounts!

Just imagine what it's like to be a young medical student and going with your brother on holiday to England in the summer of 1914, and writing home to your parents saying: 'I'm terribly sorry to worry you but there's a war on; shall we come back?' And Dad writes back to say: 'Take it easy son; stay put.' So

Herbert managed to cadge an entrance into St Mary's hospital to keep his hand in with the medical world with which he's already absorbed. At this time they started recruiting for the army. This didn't directly affect him, but he felt he ought to do something and, much to the surprise of brother Edgar, he joined the Red Cross, got a uniform and was sent off to Boulogne. Doesn't it seem extraordinary to join up whilst on holiday? But complications occurred: his mother's maiden name was Lórentzen, which sounds a bit German when you come to think of it; so at the moment when he was ready to start work as a medical orderly, they put him under house arrest until things were sorted out. But they were not and, irked by his enforced idleness, he got fed up and found his way, passport-less, back to Edgar in Surbiton. For this abortive bit of war service he was awarded the Mons Star which he used to keep in a drawer very diffidently.

After this trip to England and the award of the Mons Star, he returned to Russia and entered a southern university, Kiev. Once more, the war was impinging. The Russian 'steamroller' was moving from the East aiming to squash the Germans in the middle. But it wasn't successful. There was trouble in the Russian army, and it broke up. Everybody was fighting their corner and gradually the whole thing caved in. All this is pictured wonderfully in Solzhenitsyn's *August 1914*. As I write a crowd of a quarter of a million are crying 'freedom' in the Baltic States. Is this not a sequel to my father's story?

So in 1916 father was a student at the university and, just as in England, he joined another Red Cross unit. This time it was organised by a famous surgeon, Doctor Butz, who gathered a team of young medical people to go to the front. Dr Butz was already well known for a certain technique of leaving wounds open. As the wounded passed through the various casualty clearing stations, instead of constantly re-dressing the wounds, he insisted they should be covered in plaster and left until they could be operated on; this was because the re-dressing was causing endless pain and infection. Much later, when my father got osteomyelitis and was about to be operated on, he and his surgeon thought of this; keeping the wound covered for three months saved his leg.

I am fascinated by a tale he recounted of the Russian Queen Mother visiting the medical unit. She was María Feódrovna, widow of Tsar Alexander III and the mother of Nicholas II. She apparently spoke to him in English. 'Thank you very much', she said; so his Englishness was coming out, even there.

At this time – 1916 – General Brusilov was about to produce an offensive against the Germans and from Kiev the unit moved right up to the front. Some of Herbert's stories were harrowing, with hundreds of casualties and bodies hanging from trees in an awesome place they called 'Black Wood'. He talked of maggots crawling in wounds but actually doing good, destroying the sepsis by eating all the pus. A bit of Green medicine: the 'good' worms. He went up in an observation balloon to view the German lines, with the Germans taking pot shots at them. I've never visited this area; I'd like to have a really good look at Kiev and see the actual terrain.

I imagine them working away as a good medical team. Herbert never seemed to get tired at this point. He was always bursting with energy, and very excited about working with Dr Butz. The push only got so far; then things quietened down so after they'd coped with the casualties they occupied themselves by playing cards, all the time wondering about what would happen next. How soon did he observe that the Russian army was beginning to collapse, not because of the Germans but from internal disaffection? As a medical person he was not involved with strikes or confrontations but it must have been obvious that the troops were fed up.

Something different turned up about this time: a unit of Tartar doctors and nurses from Ashkhabád. We've got to imagine that South Russia heard about the war and felt they ought to do something to help. So this very exotic bunch of Moslems came to the Ukraine, and my father met one of the young nurses called Naguimé Sultán Piszóva. There were social links between the Ashkhabád and Russian units and he started to accompany this nurse on the piano as she sang her gypsy songs. Do you see how the piano always comes into it? Their romance developed right there in the Ukraine. Everybody began to notice that Herbert Alfredovich had lost his heart to the young nurse in the Transcaspian unit and, when it was sent off to work in Galicia, he started to wonder if he could join the unit to be with her. Eventually, to the disapproval of Dr Butz, he received permission to do exactly that.

Now I need to sketch in her background. Beyond the Caspian Sea there are huge desert areas, and the people of Tartar and other ethnic origin lived half in the desert and half in the towns. I'm absolutely fascinated by this. I love deserts as others love the sea. Of course the desert is sea to southern Russian people and Bedouins, and the camel is the ship of the desert. My mother, apparently, loved camels. I love them too but in a rather different way from desert people. I'm inclined to find them funny, but they dream about them all the time. The perfect picture of an evening is the camel wandering across the desert, like the seagulls on the walls of English boarding houses. And desert people have at their disposal a vast range of camel-orientated songs, one of which I know. My mother spoke three or four Caucasian languages, and always wore a Koran around her neck which fascinated Herbert, who was interested in different faiths. She was very beautiful in an exotic way, with a deep voice which excited him tremendously.

We have to remember this is a theme that Lermontov writes about. Northern Russians are entranced with the south just as we are with Spain and Italy, or as the Americans like southern California. The south haunts the north, with the gypsies always in the middle reminding people of a freer life. When you think of my father's background in St Petersburg with the English church, the family routine, all that accounting and what have you, then it's understandable that someone from the south, a Moslem who sings strange songs, was going to be romantic and exciting. After some months of working together in the

14

Transcaspian unit they decided to get married but, before we go into the amazing story of their marriage on the eve of the Revolution, the question has to be asked: what do I know about my mother's family?

I've talked a lot about the Swann family because it is chronicled and known. But as my mother died when I was thirteen, and I never got to Ashkhabád, her life disappears into the legends rather like the camels into the desert. My grandfather was a Turkoman, and mother was one of nine brothers and sisters. Naguimé, I discovered in later life is Russian for Naomi. Sultán has some connection with a Royal Line, and she was rather proud of the fact. I believe she was a Lesgine, which is yet another tribe of the Caucasian mountains. Lesginka is a famous Russian dance which is performed usually after a few drinks. Piszóv, her surname, is equally interesting because it means writer: 'pisáts' in Russian means 'to write'.

I believe my great grandfather was indeed a nomad because a family story related that my grandmother was born on a camel. That is quite natural when you think of it because nomads are always on the move, and pregnant women would be riding on the camel. As a child I used to think this was terribly funny, but now I think it's deadly serious, and often wonder if the nomadic life I've had as an entertainer isn't connected with this in some way. My great grandfather's family eventually moved to Ashkhabád which was a big town, and then to Baku by the Caspian Sea, which was even bigger; and I believe the name Piszóva shows that writing came into the family and, instead of just being camel herders, they became literate and worked as scribes.

My mother, apparently, was a clever girl: she had a gold medal from school and managed to get a nursing qualification. It would, of course, have been very unusual for a girl of her background to join such a unit and leave home, and probably she had to push very hard to achieve this. I think she wanted to do something different – coming up north was pioneering for her. So, in spite of her oriental appearance, and her different cultural background,

I believe my parents had quite a lot in common, and, of course, music was an important part of this.

As for my mother's brothers and sisters, they became legendary to me because most of them disappeared into the mists of time, except for her brother Sokólik. This means 'little falcon' in Russian, and he was the one who turned up in Llanelli, doing the sword dance outside the house. This rather remote family would only occasionally creep into my consciousness when I was a child.

We now come to the marriage of my parents. Is marriage the great climax we make of it? I have always questioned this; as a Quaker, I believe in the primacy and religious nature of natural relationships between two people. On the other hand, when I look back at my parents' marriage, it does seem the most dramatic thing, as though it is in bold capitals and inverted commas. If they hadn't engineered marriage in wartime Russia, there would have been no way they could have entered the fantastic drama which propelled them into the life that was coming.

Anyway, walking along the Carpathians one day, they decided to begin on this adventure. They took a three-week leave. But how and where would they marry? They were advised to find a Church of England priest who would agree to marry them, and set off on their quest. First they tried Kiev, only to find the nearest incumbent of the Church of England was in Odessa, some 400 miles away. (People who read this will have to look at Pasternak's *Dr Zhivago* to get the full story of how awful such train journeys were on the eve of the March Revolution.) They travelled to Odessa in the most horrendous conditions; there was nowhere to sit, and all the lavatories and corridors were crammed with soldiers, which means there was nowhere to relieve themselves. I don't know how long the journey took but I do know that they were both in great physiological distress at the end of it. And this was only the first of several such nightmare journeys; during one of these my mother fell on a buffer, causing the internal injury which led to her death at such a young age in 1935.

Now to be an officer of any sort is a dangerous pastime on the eve of Revolution, so, in spite of the fact that he had only a medical role, Herbert ripped off his officer-like epaulettes in order to look more anonymous.

They came to Odessa and found a Church of England priest. 'I'd like to marry this Moslem nurse, please', says Herbert, but the priest says: 'Impossible! You can't marry her unless she renounces her faith.' Well, Naguimé wouldn't dream of renouncing Islam, so my father worried all night, and decided to approach another denomination – the Lutherans. The Lutheran pastor was more sympathetic to their cause but wasn't sure whether this was in order. This was no time to try to get wires through for advice from higher bodies, and anyhow the lines were down. So he said he'd marry them providing Herbert got permission from the Governor General of Odessa. This seemed reasonable enough except this was during the first days of the New Provisional Government, and a new Governor General had just been appointed. This was Nabokov – either father or uncle of Vladimir Nabokov who wrote *Lolita* and he was up to his eyes sorting out his new administration with hundreds of people waiting to see him, including the mayor; and there was Herbert with his torn-off epaulettes! But eventually he got his audience with Nabokov who seems a cheerful bloke, resplendent in uniform and sword. 'Excuse me Sir, I would like your permission to get married', says Father, at which the Governor General bursts out laughing. Can you blame him? I mean, it's like a scene from Gogol, isn't it? 'I'm supposed to be sorting out this entire area', says Nabokov, when he's stopped laughing. 'I've nothing to do with matrimonial matters.' But Father was desperate and persistent and eventually the secretary was instructed to write on headed notepaper: 'I have no objection to Herbert Swann marrying Naguimé Sultán Piszóva.' Nabokov seemed amused by the whole business. I suppose it made his day.

Back goes Herbert, clutching his precious document, to the

Lutheran pastor who was prepared to perform the marriage immediately; but my mother-to-be wanted to leave to put on a clean uniform. Fortunately my father had a premonition – it was now or never! So they were married. At this point, in came the pastor's worried-looking secretary saying 'I've just read this document, it says nothing, apart from stating the Governor General has no objection.' But by now they were getting out of the door.

This was 27th March 1917 which coincided with the issue of the 'Freedom Loan' issued by the new government. Herbert bought a fifty-rouble note which he always treasured, although presumably it was totally valueless. You might say it was the beginning of what was hoped to be a new Russia, which perhaps is happening only now – more than seventy years on, a new free Russia. Dare we hope? Also, apparently, my father promised that Lutheran priest to baptise his children as Christians. I was confirmed at an incredibly early age of eleven and a half at the Elephant and Castle. I did not know then that he was fulfilling a promise.

I am amazed by my father's story. Time and time again, I see the film of it, called either *The English Zhivago* or *I Was Dr Zhivago's Anaesthetist!* I can't think of anything more dramatic than this Englishman trying to get married in Odessa during the turmoil of Revolution. As a result he renounced his Anglican faith, but I don't think it worried him too much. He had quite a reaction against Anglicanism, not only from that incident, but from the Church of England in St Petersburg which he remembered not as preaching the gospel of love, but the gospel of get-on-and-do-what-you're-told-to-do; and in later life he could never get down on his knees and pray. In fairness to Anglicans, I've since met a priest in a chapel by the United Nations building in New York who said 'If your parents had come to me I'd have married them straight away', but in those days it was impossible.

The newly weds returned to the hospital unit, now at Kaloméa, and Naguimé wired to her family about the wedding. She was heart-broken when they responded: 'Renounce Naguimé for ever.' They assumed she had abandoned her faith. But the married pair wired back explaining she had remained faithful to Islam. All was forgiven; Herbert was accepted into the family. Sadly, the Revolutionary and civil war events prevented him from ever meeting them.

By getting married, Herbert established two things: credibility with Naguimé's family; and he also conveyed British citizenship on her which was absolutely crucial to her safety, and to their future life.

2 Via Kiev to Tilbury

As I continue my parents' story it becomes ever more vivid. The young couple set up home in Kaloméa, sharing a house with another couple working in their unit; they are deeply in love, but life is far from idyllic. Although the Bolshevik Revolution has not yet happened, there is a tremendous amount of disaffection in the army, and local 'soviets' of soldiers are being formed. All organisations in the area are expected to send a representative, and Herbert becomes the unit's delegate and has to attend these stormy meetings. Now, that's quite something, isn't it? A British subject, yet a member of a Soviet! They are all fired with enthusiasm and idealism, really thinking that the Germans would join them leading to an international brotherhood of man. He really seemed to hope, at this stage, that all the turmoil and chaos might work out in the direction he'd always hoped for – a free and democratic Russia.

Life goes on like this for some months, then he decides that it's time to visit his family in Petrograd: the city, of course, has a new name; everything's changing. So, they're setting off again on yet another epic journey.

Do you wonder that I tell the story of my father's adventures and continue at length? When your father is taking his bride to meet her in-laws seven days before the Revolution and during the period which John Reed calls 'ten days that shook the world', then the story should be told.

After another horrendous thirty-six hours by train, they arrive in Petrograd. Nothing much is happening in the city; everything seems very calm. Great joy! The in-laws welcome Naguimé.

Alfred and Edgar are there too and they are all entranced; she is from the south and seems completely different. Out comes the great family Bible and all the peculiar Turkish-sounding names are written in by my grandfather alongside the Swanns and Hynams. The son has renounced his Anglican faith to marry into a Moslem family, and the names of this family get into the Bible. I don't know what the Lutheran pastor would have made of that. A week passes in blissful family surroundings. Naguimé is singing her gypsy songs and charming them all, and the Bolshevik Revolution is about to start.

There are rumours: Lenin himself is said to be in Petrograd organising an armed uprising. But they sit there through it all, no thought of going into the centre to see for themselves what is going on. Although there is much apprehension and tension, they don't seem particularly threatened or frightened. My grandfather apparently said: 'Well, if there's another Revolution, the Bolsheviks just won't last', and they all assume it will go away. It reminds me of the people who slept through the October hurricane in England a few years ago, woke up to find a million trees had disappeared, and had no idea what had happened.

On the 7th November the family hear firing from the direction of the Winter Palace, a couple of miles away; and, around midnight, the famous shot from the cruiser *Aurora*, which had come up the Neva to support the Bolsheviks. But still they don't leave the flat, but have their supper and keep the samovar going; and it was great grandfather Lórentzen who predicts at this time: 'Kerensky will crush them like lice!' They really did think the Provisional Government would put the coup down. But my father himself wrote that from that day social democracy in Russia was finished.

When they venture out on the 8th November, they find an electric atmosphere with victorious soldiers and sailors rushing around in cars and lorries, in command of the city; and with people scurrying around buying up everything they can lay their hands on, anticipating the hungry days that awaited all Russians.

21

Grandfather Alfred goes off to his factory. Who's in charge? The porter! The porter is now running things in his capacity as 'worker'. I'm sorry, that sounds a very snobby sort of remark, and perhaps the porter should have been running things all along, but for my grandfather it was a bad moment. I suppose he could see his investments, such as they were, all slumping; indeed, they did slump, and we can imagine the effect this had on him – he'd always been worried about his accounts, even when things were calm. Now, his salary became minimal and worthless. For him, this incredible upheaval was too much: he was absolutely locked into despair. But the brothers, whose stories we'll come to later, had the alertness and resilience of youth; and the unbelievable excitements and traumas they went through were to be a counterpoint to their new lives.

You would have thought that the wedding was enough drama and that my parents would hasten off to England, wouldn't you? But what does Herbert have in mind? Somehow he has to finish his medical studies. Survival to him means passing his exams. People are fighting, suffering and dying, but he needs to press on; and he wasn't far wrong, was he? He did desperately need his medical qualifications.

So, back they go to Kiev in the throes of the Bolshevik Revolution. The train journey tests them to their limits. It is packed to suffocation, and they have to get off in the middle of a freezing night to cut wood for fuel. Back in Kiev they work on an ambulance train bringing wounded soldiers from the front, until the Armistice, signed at Brest Litovsk on the 3rd March 1918 brings the war to an end on the Eastern Front. The Transcaspian unit is ordered to return to Ashkhabád, so Herbert then presses ahead with the urgent task of completing his medical studies.

The civil war is beginning to wage all around them, and I can just picture him studying anatomy and physiology, with the guns rumbling outside as he sharpens his pencil. Life is terribly hard for everyone in Kiev, especially finding enough food to keep them alive. There is now famine in the area. At one stage he even parades up and down in the market place with his long underpants draped over his shoulders, bartering them for food.

In turn, they both get very ill – my mother very seriously with a severe attack of pneumonia. In fact, at one critical stage Herbert is instructed by the doctor to take her measurements and order her coffin from an undertaker. But he manages to get some horsemeat, which builds up her strength. I suppose that much of the serious illness then was due to severe malnutrition. Herbert himself has what appears to be typhoid, but somehow survives.

The political situation in the Ukraine was chaotic. Herbert describes it in his book *Home On The Neva* as being 'a grotesque tragi-comic opera'. Kiev changed hands several times, and there was always threat of attack from the other side – be it Reds, Whites, or Greens – with the numerous anarchist bands making things even more confused.

Fearful things are going on all around them: on his way to the hospital, he sees a man being lynched in the street, and corpses are hanging on street posts. In the middle of the night, five soldiers raid their home; they sit shivering by the door while their flat is ransacked and all their stuff pinched, or 'confiscated', as the soldiers put it. He lodges a complaint with the city commandant's office, only to be told they are lucky to escape with their lives. Who knows who these people were: Red Army? Whites? Some marauding gang posing as soldiers?

One memorable day Trotsky comes to speak. Herbert, curious to see the famous but dreaded Commissar for War, ventures out to hear him. Trotsky harangues the crowd, urging the workers and soldiers to rout out the bourgeoisie and give them their due. Herbert thinks: 'Is this us? Is he after our blood?' Trotsky is given a tremendous ovation after this speech. Recalling the expressions on peoples' faces, Father wondered how many lives were lost as a result of this terrifying and electrifying speech. It's very strange; even there his Englishness came out. He spoke of lack of partisanship, that he was 'just an Englishman caught up in the circumstances'. But I can't think of him as a mere observer, he was so inextricably enmeshed in this incredible drama which, obviously, had a deep effect on him. In his notebook he wrote that although all war is cruel, civil war is the cruellest of all.

It was in the midst of all this that he actually passed his medical exams, and there is a legend about the problem of finding paper to write his treatise on. But he passes, and then joins Dr Anders in another Red Cross unit; and it was this time – July 1919 – that he volunteers for the task of helping Jewish victims of a terrible pogrom that had just occurred in a nearby place called Malin. Jews, as usual, were having a very rough time from every quarter, with all the economic troubles heaped on their helpless heads. The area the Red Cross unit is sent to is completely anarchic, and a terrible man, General Lokatósh, a freebooter surrounded by a gang of cut-throats, has the upper hand there. They find the area devastated with streets strewn with rubbish and all the houses gutted. Violent pogroms had taken place and hundreds of Jews slaughtered; the pitiful remnants of this Jewish community had been assembled near the general's headquarters, and Herbert is ordered to pass them fit for manual labour. This he will not do. They are in a terrible state: old, debilitated or injured, and frightened to death. He is then arrested as a saboteur and counter-revolutionary, and only escapes being shot by the intervention of another officer who recognises his scarcity value as a trained doctor. Surprisingly, when he wakes up one morning, General Lokatósh and his band have moved off. So back he goes to Kiev where, as he told me: 'Your mother ticked me off for this escapade.' But there's more . . .

Around this time he receives a note ordering him to present himself, with his British passport, to the Bolshevik commandant in Kiev. Like it or not, he has to go; his passport is taken from him and he's told that he can now consider himself a Russian subject, and is recruited into the Red Army. This drastic situation clinches a plan that has been forming in his mind: General Denikin's forces, with British support, are in the south; somehow he has to reach the British. But how? As

24

a Red Army man, he's now in real danger. Also, the loss of his passport is a major disaster; but he visits Mr Thomas, the British vice-consul – probably the only other Britisher in Kiev then – who gives him a paper vouching that Herbert Swann is a British subject; and this precious document is sewn into the lining of his coat.

Meanwhile, Dr Anders and other medical colleagues have devised a plan for Herbert to go north with a section of the unit before his marching orders from the Red Army arrive. The idea is to detach himself from the rest of the unit *en route*, and find his way back to Kiev and, hopefully, to the Whites who are tightening their grip around the city. He boards the train as planned. It crawls along slowly, which enables him to hop off. He then finds a steamer going down the Dnieper to Kiev, and in the throes of all this anxiety, a marvellous lyrical passage from Gogol floats into his mind:

> Lovely is the Dnieper in still weather when, freely and smoothly, its waters glide through forest and mountains.

Just imagine the people in this boat: all the couples hiding away in little amorous huddles; people knowing that their lives are probably coming to an end; nobody knowing who is in charge of Kiev, and what they're returning to. Then the boat is stopped by a Red Army patrol and they're all ordered out. The captain of the steamer, half obeying orders, parks the boat near a forest and a large number of passengers, including my father, walk out into the forest, wondering if they're going to be shot in the back as they walk away, not daring to look back. But nothing happens and he walks and walks through the night to find that he can walk straight through a deserted Kiev to the hospital where his unit is based.

He arrives at the hospital thinking, 'I have cheated destiny again' when he's stopped at the door and told he can't possibly go in as the place is full of spies and commissars. He bolts, and runs to a house a short distance away where he asks for shelter with friends, the Mathiesen family. Mr Mathiesen is a really fine Samaritan. He has a wife and daughter, and they're all very nervous because searches go on all day. They put Herbert in the garden house, and he stays there for about seven days, by which time he's grown a ginger beard and got false papers. All the while the Mathiesen family are petrified with fear, as they would be in the most terrible trouble if a search found him. In the end they beg him to move on. He then remembers an hotel in a suburb, which is owned by some distant relative of his brother, who by this time had married too. He rents a room in this hotel which is nothing more than bare boards, and feels completely disorientated. Then comes another dreaded knock on the door and another search. He considers jumping out of the window, but it's too late and he is arrested and taken to a place already known as 'the place of no return' – some sort of interrogation centre. During the night, he seems to have improved the shining hour destroying bed bugs; but what he is waiting for, with dread, is interrogation. He describes a wonderful moment when a woman, just before him in the line, starts cursing and swearing at the interrogators, and what a marvellous feeling of relief of tension this was, that somebody actually had a go at them. I think that's a remarkable detail, because the passivity of people facing death has always worried me; it's fantastic when some people, on the brink of total disaster say: 'OK, you can take me, but before you do, this is what I think of you and what you're doing . . .'

It comes to his turn. Remember, he has a false identity. Somebody calls his false name, and he fails to react in time – he's getting exhausted and careless. So, the first question is: 'Why didn't you recognise your name?' They then point out that his papers seem suspicious. The officer in charge says: 'I'll just have to give this a bit of thought' and goes out; then another chap in the room who is wearing red trousers says, pointing to a small door: 'Quick! Out through that!' So Herbert leaps out like greased lightning and doesn't stop running until he's completely winded. Who these men were, and why they helped him, he was never able to work

26

out. His one hope was that neither suffered because of his escape.

He runs back to his Good Samaritans, the Mathiesens, who can't but help him although they're more worried than ever about searches. They pass the news to the hospital. Everyone is amazed that he's still around, and another plan is cooked up. He becomes a typhoid patient and is taken by wagon to the typhoid hospital where he is to lie low, without anyone knowing he's faking except the doctor in charge. He knows the symptoms and imitates them; what he can't imitate is the temperature, but he says things like: 'Maybe I've got a relapse; maybe this is the critical moment when the temperature goes down . . .' and he stays there for a week or two. Suddenly there's news that the Red Army has left. All the patients stand up and start rejoicing – all malingerers, it would seem. Some of the nurses must have known, others must have turned blind eyes to it; but now Father was able to get back again to my mother and they had a few months in which to plot a real disappearance, a final vanishing from Russia. I ought to explain that they had been advised to seek repatriation in July 1918, with the handful of British subjects still in Kiev, but they were both reluctant to do this: Herbert was anxious to finish his medical studies, and Naguimé had hopes of visiting her family in Ashkhabád. But now, the writing was on the wall, and I think I'm right in saying they must have been the last British subjects to leave Kiev, in late 1919. They even managed to have a bit of a farewell party in Kiev. I'm really astonished at the ability of people to survive such events and come out the other side with such normality.

They left Kiev, on 5th November 1919, leaving behind many of their possessions. There was yet another epic train journey, this time to Rostov, south-east of Kiev, near the Sea of Azov. It was only 450 miles away, yet the journey lasted seventeen days – you can imagine the conditions. This time, not only did they have to cut their fuel, but they also had to leave the train to forage for food. But they made it, only to be re-directed to Novorossisk, further south on the eastern shore of the Black Sea,

27

where the British Consul, Mr Brown, was still operating. How these consuls survive. What a job! Mr Brown was kindness itself and gave Herbert not only a letter to the High Commissioner in Constantinople recommending his repatriation to England, but also a fiver for expenses – a large sum in those days.

Novorossisk was teeming with refugees of all nationalities, all pitifully anxious to get places on any ship willing to take them to safety. A British submarine arrived in port, in full naval glory, showing the flag. Russian girls were frantically making friends with the sailors and having instant marriages in an attempt to get to England. As for Herbert, he was feeling better: the sight of the Royal Navy was reassuring, he still had the semi-passport written by Thomas, his birth and marriage certificates and his medical degree, and now this paper from Mr Brown recommending repatriation. They waited three weeks in Novorossisk and then were instructed to board a British sloop, the SS *Kursk*. They couldn't help feeling excited stepping, as it were, on British soil; yet this was mixed with deep sorrow that they were being forced out of their country of birth, which they both loved. Naguimé, in particular, was leaving behind her entire family, whom she hadn't seen for over three years.

The ship was packed with refugees. Naguimé and Herbert were up on deck waiting for their cabin to be prepared which, as British subjects, they found they were entitled to. Their luggage was carefully stacked with the Gladstone bag containing all their documents tucked between the suitcases. Herbert left for about twenty seconds, and when he returned the Gladstone bag had disappeared. You can imagine his anguish: just as he was hoping to enter a new country, all his accreditation lost except for his semi-passport which he always kept pinned in his coat lining.

According to his notebook, they were in Smyrna on Christmas Day 1919, and had a game of football, the crew against some local Turks. The ship held a great boozy party to celebrate their victory. Is it possible he could enjoy this? It seems to me he would have been a very worried man wondering what would happen in Constantinople and whether they'd be sent on to England. But the British High Commissioner there believed his story and gave them permission to leave – an extraordinary moment of relief. The next ship to arrive was the SS *Borodino*. The captain looked familiar, and it turned out that he was Captain Norton, Herbert's old friend, who took him to Tilbury ten years ago, in 1909. So the captain really made them feel at home, and at last they felt safe, although Herbert had no way of proving they were married, or that he had a medical degree of any shape or size.

I suppose it's inevitable that my father, Herbert Alfredovich, has been central to this story, and my mother, Naguimé Sultán, is slightly short on details. I'm aware that there is a sort of silence coming from her because she died when I was young and she never recorded her story. I just can't describe her in the way I've described my father. But I hope as this book progresses, something of her story will emerge, and what she did for me as a musician. She was by no means a shadowy figure even though her war story has to be seen through my father's really eloquent account. But when we look at my uncles' experiences, they almost occlude Herbert's story.

Alfred was the eldest by a few years. His story has never been completely told, as there seems to be no end to its permutations. Apart from becoming an expert on Russian music, he had his own list of anecdotes: he had slept in Rachmaninov's nightshirt; the Rasputin story I've already quoted. Once in England he lectured on his special subject to a community of Orthodox nuns in Harley Street. When he arrived, there was only a small number present, but he was a modest man and he started his lecture promptly at 8 pm. The sprinkling of people were attentive. After ten minutes a lady in a white coat came in and said: 'Will you see the doctor now?' He was giving his lecture to the patients in the doctor's waiting room and the community of Orthodox nuns was waiting upstairs on the third floor. He was a close friend of Nikolai Medtner, and knew a Russian folk singer called Loggin-the-Cow. Alfred was sent from Russia to study music at Oxford University where the story goes that, after being granted a place in Balliol, he declined and moved to Exeter College because there they allowed him a piano in his rooms – all arranged in one morning.

But at this point, our minds are still on Russian revolutionary times and Swann adventures in them. If you were sitting talking to Alfred now, you'd forget all about me and my life. As far as I understand, he had some sort of document from the Tsar saying that he was a conscientious objector or something similar. He became closely involved in a strange escapade in May 1918, whereby 800 Russian children from Petrograd were evacuated to the Volga area because of the troubles and famine in the north. Their parents let them go because the southern area was more secure and, being near the harvest, there was more food. They went to the Volga and lived in camps near the river; but, again, everything collapsed with the Bolshevik Revolution, and the adventure became a nightmare when they were caught between all the different warring factions.

Fleeing from this chaos, they got on the Trans-Siberian railway and pushed eastwards across Siberia. They went through one fantastic incident after another: plagued by snow and ice, storms, starvation, boxcar fires, bandits, typhus epidemics and all the hell of civil war. On they went through Omsk and Tomsk, getting on and off the train, living from time to time in the little villages beside the railway. Eventually they reached Vladivostok and were totally marooned. The American Red Cross was pumping money into this extraordinary odyssey, and American doctors were there with the Russian teachers; my uncle Alfred and his wife acted as interpreters and general helpers.

The finale is no less fantastic: a Japanese ship was chartered to take the children to Yokohama and then, amid great triumph and celebration, they sailed through New York harbour with all the people cheering and headlines announcing: 'Russian children arrive in New York'. Bolshevik sympathisers there were saying the children were being held hostage by the 'Imperialist' American Red Cross! Two years after leaving home, they were repatriated having continued their journey across the Atlantic, full circle, to Finland, and to the place which by then was called

Leningrad. (Now about to become St Petersburg again.) Imagine the surprise and relief of their parents. My uncle's second wife, Jane, has been charting the history of these children and has just published a book called *Children's Odyssey*. It would make a fascinating film – I can't wait to see it! I've always thought of uncle Alfred as a composer and an American professor of music, but now this extraordinary drama has been revealed. I must ration myself with these stories about my relatives, or else it will be a book about *them*. Let me just say that uncle Alfred having thus acquired his own legend, died at the age of seventy-nine in Haverford, America; but he will certainly come into my story again as an influence on my music.

Now I'll turn my attention to uncle Edgar of whom I was extremely fond. Like my father, he'd also been press-ganged into the army, but the Imperial, not the Red Army, and he was an officer. This was about the time when one of the first edicts of the new Bolshevik government was promulgated, saying that officers are now finished with and privates are running the army. The story goes that he was playing bridge with his fellow officers when the soldiers barged in announcing that the officers' time was up. They shot the lot, except Edgar, whom they liked. He was a very personable young chap and had treated them decently. They told him: 'You are now the commander-in-chief of all the armed forces. Please take over.' But he took his sword, and ran home and hid. Somehow he survived until 1933 in Leningrad, always being in great danger. There was no safe place for an ex-Tsarist officer in those days; but, again, his Englishness helped him to get through it all.

The searchers would come thick and fast, and we all used to laugh about the time when his wife put his sword down the toilet when they arrived. For those who like silly jokes, this proves there was no 'S' bend in the 1920s. It would have to be an earth closet, wouldn't it?

Edgar was actually under arrest as a suspicious character for quite a while. He had a ring, given him by my mother. Evidently, she was somewhat psychic with her gypsy connections, and she told him if ever he was in danger, to turn the ring three times and he would remain safe. So he used it as a charm in prison and lived to see the day when he could thank her for it.

He worked with Famine Relief during the dreadful days of 1923 and later; he had been taken up by American benefactors and worked as an interpreter and translator. In some ways his story resembles Alfred's, but it is not so well documented. He eventually emerged from Russia when his brothers in the West clubbed together a sum of £150 – a fortune in those days for them – and bought him out. It was possible to do this in 1933. He had the same claim to being British although he'd long lost his passport, and was effectively a Soviet citizen because he'd served in the Russian army.

I met him for the first time when I was ten. He was naturalised when he came to England; then later his wife, my aunt Mourasha, joined him travelling with, of all things, some of the family furniture from the parental flat in St Petersburg, including the Hynam clock which is now in my drawing room. Mourasha was a great character, a Ukrainian wit, and in her later years was the life and soul of Shepherds Bush market, selling trinkets.

So there they are, these three brothers: Alfred, Edgar and Herbert, sitting in England with their four-hand music, having emerged safely from the seething cauldron of Revolutionary Russia. The last brother, my uncle Freddie, is going to have to remain a bit of an enigma.

He joined the British army – don't ask me where or how – and became a colonel in Intelligence. He retained a certain mysteriousness until his last day. Like the other brothers, he was tri-lingual, and was reputedly recruited into MI5 at some stage. After the army, he became an equally enigmatic businessman. He did the most peculiar things, promoting independent projects; I think he had something to do with the invention of the safety razor blade, with Lord Hardwicke and David Niven. Once he hired a yacht and sailed round the world with an aristocratic drug addict who was kicking the habit. He was a fantastic dancer and lived in high society in Mayfair. His exchange was

MAYfair; ours was HOP. He could hardly bring himself to dial HOP which to him seemed monosyllabic and definitely south of the Thames.

I am not at all sure about the MI5 connection but recently I met Michael Mates, the MP. He knows a famous bridge correspondent called Rixie Marcus – now a very old lady, but number one in the bridge world – and Michael said he'd ask her what she remembered of Freddie at Crockford's club. She remembered him very well and told Michael that, as well as being an excellent bridge player, he was a colonel in MI5, and a great charmer. Freddie never let on what he was up to, but I gradually got to like him very much. He was the only brother who didn't play four-hands, and I think it made him feel inferior and slightly less cultured than his brothers, and not quite of their scene. But he was brilliant and charming with a great aura of mystery surrounding him.

The brothers emerged in their various ways from this great cataclysm. As for my grandparents, my grandmother had gone to England soon after the Revolution, then my grandfather a bit later. They went to stay with Anglo-Russian relatives, the Sevier family, in Barnard Castle, Durham. I pity my grandfather very much: he had been desperately shaken by the end of the Rubber Factory and the way his whole life – his family, his flat, and his possessions – had all disappeared. He'd had a breakdown, and suffered ill health before the Revolution, and the terrible upheavals from November 1917 finished him off. In 1919, broken in body and spirit, he died of pneumonia in England. He seems like the family casualty. Although the brothers endured terrible traumas, they escaped with their lives, and perhaps with standards with which to measure subsequent experience. It's hypothetical to say my mother would have lived longer if she hadn't fallen on the railway buffer during the revolutionary chaos. And my grandmother, I remember, went on playing vint. Having lived with us for a bit in Llanelli, and then in the Elephant and Castle, she went off to Riga – she was of Baltic extraction – where, as far as I know, she was still playing vint

33

until she ended her days. Rather shadowy figures to me, the grandparents.

As I end this part of the story, for some reason or other it's the three uncles who are to the fore on the stage. They were to be a very powerful influence; but the things I've been telling you about them were less prominent in my early life than the fact that they were just about. My friend Sydney Carter has read somewhere that all through life, we enact, year after year, the role of one of our relatives. For a time you become an uncle or an aunt, or a grandparent as their persona takes you over. I find that plausible. When I started this book I thought 'It's all history. Aren't we just sifting through papers?' But having thought it through, I realise this isn't just history, but an essential part of me. The medical part of my father, for instance, drew me into the Friends' Ambulance Unit when I was searching for a role in wartime; the four-hand music drew me into piano playing; uncle Alfred's music has drawn me into religious music; and uncle Freddie has been a sort of Joker and mystery: although I hardly knew him, he made me his heir. I've inherited not only stacks of mysterious papers, but ten vast albums of pictorial mementoes from 1914 to 1954: programmes, cuttings, memos and photographs galore, like a picture history of the time – from Germany, Russia, USA and all over the world. He was a globe trotter, jet setting before jets. The photos show generals and glamorous women posing out of the twenties and thirties era; and the most striking photo of all is of his wife of only eighteen months duration, heiress and parachute jumper, who achieved celebrity by being kidnapped. This was my American aunt Louise.

Throughout my life my relatives have played a strong role, and I wonder if this is borne out by others: do they pension their relatives off as mere forebears; or do they say: 'No, these are really part of me today and tomorrow.' As I'm remembering all this, it seems that Russia is changing dramatically. Who is to know whether these refugees – these very early dissidents, if you like, have made contributions to the fight for freedom in Russia today? My father, for instance, struggled for years to overcome a tide of fears so that he could return to Russia when he was first invited in the early sixties. When he began to write up his experiences from his notebooks for his book, mentioned earlier, this acted as a kind of therapy that cured him of his dread of the place. From then on he was an enormous advocate of medical exchanges; he translated many Russian medical books and journals and, once more, became a friend of the Russian people. He had a great sense of kinship with Chekhov, the doctor-writer, and managed to visit his home town. So it seems that Herbert too found a rebirth in the very beginnings of what we now call Glasnost. I think my uncle Alfred's settings of Russian church music could well be used now in the new Russian church. Sitting in America, he wrote beautiful liturgical chants in Slavonic which show a genuine yearning for this country of his birth. So I don't see the Swann family now as ancient characters, dead and gone, but living spirits, almost forerunners of the new Russia.

What does Russia mean to me? Obviously I lived in a bi-lingual state for my first twelve years; I also studied Russian for three years at Oxford and got enormously wrapped up in the literature. There is no doubt in my mind that the music I write is influenced by Russian melody. If my uncle slept in Rachmaninov's night-shirt, I was forever playing his music. I remember Rachmaninov playing in his last concert at the Queen's Hall, and coming on the stage for his tenth encore, the famous prelude in C sharp minor, and saying in a loud voice: 'First performance.' Rachmaninov, Glinka and Tchaikovsky were the heroes of my early life. My mother's Transcaucasian music, especially the gypsy songs, has meant a great deal to me. She was the first person I ever accompanied on the piano in my very early years, and she certainly edged me towards song-writing. I think too that this business of being philosophically minded is very Russian.

Also, I'm now grateful for innumerable new Russian influences: my recent re-discovery of Shostakovich, and the films

35

of Tarkovsky. I am reborn in Russian writing as it comes again and again into my life: I've set Pushkin to music and have just gone overboard with a setting of a Tolstoy story; and of late, I've been setting Pasternak and getting more interested in post-Revolutionary poets. The Russian musical and literary ideas keep coming through. Here, I am at one with many other Europeans who are rediscovering or discovering for the first time this stimulating part of European culture. It could be that we're entering a time when the Russians and Europeans are going to be as one. I am losing the sense that they are they, and we are we: we're beginning to merge. Of course, this is to do with the privilege of being alive in 1991.

On the other hand, I have to admit that I've had feelings of outrage and horror about Russia – or the Soviet part of it. Russia as a country is a formidable conspiracy of violence; it's difficult to describe the horror that's been perpetuated there over the years. I have a real loathing, a sick disgust for all the things that happened to my family: they had decent and good lives that were chewed up in this overwhelming catastrophe. On my mother's side who knows how many of them suffered unbelievable hardships or were massacred. I think the beginnings of my pacifism can be traced to this: I've always had an acute distrust of violence, revolution and the war system. It also had an influence on my humanitarianism. In the throes of war, revolution and civil war, my parents – the nurse and the doctor – strove for a neutral position. My father always hated violence and saw himself as someone who came on the scene to look after those who were suffering, in the best way he could. Although I might not have recognised it at the time, I'm sure this was to prove important when I was faced with the prospect with serving in World War II.

My Russian roots also gave me the feeling, which I've had until fairly recently, of an outsider sort of isolationism. My father continued to dwell on his Russian predicament and was constantly asserting 'I am not a refugee!' Paradoxical really, because you'd think he was. And he went on to write a book about what it was like living in a foreign country. I inherited

36

that feeling, and still feel – just a little bit – that I'm living in a foreign country. When scratched, I'm still an Anglo-Russian and if ever I had a phase of life where I could live in Russia, it is possible I could take it on board as a home country, including the funny food which is a real draw to me. But, until now, I've never wanted to be part of such a country: I have strongly identified with those pleading for liberalism from the beginning, including writers like Pushkin and Tolstoy. What happened in November 1917 and since was a con trick played by history against ordinary people who were abused and let down by their rulers. So I rejected Russia and, although I've had opportunities to go there, I have barely taken them up. I think I have a block about the place which is to do with this feeling of being thrown out. There is a real feeling of intense loss, which was accentuated when my mother died. But there is one Russian adventure that you might be interested to hear about, since it concerns the shadowy Piszóv family.

In 1974 I took a whistle-stop tour of the Soviet Union with Intourist, visiting Moscow, Leningrad and three Caucasian capitals. At this time there had been no communication with my mother's family for a very long time. We'd informed them of her death in 1935 and they sent an Islamic inscription for her grave, but soon after they'd written saying: 'Please don't write any more, it's too dangerous.'

I was travelling with my daughter, Rachel, and sister, Marion. When we arrived in Baku, we started searching for relatives. We arrived on a Sunday; although Russia had become atheistic, the place seemed more deserted than Llanelli on the Sabbath. How were we going to find them? I remember someone saying: 'If we're going around Baku shouting "Piszóv!" somebody's going to arrest us!' We were warned off going to the police, and there weren't such things as telephone directories; so we were advised to wait until Monday morning when the Address Office, where everyone was registered, was open. At this time the Russian food had proved too much for me and I was in bed with food poisoning.

37

Marion, who looks oriental like my mother, queued up in the Address Office early Monday morning; when she got to the front, she pointed to the pigeon hole marked 'P' asking for the addresses filed there. Out came a card with the name Fazilé Piszóva, who was my mother's youngest sister. 'That's my aunt!' she shrieked, at which everyone recognised her as a British tourist, but when she explained our quest, the place became electrified. The taxi-driver put down his flag – no more charge. Marion rushed back to the hotel, dragged me from my sick-bed, gathered up Rachel and we dashed off in the taxi to the Ealing of Baku, as it were; and arrived in a place where the houses all had wooden balconies.

The taxi-driver rushed up the stairs and there was an old lady sitting with her head leaning on her hands. 'Your niece and nephew have arrived from London,' he shouted. She was flabbergasted, absolutely amazed. We rushed up the stairs to greet her; fortunately Marion's colloquial Russian is better than mine and she could really keep a conversation going. So we had thirty-five minutes to cover this lost thirty-five years. The Intourist flight was leaving for Tiflis at 11.15 and it was debatable whether we'd tell our tour guide that we'd found an aunt and would wash our hands of the trip because we had family business to do; but it didn't seem right, we knew it would cause great consternation and possibly a black mark for the guide of whom we were very fond by then. Something that influenced the decision was that aunt Fazilé seemed totally thrown by the British invasion and we had a feeling that if we stayed around it might embarrass her very much.

She told us that all the family had died, with the exception of herself. She couldn't give us all the details of what had happened, but we gained the impression that it was very hard. We had a few bits of news for her including some details of uncle Sokólik's experiences; but, just as I was beginning 'Well, as for Sokólik . . .' she put her hands up to her lips quickly and fearfully and pointed to her flatmate, another old lady, who was just through the door. Obviously, Sokólik was a non-subject.

38

Isn't that tragic? She just couldn't listen to what had happened to her brother. Hopefully, things would be different today, but she just couldn't let us talk about him. So we went on talking for a bit, and we struggled to find something to give each other: the Russian way, when meeting a friend or relative, would be to make a gift. In the end she grabbed a flower vase, took the flowers out, and gave us the vase to take home; and my sister emptied her bag, put all the things in her pockets, and gave her the bag. We couldn't think of anything else.

We corresponded with her for a while, but she died a few years later. I remember her as being amenable and friendly. She remembered me by my baby name of *Dutzik*, which means 'a little pipe' in Russian. This is how my mother spoke of me when she wrote in 1925. In 1974 my aunt thought of me as a child of three. Very strange, isn't it? Very moving. The thing that really haunts me is that we never heard the full story – the gap remains.

The relevance of all this is that I've felt a barrier, an unscaleable barrier. However many times I play, or write songs with a Russian flavour, I can't restore the link, as my father did. Maybe with me the link has to be musical and intellectual, rather than physical. It would be interesting to know how other second-generation refugees feel. I've known lots of Americans in this situation, and it's often the older generation who know and pine for their country of origin . . . Poland, Sweden, Lithuania . . . and the generation that became Americanised, as I became Anglicised, doesn't feel the same and doesn't need to go back to the Old Country. They feel their greatest conquest was that they became Americans; or, in my case, English, becoming sort of Christianised, and public school-ised and then going to university. And I think that much of my effort was put into becoming as English as I possibly could. Many people don't recognise my Russian-ness – but it's been a real treat to talk it through because, now I have confronted it, I can feel the power and strength of it.

3 Llanelli, the Elephant and Castle, and Over the Bridge to Westminster

My parents arrived in Tilbury, minus papers and penniless, but a kind chap on the boat lent them some money so they could go and find Herbert's mother, now living in Barnard Castle. They must have felt rather lost, but Father, at least, had a memory of living in Surbiton for a brief spell before the war, and various images of St Mary's hospital. He also had the refugee's urgent desire to restart. It was important that they were both young enough to be reborn – in a new country.

During their first year in England, my parents were quite destitute. They existed on a little money from various refugee societies including one connected with Sir Samuel Hoare, and the Salvation Army. Because they were so poor, Herbert took the cheapest and shortest medical degree, the LMSSA (the diploma of the Society of Apothecaries). I remember he always used to speak of it with some modesty because it is the mini-minor of degrees which one took when you couldn't afford anything higher up the scale. But it enabled him to practise. After about a year, he secured locum work in Yorkshire, and then was offered a proper job as assistant to Dr Davies in Llanelli for the sum of £500 – a real windfall.

By British standards, his degree might have been a lesser one, but we have to remember he was a very experienced young man. You could say he'd seen it all. His time with Dr Butz, for instance, a really innovative doctor, would have given him some surprising knowledge compared with his English counterparts. He would have been sensationally qualified having been through the war on the Eastern Front, as well as Revolution and civil war. In better times, with real choice, he would have been a surgeon; but, in fact, I think the social aspect of GP work satisfied him greatly, especially the human relationships side. He spoke very fluent English, but retained a Russian accent to the end of his days, not very marked, just a little difficulty with one or two vowels. Of course, my mother's English was far less good. I heard only recently that she went to Morley College for lessons, and she did her best; but she didn't really have much time for study.

By 1921 they were in Llanelli with their new-born daughter, Marion, my sister. Dr Davies, 'Reggie', soon became a very close friend and, when I was born two years later, his wife Annie became my godmother. Herbert really loved Llanelli and the Welsh people. I think he recognised something of the outsider in them which gave him a sense of kinship. So far as he was concerned we could all stay there forever, but my mother yearned for London where her *émigré* friends lived.

A couple of weeks after they arrived in Llanelli all the partners in the practice were taken ill, and this young fledgling of a doctor took over the whole of the town, working all hours but gaining useful local experience. There were lots of tin-plate workers there and many had eczema and TB; he liked working among poor people and later, in the Elephant and Castle, really relished a brotherhood with south Londoners, just as he had with the Welsh. These were the days before the National Health Service, but some doctors were already working hard and imaginatively at insurance schemes. By the time Herbert arrived in Llanelli, Dr Davies and his partners had worked out a system under which patients were not having to pay. This appealed enormously to Herbert: he was mad about the idea that nothing should stand between doctor and patient, and certainly not five bob, or half-a-crown. That was anathema to him, and he lived for the day when the NHS was finally created. Such was his interest that he knew several of the founders.

How was this Moslem lady getting in on Llanelli? Not too well:

42

the culture shock was enormous. The thing that finally got her down was not being able to hang out laundry on Sundays because the Sabbath was sacrosanct. Her Sunday, of course, would have been on a Friday anyway. She was indignant, and thought this the ultimate nonsense, which of course it was. I hope nowadays people can do what they like with their washing whatever the day. Another thing was the peculiar food; although she cooked her own, probably the range of food was more restricted there than in London. But the thing that really astonishes me is that my father accidentally poisoned her very early on in my life. I was, apparently, a whining child; from the first day of my life I was either grisling, or screaming my head off. That was bad enough for her, but when I was about nine weeks, my father, about to give her some sedative, picked up the Lysol bottle by mistake. I don't think Lysol is much around now, but it was a horrible, poisonous thing used as disinfectant. She was rushed to hospital and only just saved. Awful for her, but not good for me either because her milk dried up, so I was weaned in one night. What would Dr Spock make of that?

Another bit of drama concerned uncle Sokólik, my mother's brother, the only member of her family to turn up, and on the day of my birth too – just like the fairy stories. He had been an officer during the war, but had managed to leave Russia after the Revolution and had roamed around Persia and Turkey until his three-week stay with us. He caused a tremendous stir in Llanelli and was certainly remembered there twenty years ago when I made enquiries. He was called 'the wild brother of Mrs Dr Swann' and his like had never been seen before. He entertained the people of the area by singing rousing songs and playing his guitar, and dancing exotic Eastern dances whilst brandishing sabres and knives. I was also told by one old chap that Sokólik had psychic powers. Evidently, he was once asked to sit down, but said, without having examined the chair, that there was a great hole under its cushion – and indeed there was. I always called him uncle Mohammed because he later changed his name in Persia.

After his visit to Llanelli in 1923, he surfaced again in 1925. I've got photographs of him with uncle Freddie taken on this visit. Then he vanished completely for thirty-five years. When he reappeared he was living in South Persia in a town called Ahwaz, about fifty miles from Abadan across the desert, and as far south as you could get from the Russian border. He was working as the director of music in the hotel Shoush. Various oilmen came to the hotel, and he asked one to try to trace his brother-in-law, Dr Herbert Swann, living in London. This oilman went back to London, found there were eight Dr Swanns listed in the Medical Directory, wrote to them all and one of the letters found Father. From then on Herbert corresponded with Sokólik, who had changed his name to Mohammed Zadek. Fascinating letters would arrive and how I'd laugh at some of the things in them. At Ramadan, he would turn his hand to interior decorating because music was frowned upon; and the fact that he tuned pianos tickled me – I mean what scale? Was it the well-tempered mode? Or some oriental Persian scale? Then one day he promised to write the whole story of the great gap between the sword dance in Llanelli and his present life. But it never arrived, and the next time we wrote, a note came back: 'deceased'. I feel deprived of his lost story to this day and ruminate on that Persian pillar box where it went missing.

There is a sequel. In 1964, I went to South Persia and took my wife and two small daughters by taxi from Abadan to Ahwaz. I started asking around about him and, after a long time of getting nowhere, someone suggested the Hollywood shoe shop. Again, we kept repeating the name Mohammed Zadek – no luck. Then I let slip the name Sokólik to the taxi-driver who was interpreting, and the shoe man said: 'Oh, we remember him; he was a musician who used to work in this town, a nice old gentleman, then he died in hospital.' That was just eighteen months after his death.

The final part, which also touched me very much, was during an autobiographical entertainment in Cambridge. I'd been making jokes about Mohammed and sang about the camels and the desert. The professor of Persian in King's College came up to me afterwards and said: 'I was in Ahwaz and went to the hotel Shoush, and a tall gentleman came up and spoke to me. Obviously, he was your uncle.' Now, isn't that absolutely amazing? So, he's real, isn't he? This legendary uncle, in spite of the embroidery of camels, wild dances and songs, is real! And I've two framed photographs of him in my home: one playing the balalaika and another which you can see in this book. He's doing a Russian-style dance, with a big fur hat on. There he is: a professional entertainer, just like me.

We had other things in common: Moslem names were passed on to us; my sister's second name is Fatíma and mine is Ibrahím. My mother opted for two popular names to remind herself of her people. There it is, on my passport, just an exoticism to which I never paid much attention. But things like that come back and joke at you from time to time. There was the moment on an El Al plane when they looked at my name and said: 'OK Mr Ibrahím – we're keeping an eye on you!' That was quite a good moment. Then, only recently, I took a Turkish bus from Salonika to Istanbul. For fun I had booked on as Mr Ibrahím and having arrived, went off to admire carpets. I let my name slip to the carpet dealer who exclaimed: 'Ibrahím Pasha, you are one of us! How about one of these?' He'd got me beaten. I had to buy one. So every now and then my Moslem name comes back. It's nice to think it's Abraham too, and I'm always cheered to think it's as much Jewish as Arabic, just the other side of the language really.

I became rather proud of the mix of religions in my family. There is the Moslem part on my mother's side; my sister is married to a Jew. My uncle Alfred became a devout Russian Orthodox; later, at school, I was plunged into high Anglicanism; and now I'm a Quaker. All this gives me the feeling that religion is a kaleidoscope where all these strands merge to form a beautiful pattern.

It's disorientating, but the 'film' I've been watching of the old Swann family is fading. Reality is taking over. Is this because I'm now 'in the picture'? I'm now talking of 1926, and my family returned to London when I was three. This was to a part of the Harrow Road where my father worked for a very unsatisfactory doctor. Fortunately, after a year or so, he managed to buy a practice – in those days they changed hands for very small sums – at 92 Walworth Road in the Elephant and Castle, just four miles away from where I now live. I pass the house regularly in my car and there's a notice on it saying 'Tattoo Artist – all hygienic methods used'. Before that, it was a pornographic bookshop, but at least it's stood the test of time and hasn't been bombed nor pulled down like so much of the old Elephant. That's where I lived until the blitz of 1941.

Whenever I remember the Elephant and Castle I immediately think of the Southern Railway, as it was then called, visible and audible right outside our flat roof at the back. Underneath was the tube train. I loved the tube train; it seemed part of my home rushing and rumbling away beneath us. Outside was the tram. I adored the tram; if only we could find a tram map and put it into this book! There was the 33, the 35 and the 37 and they ran right past the house. As the tram drew near it made a sound to wake the dead, but to me this was like a lullaby. It started faint, and clanked nearer to reach a gigantic forte; then faded away as it rounded the corner to the Elephant and Castle. All this was part of my boyhood romanticism.

Now, the house. It's tall and thin with a flat roof. We had two lodgers: a clown's daughter who was a washer-up in the Union Jack Club in Waterloo Road, and a very old, poor, distressed lady whom I never saw until she died. She was right at the top of the house and I don't recall her ever going up and down the stairs. When she died her flat was fumigated. Our landlady was most peculiar. She had a box which said 'For the Blind', and I used to put my farthings into it. When it was full, do you know what she did? She took all this money and put a blind up. She actually used it for a window blind; she conned us!

My father worked very hard in his surgery on the ground floor, and we lived on the two floors above. We ate Russian food which was wonderful: kasha, bortsch, but mostly macaroni.

I don't know why macaroni comes to be so Russian, but I collected all the macaroni dockets and we got a whole heap of saucepans with them. Patients would come and go; in those days they would pay my father 1/6d or half-a-crown. I used to help him in the surgery dispensing medicine, pouring water on to coloured powders which we pounded with a pestle. (Is this a song?) I said earlier that he liked working with poor patients, but he also liked the rich ones. I don't think he was discriminating about this, but he was very much at home with the people of the Elephant and Castle.

The rich patients were occasional, but they were always welcome. Because we were poor, if they could pay half a guinea it was really good news for us. There was a Grand Duchess he treated at one point: Xenia, Nicholas II's sister. I think she was living in a grace-and-favour house in Richmond, and father would go off to visit her dressed up in his suit, and I suppose she was tickled pink that he could speak Russian. Every so often the richer *émigrés* asked him for medical advice. I should think Russian-speaking doctors were few and far between.

I'm trying to picture our lives there, and the high days when musical friends would come round. One fine day a piano was bought with some of our first savings. It was an upright, a Gerhard Adam, an excellent instrument, until recently in my stepmother's home. The stairs to our flat were extremely narrow, and the piano got stuck on the way up and looked as if it would never leave the staircase. Then the old piano heaver said: 'Leave this to me' and he just lifted the whole thing on his shoulders and inched it up, bit by bit. I was enormously impressed, perhaps even more so because what had arrived was a pearl of great price: my father's talisman, right there in our home. As soon as it arrived, he opened up his volumes of four-hand piano music; the whole classical repertoire, all the symphonies and quartets arranged for four-hands. Where did he get this music? He couldn't have brought it from Russia, could he? Somewhere along the line someone had produced it – probably one of his brothers. So, from then on, at the age of seven, I became a putative four-hand player, and began to play little bits to fit in.

Some quite grand musical friends would come: the conductor Lawrance Collingwood, who was to bring many beautiful Russian operas to the Old Vic and Sadler's Wells; the first-class piano duet team, Ethel Bartlett and Ray Robertson; and on occasional Sundays we would visit the Russian *émigré* families for more music and have yet more rice and cabbage tart. This is like an apple tart, but with cabbage in the place of apple, and you take a great chunk of this and feed it into the bortsch – absolutely superb stuff! It was very good to share this Russian food. One of the *émigrés* was the composer Nikolai Medtner who, to some extent, was like another Rachmaninov – he composed wonderful piano music. I remember once I cracked a walnut with my hand, and he said: 'Never do that, you'll ruin your wrist.' Of course, he was quite right, and ever since I've used a nut cracker. I've mentioned that we heard Rachmaninov play; we'd also go to Sadlers Wells and the Old Vic to watch the opera and listen to all types of music, Sir Thomas Beecham being a favourite. I even saw Anna Pávlova as the dying swan – her last English performance.

We also had home music. From time to time, when she felt in the mood, my mother would invite Alexis Chesnakóv, a guitar player of our acquaintance; then she'd throw a colourful shawl around her head and sing Russian gypsy songs. By the age of eleven I had learned a lot of them and could put the chords in, and was beginning to accompany her before she died. There really was a lot of home music – in fact it was the main pastime. The rest of life was pretty hard. We didn't have a car and it was all hard work for my father, with surgeries and home visits by foot or public transport. Mother would have been confined to the house; and, for the children, school. We were speaking Russian at that time although I was being heavily Anglicised by school and, with my early confirmation, by the church. So, you can see, I was beginning to move swiftly into English life.

I've mentioned earlier that my mother died when I was

thirteen. It's strange how I can never visualise her with any certainty. Recently several of her letters were passed to me by a relative; even reading them in Russian doesn't give me any recognition of her handwriting or her presence. So much about her is secret: her Mohammedism, for instance, which I hardly knew about. She wore a silver Koran around her neck and was buried with it. But was I ever told about Islam? No. The only thing I knew about it was the Islamic inscription on her grave sent over by her family: 'From God we come, to God we go.' And now, as I have the opportunity to think about her, it occurs to me that her language was Russian and, before she died, I was about to lose that language. I was getting weaned again, not through the Lysol bottle this time, but through being thrown suddenly and unexpectedly into a new cradle; and this parent who, everyone tells me, was the most caring and loving mother, was beginning to evanesce. She was ill for long periods with asthma, which could well have come from the trials and tribulations of the war; and she eventually died of cancer at home, which was horrifying. She was buried in a Mohammedan cemetery in Brookwood, outside Woking.

I deeply regret this lack of psychological, inward understanding of my mother, nor do I recall any physical awareness of her; probably I felt very much an orphan because of this. But when I compare my story with the stories of others who've had enormous tragedies in their early lives, I know how lucky I was with a loving father and many people to care for me. Nevertheless, the shock seems to be there, and, even today, I seem to have a block about her: I can't describe her facially, or otherwise, as I would like.

However, very gradually, it dawned on me that my mother conferred on me the gift of releasing my emotions at the piano; of putting music to ideas, which is to me the heart of song-writing. I can say, without any doubt whatsoever, that my love of the piano is tactile. I wanted something to touch and stroke, and I found it – eighty-eight keys! From an early moment, without playing any tunes, I started feeling my way around the piano.

Later on I would clean the keys with Thawpit, an essentially tactile thing. Even now, the moment I play, I feel comforted and consoled. On the day of my mother's death, I wrote my first tune: a lament for her passing. I have it here in my file: Opus 1, number 1.

What a parting gift – a mother's gift. I never lost the feeling that the piano was an act of consolation; and with my father's music and all the musical uncles and friends, I was put into the right frame of mind for an artistic existence. So I bless my mother and her Russian folk-songs which are as strong an influence as any serious music I ever heard. Later on, it turned out that I transformed them into Greek songs, but that's another story.

My education was proceeding throughout all of this. I went to Dulwich Prep school which cost my parents tens of pounds annually. Now it's thousands. I travelled there with someone who sold Cornflakes: my parents found a lady who regularly took my train, the 8.21 from the Elephant and Castle to West Dulwich, who acted as chaperone to little me in my uniform. She carried a huge suitcase full of Cornflake packets. Isn't it odd? Have you ever been approached by a lady with a large suitcase who says: 'Would you like to buy some Cornflakes?' It brings back another world. In the twenties and thirties lots of people travelled in such things.

So, a journey to West Dulwich, a walk up the hill playing a yo-yo and then classes. I was rather keen. I liked lessons and wanted to get on. In those days you sat in form, positioned according to your marks. To sit at the back was a real disgrace, but if you managed to get a few answers right, you were moved up and got a better seat. From the beginning, parts of English education scared me. Much of it was very alien, and when later I went to Westminster School, much of that was very peculiar indeed, especially the food and some of the habits. My father's school in St Petersburg had been so different. He had a horror of physical punishment, so had I been beaten, I wouldn't have dared tell him. I'm rather ashamed of that, because all my efforts went into not getting beaten or punished. This probably encouraged me to get more marks, and push ahead yet more. We had some good language teachers at both schools. I remember at Dulwich one was a Nazi who wrote 'Deutschland über alles' in my autograph book. This must bring us to the early thirties. Another teacher was an ex-policeman. I can't remember anything he taught me except escaping from pursuers: 'Go above the height of the person tracking you', he said. 'People always look along and never up. If you sit in a tree you'll be safe.' Another thing that appealed to my verbal sense of humour was that the Headmaster and his son were called Leake, the assistant Headmaster was John Leakey, and the school secretary was Miss Leech. Delightful.

I've kept one friend throughout my life from Dulwich Prep: John Amis, the musicologist, entertainer and singer. He was cutting his teeth on music at that time, just like me. We discovered our mutual interest in music during the last year. By that time I was playing a bit more and had been taking lessons from an elegant Sussex lady, Miss Bengough from Wisborough Green. John was the first of the musical friends of my early life, apart from my father's generation. He would come to my home after school. He writes about it, eloquently, in his autobiography *Amiscellany*: how we would move between piano playing, ping-pong and eating peanuts, and how we chewed up the music. Everything seemed fascinating and interesting.

John is a funny man, and he was a funny boy with some of the verbal humour Michael Flanders excelled in. I must include a little gem from John. He later worked at EMG – Electrical and Mechanical Gramophones – and he would pick up the phone and say: 'This is John Amis from EMG E for eczema, M for mange, and G for gangrene.' Typical of his school-boy humour. We were always laughing. Everything was funny, especially words which were either funny or slightly dirty. It could be that my love of linguistic humour was to do with being bi-lingual, although John was not bi-lingual. Maybe children just do find words funny. The greatest response to Michael Flanders's lyrics was often from children who love all the word-play about Gnus and so on.

By the end of the Dulwich period, we older prep school boys were all working ourselves up to go on to the next stage. My case was comparatively unusual. I don't know who suggested that I should go to Westminster, because most of the boys went to Dulwich College proper, just a couple of hundred yards up the hill, towards Sydenham. The story goes that my mother saw a Westminster boy walking about in a top hat, and thought: 'This has to be it!' In those days Westminster boys were clad in full morning dress. So my parents signed me up. This reminds me of an anecdote. An ex Friends' Ambulance Unit chap wanted to get his boy into Westminster and went to see the Bursar. He was asked: 'What did you do in the war?' He replied: 'I was a conscientious objector.' Then he was asked: 'What is your religion?' He replied: 'I am lapsed Armenian Orthodox.' Finally the Bursar said: 'What is your income?' 'Unemployed violinist', he whispered in reply. He was shown the door. But my case must have been a bit better because somehow my father did get my name accepted. I was then invited to take a scholarship called 'The Challenge' which I just scraped through, and this gave some financial support for me to enter this imposing school.

Dulwich to Westminster felt like a great change. It was a pretty peculiar time for me, going to this big public school at the time when my mother was becoming seriously ill. When she died, and I became a boarder, it was even more frightening. Suddenly, I lost the Russian environment and the home atmosphere. Of course, Westminster was a home, but it was so completely different; to suddenly lose my mother and become a boarder at the age of thirteen was traumatic. To qualify for my scholarship I had to live right in the middle of the school, and although it was, and still is, a very privileged place – quite glamorous by English standards to be right in the middle of Westminster Abbey precinct – I missed the Elephant and Castle very much. Later, I wrote a song which expresses my feelings for the place. It's called 'Conurbation' (with the subtitle 'More's Subtopia'). Here's a snippet:

The aerials
Are ethereal
Above the densely crowded flats:
The outlook is
Funereal,
There's a smell from dogs and cats.
But if you look along a disused gutter,
Which is covered with an inch of grime,
You'll see the clover-
Leaf fly-over
Every time.
    Conurbation, conurbation,
    It's to you I've lost my heart . . .

Not exactly Ira Gershwin; but there's no doubt that you become part of your home and identify with it. Despite all the sordidness, it really fills me with a great deal of pleasure to think of the Elephant. It seems wrong, doesn't it? Pleasure? With people dying of TB and goodness knows what because of the smoke and filth! I can remember a really foul pea-souper fog which stopped me and the Cornflake lady on our journey to Dulwich. There were smoke signals on the lines during these fogs which made strange, haunting noises. I would pine for all that during my early days boarding at Westminster.

Imagine what it's like moving into a curious, long dormitory with forty beds in different compartments, the boys being graduated from top boy to bottom boy, twenty each side. Monitors strode up and down the corridor between the rows of beds with their tanning poles. They didn't use them prodigiously, but we got the idea. And there was the 'John', the school servant, who cleaned the boys shoes – can you imagine it? Antidiluvian. The school historians write that from 1939, when the school was evacuated, it changed abruptly to being quite a modern school, but during my first years there it was still locked into the Victorian age with a very strict hierarchy.

As you can appreciate, all this was a far remove from the Elephant and Castle. I had to wear school dress which, for King's Scholars of up to 5′4″ was a mortar board, an Eton collar and white tie. Then you graduated into a morning coat

53

and gown. Bad enough, but when I went home I had to wear 'town boys' uniform' which included the top hat and stick. I was deeply embarrassed by the top hat and would shove it under the seat as I hopped on a tram across Westminster Bridge; back in the Walworth Road the local boys would enjoy themselves throwing pellets at it. I never got used to wearing that hat. One of my profound resentments about public school is connected with this uniform. They've abandoned it now, of course, except for the gown. All this was an enormous jump: geographically just a mile or two, but culturally, a great leap.

My father was incredibly pleased that I'd got into Westminster. He just loved it. I was reasonably pleased to think I was part of it. I suppose it's the *émigré*, isn't it? Here I was a King's Scholar! Westminster was an incredible place. It had then and still has, enormous eccentricity. It has always been very open minded. I am told what clinched my scholarship was my reply when the Headmaster, who was examining me asked: 'Who is the current Prime Minister of France?' I replied: 'Well, there are so many of them, it's impossible to remember their names.' This was 1935. Now he thought this was a little bit witty; so I think they were looking for the unexpected, and far more eloquent people than I have spoken of it very amusingly. Peter Ustinov is one, though he disliked this very Headmaster so much because of a terrible beating he gave to a boy, that he caricatured him in his play *The Unknown Soldier and his Wife*. But there's a great deal about Westminster that I found enormously attractive, especially its idiosyncracies and funniness. Not so long ago I gave a concert to the Westminster Choir school, and I told the boys some of the things I remembered – the top hat, and the peculiar rules we had. For instance, there's a particular stone in one of the cloisters, marking the grave of Samuel Flood, a school benefactor. If you trod on it, or even touched it with your foot, you got beaten or some other punishment. Treading on graves is mythologically dangerous; the Westminster monitors could have been right.

There's something about the Abbey itself which is also a bit eccentric. It may look a very Establishment place with the lovely architecture, stained glass and grandiose monuments, but when you start looking around – poets' corner, for instance – there are some way-out people there: how about Dylan Thomas? I think we realised we were not only in a privileged place, but in a place where some really interesting and original ideas came through, and I cherish the Abbey connection very much. I've had contacts with some of the Deans and have worked with several of the choristers.

Mainly, I was a language student and particularly admired a philosophically minded teacher called G C Claridge who would stop the class to give us a talk on 'the meaning of meaning'. Once he wrote the phrase 'A waste of time is worse than death' in seventeen languages on the blackboard. One was Phoenician. We had a total 'school language' and were examined in it. All the masters and all the activities of the school had pet names, nicknames that we had to memorise. The lavatory was called 'the Japs' – I can't think why. 'Station' was compulsory activities; things were either voluntary or 'station'. 'Election' was the word of order. Just as when you order a dog to do something you say 'Sit!', they would say 'election Swann!' That would mean 'Swann, come and speak to your monitor!' Of course Latin was the language we really had to get to grips with, along with French and German which I took to later. Prayers at the end of the day, which were 'station', were in Latin; and they even had their own Westminster School Latin pronunciation which is different in that being highly Anglicised, it makes no concession to the original Roman sounds.

We also had Latin plays. All the dialogue was in Latin. The monitor would sit at the back with a huge great stick and when he waved it we all had to laugh. We had no idea where the jokes were, you see, and if we didn't laugh then we were punished or beaten.

Like at any public school, we had endless school jokes. Shall I tell you one? Actually, I think it's from Marlborough. A man goes to the school to preach a sermon including the text: 'I will

55

pull down my barns and build greater.' He can't think why all the boys are laughing their heads off; it turns out that the school language for trousers was 'barns'.

I remembered a story which amused the modern Westminster choir boys enormously. Our school chaplain once said: 'When you sing the hymn, keep one eye on the words, one eye on the music and one eye on God.' The other thing that appealed to them very much was that, on the last day of term, we used to go swimming naked in the Great Smith Street baths with our top hats on. That's where that hat went! It disappeared either there, or in the blitz. I have certainly lost it. Although I hated wearing it, I loved it and would massage it every morning with a special hat device.

A key moment came just when I arrived at the school: the coronation of George VI and Queen Elizabeth. As well as the formal dress I've described, we were issued then with 'coronation dress' consisting of doublet and hose and some elegant slippers. Westminster School scholars, of which I was a small example, represented the people of England. All the rest of the congregation in the Abbey were the top brass: the prelates, the ermine-clad peers and what have you. The ordinary people were all outside but, thanks to tradition, they were represented by forty boys from Westminster School – in fact by us. And in the middle of the coronation anthem by Parry, which is a most beautiful piece of music, we called out in Westminster School Latin: 'Vivat Rex Georgius! Vivat Regina Elizabetha!' It was our privilege. One of my best moments in my school life was this time; not the coronation itself, but the rehearsals – the dress rehearsal, in particular. All the peers were wandering around in their robes, and we could go downstairs and mingle with them. The music was playing, and I was immensely thrilled by the organ and trumpets and the orchestra. When we got to the coronation itself, we were right up in the triforium, a little balcony. All the big boys were at the front, and the little nippers at the back were squeezed out. I saw absolutely nothing. I remember a huge urn of milk, so my whole impression of the coronation was guzzling this milk continuously from early in the morning until late in the evening. We were given a medal for attending the coronation. I wore it when I spoke to the choristers recently. Only one person recognised it. This was the organist of Westminster Abbey who had received one for attending the next coronation. So there you are, medals are given just for being present, not only for valour. My Mons Star?

Of course, the top brass were right there in the school. One little bloke was a Peer of the Realm, an Earl. He was a fag when I arrived which meant that he was doing menial tasks for monitors. One day he was asked to go and buy an evening paper. Never having done anything so mundane in his life, he called up the family Rolls-Royce and a huge car came into Dean's Yard. He hopped in and they drove 150 yards down Tothill Street. The chauffeur got out, bought the paper, handed it to the little Earl at the back and they returned to Dean's Yard. The chauffeur helped him out from the back of the car, and the fag-of-an-Earl took the newspaper to the monitor.

My family had a glimpse of the upper echelons of society before I went to Westminster, because one of my father's patients worked at Buckingham Palace – not as a cook for the Royals, but a cook for the cooks there. He was a Swiss, called Grieshaber – shades of Mervyn Peake. He said to my father: 'Perhaps you'd like to have a look around the palace.' You can imagine, we were entranced. So we took a tram to Buckingham Palace and presented ourselves at the door to an enormous chap in a busby and said: 'We've come to see Mr Grieshaber, and we'd like to look around the palace please.' Somehow or other we got from the gates to the next portal and the liveried servant there was completely and utterly baffled. He roared: 'Grieshaber? How do you spell it? Who's he? A *chef*!' His exclamation echoed down all the corridors and we felt it would reach the Royals themselves. But my father, clutching his bald head, seemed reasonably plausible, and we were all wearing our best clothes so, although they had no notion at all of what we were about, some compassionate person must have thought us harmless-looking supplicants, and we were given a private view of the palace. We went up and down the great corridors into some of the State rooms; I remember seeing portraits of King George V and Tsar Nicholas II next to each other; and recall vividly a secret door in part of the library through which the Royal family could quickly enter their private quarters when they'd had enough of their guests. It seemed a world apart to me then, and still does; but there's little doubt old Grieshaber gave us an interesting afternoon.

My musical development accelerated during my Westminster days. I was known to be a keen musical boy when I arrived, and I remember winning the main school piano competition during the first term, thanks to Hugo Anson, an examiner of the Royal College of Music who later became my tutor at that same college. From then onwards I went downhill, and I don't think I ever won it again. I'd reached my peak at the age of fourteen, rather as swimmers do. I could both extemporise and play simpler classical music, but it wasn't too long before I discovered that the more complicated classical music was beginning to fox me more than a little. Then, of course, I began to compose my own which was fine. A simple answer to all classical music is don't play anyone else's, do your own thing. At least it's within your own compass! And I suppose my mother's folk music, although I might not have realised it then, had really got to me. I was pining inwardly for a friendly bouzouki or a balalaika, and what I got was Beethoven. I gagged on it. It has taken most of a lifetime to get used to Beethoven.

I was playing all the time: accompanying hymns, playing with the orchestra and with friends. I took up the flute, which was a disaster. I don't seem able to play it; pressing the flute keys is not the same as touching the piano at all. I tried to play the organ, but couldn't cope with the feet. My music seems to end at the waist. You'd think I could march to time, or dance, but I find this very difficult, even the two or three tempi, so it's something to do with the mind and hand. I'm absorbed with the fact that music is wrongly considered to be purely a sound thing; it's as much to do with touch and the co-ordination of the limbs, as well, of course, with words and ideas. But Westminster then was very music orientated with lots of hours slotted in for play and practice. Then my father would come during the few hours when a schoolboy was allowed to see a parent, and would take me by his first-ever car to the Royal School of Music where I became an external student with two wonderful tutors: Angus Morrison, who died only recently; and Hugo Anson, already mentioned, who encouraged me to write music. I was lucky that a boy in an English public school was allowed this connection with a main music college.

Life was very competitive in those days. You never played for the sake of it; you were always beating someone else by playing better than they did. Grants' House and the King's Scholars would have been vying with each other to emerge with the best choral song, and the best compositions, then you would win or lose a lot of points; slithering up and down a slippery pole. Isn't it odd that music should be so connected with competition?

When the biographers come round, they ask me about my friendship with some of the better-known Westminster boys. There was Tony Benn, for instance, and I certainly remember him and his brother recruiting for various socialist societies and distributing leaflets. I've kept in touch with him and respect him enormously. At the other extreme, how about the young Von Ribbentrop, son of the German Ambassador? He was also there, putting the weight, if I remember rightly. Peter Ustinov, as I've mentioned, has made good use of his Westminster experience in his comic anecdotes. Back then we played tennis together. Another now illustrious ex-pupil was young Peter Brook, whom I knew as a Russian refugee, and played games with on Bognor beach.

One King's Scholar, Adrian Adams, aroused my intense admiration. His father was in the travel business and he allowed his son to run an agency for the Batavier Line in his cubicle where he (Adrian) did his homework. You could buy from him a shipping ticket to Rotterdam, a real one. Travel mad, this boy climbed out of a school window one night, went on a train to Crewe and returned by the time of roll call. His most successful coup, however, was to reach Paris by plane when the school was rowing at the Henley

Regatta and we all had a free day, either to watch the school eight or to do our own thing. At lunch-time Adrian was sitting in the Café de la Paix and bought the midday edition of the *Continental Daily Mail*. He saw that the school had won the first heat of the Regatta and would continue into the second or third, so he delayed his plane as he knew none of us would be back until late evening. I thought this was brilliant.

Another boy, now a distinguished professor of aesthetics, Richard Wollheim, a fellow King's Scholar, started a magazine called *Bogeur* which featured all things bogus – an early *Private Eye* of a highly intellectual type – with poems and anecdotes about masters and boys. I recall a clerihew about John Corsellis:

> Corsellis
> Rhymes with trellis
> And hence
> With fence.

Puncturing the bogus was also the central idea behind a smuggery competition which had us riveted and full of laughter for weeks. A score-board hung on the wall. If you did your prep in ten minutes instead of two hours you might gain a point; if you sang extra loudly in the school hymns you'd gain a point for being vocally faithful. The idea was to be smug wittily enough to get away with it. But one day a boy put his arm round the Headmaster and said: 'Hello old chap. How are you?' This gave him twenty points; he was the overall victor and the game was abandoned.

Michael Flanders was there. He was a 'Grantite' and a town boy, i.e. not a King's Scholar, so we were worlds apart. Although we shared the same quadrangle, the tradition then was that you didn't speak to boys from other houses and we were not permitted to talk to boys two years our senior unless they spoke first. So Michael was around but was not a close friend until very late in my school life.

Unlike the Elephant and Castle, I've not written a song particularly associated with Westminster School; but I do remember a hymn Michael and I wrote years later for the Abbey which was turned down by the Chapter, – a great *cause célèbre*. 'Vivat! Vivat!' it went, just like the school song. We'd been asked by Archbishop Joost de Blank, also a canon of Westminster, to write a song for the 900th anniversary of the Abbey. Half of the powers-that-be thought this a good thing, the other felt we were too flippant. We were theatre entertainers. What had we to do with the august goings-on in the Abbey? This didn't do a great deal of good for Michael's very peripheral interest in Christianity. He wrote back to them saying: 'What you really want is "God, God, Glorious God!"'

As I write about these things, it all seems racy and exciting but there was much profound loneliness too. My growing love of modern languages, particularly German, led me to read Hermann Hesse, the perpetual outsider, who never managed to be part of any society, partly because of the impending cataclysm in Germany. A lot of this affected me and many other boys. We knew that this cocoon, with the weird school language and customs and our progression to university was not going to be a total world. It just wasn't enough, we sensed this; but little did we know that we were out on a most peculiar limb. In our privileged position, we had very little contact with ordinary English children outside the precinct of Westminster. There was a whole lot of other things we knew nothing about: I certainly knew nothing about women or girls. The only connection was one boy who knew a girl and got so excited about this that he'd write her daily thirty-page letters giving his total sequence of thought. He'd write these during prep time; so if you came in he'd put in the letter: 'Donald has just come into the room . . .' This might sound a feeble point, but it was real: we're talking of an era even before girls were invited in for a bit of tea or dancing. We were incredibly withdrawn, and the sad thing is that to a great extent I lost contact with my sister who went to a day school in Clapham. Marion, in turn, thought that I was living in a cocoon, withdrawn from ordinary society, and certainly from her.

I didn't know very much about the English countryside either.

We would go out to play football, or row at Putney and that was about it. But in the Boy Scouts, we had to get a badge by sleeping a night in the countryside. Off I went with the head of school music, a very intellectual boy called Peppin. We were on bikes and took a tent; then we saw some green – very unfamiliar to me at that time – so we parked on it, tore up the grass to pitch the tent, and bedded down for the night. After a bit an irate farmer appeared who said: 'Don't you realise you're in the middle of my hayfield?' So my friend, who is now a philosopher, said: 'I've never seen any green hay. I thought it was always brown. This is the first time I've ever been in a field.' You should have seen the farmer's face! He couldn't understand the language; this was an incredibly educated young bloke who was giving him a sophisticated definition of green grass. So in the end, we paid him ten shillings and disappeared. Believe it or not, we got that badge. We were given a badge for sleeping out in the open.

Again, this is a fatuous anecdote, but it does say something about the things that were completely and utterly missing in our education. I wouldn't want to fault the education too much. There were some very humanitarian and thoughtful lessons given to us, and the breadth was very wide. They wanted us to study and open our minds to think, and it was classically oriented: not only did we study Latin and Greek, we made jokes in these languages. This points to a great change that's come over England. We thought that boys who went on the science side had simply failed in some way – that they just hadn't the wit and breadth of mind to study ancient Greek – so poor things they had to go and do chemistry. The chemistry master was treated like a joke. He smoked crumpled-up loofah! I love art now, but in those days I didn't even find the art department. These terrible gaps may be reflected by the gaps right in the heart of me. I think there's a lot of loss in any child: in my case I don't know whether it's to do with my mother, or my Russian-ness. But it seems that we all strive to make up for the lost ground of one's childhood.

How did school end? What happened to this cocoon? Well, it burst open in September 1939 and all the boys were spilled out into the countryside because it was considered too dangerous to stay in the centre of London. So all the fagging, the uniform and mortar boards disappeared. The whole scene vanished and the boys were evacuated to Lancing College. We became cuckoos in the nest of another public school, and we had all sorts of ups and downs there. It was rather like people sharing a kitchen. Then we were told: 'Nothing much is happening, let's go back to London.' So off we went with our great tin trunks, arriving back just as the first bombs of the blitz fell. So we couldn't settle back: the Phoney War had ended and the school was about to be blitzed, including my dormitory with the forty graduated beds. So then, in 1940, the school went off to Exeter University by which time Michael Flanders and I were beginning to write funny songs together.

From Exeter we moved again to Bromyard where great country houses had been taken over for the school; and we'd bike from house to house along the long hills of Worcestershire to continue with school activities. Even then I began to realise what a survival thing war was, that we were continuing our intellectual education and studying Goethe in the midst of world upheaval. I went to have music lessons from Sir Ivor Atkins in Worcester cathedral. We called him 'Saliva'. In this new environment it felt a vastly different school, and the boys, masters and monitors suddenly seemed to become more egalitarian. By this time I had grown to be one of the senior boys, and I remember how we voted out corporal punishment in our last year. It was our own little bit of pioneering according to our consciences. At this time I began to acquire my pacifist convictions.

When I stop and think about it, thanks to Tony Benn and others like him, there always was a rebellious streak at Westminster. Our world was never completely stratified by the monitors, lessons and peculiar customs. We all sensed the world beyond was a very different place, and knew we were going to have to learn much more. Although I laugh and joke about Westminster, there is a part of me deeply enthralled by it. But it was time to say: 'Goodbye to all this – I'm going off on my own safari.' That's what I did.

4 Can You Fight War with Peace?

I laugh ashamedly at the end of the last chapter. There stands the schoolboy 'going off on his own safari'. My own? The world was blowing itself up. The safari was not shooting leopards, it was a civil war among the nations, the second in my family's lifetime. However, like my father and mother I was able, up to a point, to select my own footsteps.

I've mentioned my hatred of violence and how this related to my parents' experiences of World War I in Russia. When it came to public school, I never adapted to the ethos that a beating should be given for the slightest misdemeanour, and I managed not to get beaten. Three years of solid evasion, presumably funking to do brave and rash things. If I've boasted that when I became a monitor I helped vote out beating, I also vividly remember that I didn't want to join the boxing bouts. I had a real reluctance to get in a fight. Had I reached the crossroads of cowardice and an impossible dream of a better world?

Then came the issue of the Officers' Training Corps, the OTC, which most schools – certainly all the major public schools – had then. By that time I knew where I stood. I just loathed the idea of being a young soldier, and I knew I wouldn't do it. I refused to join and opted instead for the Boy Scouts, hence my 'countryside badge'! There is a wonderful story of the day a general came to inspect the OTC. One of our King's Scholars, a very eccentric boy, put his PT shorts on and ran in front of the general during the inspection. Heresy! King's Scholars then had a tradition by which no master was allowed to go into a certain part of the school; so the boy ran to seek refuge there, clung to the horns of

65

the altar, and had to be winkled out by other means, after which he bargained with the Headmaster. We thought it marvellous that someone had cheeked a general. Later, somebody saw the general's report where he wrote that Westminster OTC resembled 'Popski's Private Army'. It would have been around this time that the 'King and Country' resolution was passed, at Oxford, where many of us were bound, and I remember it as a time of intense turmoil and extreme excitement with lots of debates, discussions and visiting speakers on the theme of whether or not it was right to fight for King and country.

My developing pacifism was not just physical and psychological, it was also political. We're talking about the period of 1936–39 and there was a lot of hard news about the place. Look where we were! Right next door to the House of Commons. We had radios, and there was always gloom: Mussolini, Hitler, the Anschluss, Czechoslovakia and all the other things were coming thick and fast. I remember vividly the pile-up of most disastrous news and a sense of impending doom and catastrophe; and the very helpless feeling that something had to be done about it. But what?

There I was, a scholarship boy in this wonderful school but the whole thing was disintegrating. And Germany! My father was a fluent German speaker with many German connections, and so German things were really fascinating to us; and this was all falling apart. I remember the relief I felt when Chamberlain returned from Munich with his piece of paper, but I think I also felt that very probably there would be another war in any case. It's as though we were all on a spinning compass of impossible decisions. I'd got one brooding inside me; Chamberlain had another brooding inside him. What would I have done if I'd been sitting in his shoes? Would I have shaken hands with Hitler?

At least one of my relatives knew a great deal about Germany because he was of German extraction and was violently anti-Nazi. I was not unaware of the pogroms and of the rising brutality and bestiality of Germany. That's where it really hurt: was I going to

66

go out and fight them, or was I not? If you decide that you are not going to fight and kill your enemy, even when he's evil and horrible, you've got something to think over, haven't you? The intruder's going to come smashing through your door, and you don't know how you'll react. At such dark times, I turned to the piano for solace, and remember playing and playing during the last months leading up to the war.

At this time my sister Marion, older than me by two and a half years, was growing strongly in ideas. A member of the Peace Pledge Union at fourteen or fifteen, she was shocked by the Spanish civil war and collected for the children of Barcelona. I shared in the rising horror of fascism and agonised as to the correct response. I had not realised, until she recently told me, that we were all to go on a family holiday to Spain in about 1936, but it was cancelled owing to the civil war. We went to Germany instead. In a few pages I describe an incident from that holiday. Later, my sister married Bert Stern, a Jewish German refugee and learned to speak German fluently. When as an act of conscience she left pacifism to join the ATS – Auxiliary Territorial Service – we debated this intensely. (As siblings? Yes. As Ideology? Yes.)

Marion has become an enlightened magistrate and her views arrived at by socialism and a deep humanitarianism; and mine, arrived at by a glimpse of pacifist Christianity, have been massively equated by our experiences of life. It is as though our family 'Russian-ness' led us to two parallel and complementary paths. I would add as a postscript that I'm talking about 1936–37 and only now has it sunk into my mind through reading Nadedzda Mandalstam's *Hope Against Hope*, how these years were the height of the Soviet purges, the years of the total incarceration and terrorisation of the Russian people by their leaders. How, how were two idealistic Anglo-Russian teenagers to assimilate the enormity of Hitler, Franco, *and* Stalin? It occurs to me that we took our 'A' levels in evil . . .

There is also a religious dimension to my pacifism. Or course it's very much part of the Christian Pacifists' curriculum vitae

67

that you have to know your Bible texts; what you'll do about the line: 'I come to bring not peace but a sword.' And what did Christ say to the centurion? I think by that time I was working my position out; but I was coming to the conclusion that Christ was number one non-violent person. He made that point very clearly during his last days – he didn't bring in the legion of angels to defend himself, but knuckled down and turned the other cheek. But this was not the prevailing mood of 1939.

I remember the announcement of war and the air-raid siren that immediately sounded and became the most vivid aural memory of that year. By the time the school was evacuated, I knew what I really felt. My point of view was found, which was a great relief, and I changed abruptly from being very intellectual about it to being rather practical. I remember going about with a pacifist demeanour and asking questions such as: 'Shall I wear a gas mask? or 'Ought I to go into the shelters?' I was always drawing back because, somewhere along the line, I sensed I would get more unpopular. There was no persecution of pacifists at Westminster, but nevertheless I was driven into a corner. The Headmaster was disapproving especially when we objected to things like the Home Guard, saying: 'All this stuff and nonsense. Why do you do it?' The debate did get pretty fraught, but the small group of pacifists stood firm. You'd think that with this terrible Nazi onslaught: blitzkrieg through the low countries, the fall of France and then the blitz, we'd have a few second thoughts at least, but there was no wavering whatsoever. I suppose too, we were very, very busy; always on the move, running around doing chores like carrying water from the well. The food changed too. All very primitive, but some very good like the dried egg – I was riveted by that. I remember incredible cold at Lancing College – and chilblains. It was there we were all issued with gas masks. One of the Lancing masters had a lisp. We wrote on the blackboard before he came in: 'A gath mathk ith not a toy.'

It was during the school's evacuation to Exeter that Michael Flanders suggested doing a revue called *Go To It!* – one of the great slogans of the war. His mother actually wrote a song with the line 'Go to it, that's the order of the day!' I was known to be one of the school pianists who could extemporise on hymns so he asked me to accompany the show, with his mother playing the violin. This was our first collaboration. Michael played most of the parts, and dear old Tony Benn was the stage manager. I think he's rather proud of that. He appeared on a *This Is Your Life* television programme for Michael and recalled it.

Michael, of course, was not disabled then. He was already extremely funny and it was in *Go To It!* he emerged with a first example of verbal felicitousness. In 'The Quartermaster's Store' there is a line:

> My eyes are dim I cannot see,
> I have not brought my specs with me.

Michael rewrote this as:

> He cannot see his eyes are dim,
> He has not brought his specs with him.

Gerald Cooper, song-writer at the piano, was the professional guest artist in *Go To It!* He has his own felicitous line in a 'Spanish Fandango':

> I've been bursting to do a Bolero all night,
> He said: 'Straight down the passage and first to the right.'

There were some very funny skits about news reporting and suchlike, but it wasn't acutely political. Maybe Michael was already showing his ability to keep things humorous and lively without being intensively involved in politics.

Rather daringly, we moved the show up from school in Exeter to The Everyman theatre at Hampstead during the first full week of the blitz. There was an air raid just at the end of the show, and I spent all of one night in the nearby Hampstead shelter. Apart from the Revudeville of 'We Never Closed' fame, ('we never clothed' was another lisp joke of the time) we were the only show on in London. Everything else had shut.

I was glad to think I'd found a role at the piano, to be part of giving some entertainment right in the middle of all the horror of war. I felt that I was 'going to it' in my own odd sort of way.

Back in the Walworth Road I experienced the first of the London blitzes. My father, being a doctor, was on call all day and all night. Surely, as a healthy sixteen-year-old I could have been doing something useful, down the shelters, for instance? But whether it was the public school ethos or just getting on with life, I knew I had to go back for next term. Isn't it strange? All over Europe children stopped thinking they were children at all, and they got on with what was immediately around them; but I only started worthwhile practical work when I joined an ambulance unit a year later. But in 1940 I was simply following the school year. I was listening to a great deal of music too. It seems weird, listening to music while bombs are falling on your home. But that's what happened.

Another preoccupation during wartime was my rite of passage from school to university. I managed to get a 'closed' exhibition to Christ Church, Oxford. Later I learnt that the music professor, Dr Armstrong (now Lord Armstrong) had actually failed me on a full music scholarship, but thought my playing sufficiently interesting (a 'Disney extemporisation') to recommend this scholarship by which Westminster helped me financially. I doubt whether I could have attended Oxford otherwise.

John Christie was Headmaster of Westminster at that time. He was very authoritarian and many disliked him, but on the whole I admired him, although he frightened me. On my last day of school I remember going to see him and told him that, as a pacifist, I would be a conscientious objector. He strongly disapproved, and made his feelings very clear.

My father was immensely pleased about Oxford. It pleased him greatly that I was still working along the lines of being baptised, confirmed, attending public school and now Christ Church – all the 'good' things. All along he was puzzled by my rising conscientious objection. He once told me his bank manager was embarrassed. I'm wondering what his relations with the bank manager were? We were never rich. Maybe he wanted the bank manager to think that I was a model son; that he might feel there was something odd going on, that this youngster, as well as getting the exhibition and playing the piano, was somehow managing to feel very uncomfortable about the war.

I had what's called 'a wartime year' in Oxford. Oxford was very depleted. One of my earliest memories of the place is walking into a room and a youth complaining: 'We're finished.' I said 'What do you mean, "we're finished"?' He said 'the aristocracy'. Of course they weren't finished, but he wasn't to know that.

Michael Flanders was a student too. He was a keen actor, doing very well. He joined all the political societies – Conservative, Liberal and Labour – in order to act with their drama groups. One of my close friends was the marvellous detective writer Edmund Crispin whose real name was Bruce Montgomery. He was also a composer and very fine piano player. We played together on two pianos. There is no question about it, war or no war, I was deeply involved with my music now, and loved it.

I was also deep in the study of my home language, Russian. It had got very rusty but now it was brought back to life again. All of a sudden, I discovered that the Russian writers had a message for me. Being able to read *War and Peace* and *Anna Karenina* at last in Russian, I met for the first time the pacifist Tolstoy – what a treat! To me this was double-truth pacifism: an intensity of purpose combined with historical perspective. Here was a violent country that had thrown my family out, turning up a Peace Pledge Union point of view. I liked his way of life, attitude to his serfs, his whole Christian ethic. I took it all on board. I still think it's incredible that there were Russians who could think so deeply about non-violence. It's not what they're basically known for when you think of it.

All through my pacifist experience I've had the support of others who've felt the same way. They were relatively few in number (but never less than one in ten!) but we would meet and discuss things, and this helped enormously as I was made to feel very uncomfortable at times. I was certainly called a coward and accused of being utterly idealistic, as though I'd got some imaginative picture over and against the realists. I remember the insistence on certain questions like: 'What would you do if they raped your sister?' I would wrap up my arguments, in this case, with something like: 'Who knows how I'd react, but I certainly wouldn't go and bomb the rapist's wife.' Then they'd quote gobbets from the Bible which illustrated Christ the 'tiger', and it seemed to me that you can interpret these things in very different ways to suit different views. My essential conviction is that nothing is achieved by meeting violence with violence, most especially in the hideousness of war. There is another way.

All this deeply affected me. It made me feel as though I was pinned back in some way, that I was diminished into some sort of minority. This is still with me. Being the one in ten means your vote is never going to mean much. As a result, I was trying to develop a belief system, a philosophy that the little man at the end has something to say, that the rodents can topple the world. But it wasn't pleasant, no, certainly not, because some of my friends were joining up and were about to go to very dangerous places and even get killed. I sensed there was something I could probably do in a non-violent way. I wanted to find a position where I could say: 'I'm going to do something at least as brave as you lot.' I was ready and eager to participate in a non-violent, humanitarian war effort, and sketched in my mind the possibility that I would find a recognisable stance and status. I had a sure glimpse of it. So my war year at Oxford was mixed: the joy of study and music, a terrible bleakness with all the young men going or gone; and, of course, the approach of my own conscription.

I knew what I had to do when the time came: turn up at some office and register as a conscientious objector. This seemed straightforward. I then had to wait until called before a tribunal which would judge my case. This was going to be a moment of considerable importance and I tried to prepare myself as best I could. I had a long discussion with the Dean of Christ

Church about pacifism, and he gave me a supportive letter for the tribunal as a result of it. I also discussed it with my father and friends. Donald Soper, a prominent Methodist pacifist preacher, gave me an hour of his time. I'd already heard his sermons and thought they were quite something. I suppose my pacifism was always associated with doubt: 'Why am I doing it? What is it all about? Is it a dreadful thing?' Then to discover that people like Donald Soper were so confident and open minded about it, and that they'd all sing a few hymns and enjoy themselves whilst debating these vital issues, was very reassuring. Donald Soper was up at Speakers' Corner uttering prophetic oratory, with a gift for repartee, very English and funny.

During this time of waiting I was working out my statement for the tribunal and rehearsing it in my mind so that I could respond to questions; and getting worked up about the whole business. My statement was about two pages, and the Christian witness featured strongly. I said: 'Christ would never sanction a war', and gave evidence from his teachings to support this. When I think of it, it seems to me that repeatedly referring to Jesus is name-dropping. It's something that Sydney Carter is always talking about; he wishes Christ was anonymous. But he does sound good when you produce him out of a hat, doesn't he? On the other hand, Christ would not have sanctioned the war. I wanted to follow his path.

I mentioned my belief that had there been enough pacifists in Germany in the early thirties who totally refused to go along with the Nazis, things would have worked out very differently. I'd been in Germany before the war with my father, and I'd seen signs like: 'Speed limit thirty miles an hour. Jews may drive at seventy miles an hour'! We knew what anti-Semitism was. I remember my father protesting about that sign saying: 'Why don't you see that sign is taken down. It's anti-Semitic!' And being told by someone in the hotel: 'Oh we wouldn't like to interfere; that's put up by the authorities.'

To me, pacifism involves conscientious objection to cruelty at all points, and I pointed out that this was one way in which

Hitler could have been stopped. I hope I would have done my own small bit, and then I would have become a casualty of my own little non-violent war, chopped up by a Nazi gauleiter, or maybe put into a camp or prison, but I would have fought my war by non-violent resistance to Nazi ideology and practices. It seemed to me that for three or four years I'd already fought a few wars in my own little corner, and I explained that we all had a part to play to stop this ceaseless round of violence, and I did not believe that nations should war against each other, and those of us who are inter-racial and inter-faith should just get on with life and love each other rather than become martyrs to our tribal hostilities.

The final part of my statement was that I had no objections to working in hospitals. That sounds as though I'd tracked my pacifism towards my father's position. Although I had no form of training, I very much wanted to do something to help. And this brings me to the wisdom of the World War II position of the British Government *vis-à-vis* the conscientious objector: if you were willing to do something to help, this was approved. So I was never an absolutist, I was always ready to do something – though not to join the forces.

So much for my statement. I remember wondering what to wear, and the train journey to Reading where the tribunal was held, and the tremendous emotional upsurge I felt. It was like the high peak of adolescence, the point where every youth says to society, and indeed to his father: 'I won't do it your way.'

The tribunal took place in a council chamber with the judges seated behind a large rostrum. There were three or four of these formal-looking faces, judges and prelates, whose values I shunned. One could bet that one was a brigadier or colonel or something – the sort of person I had learnt to fear. Later I was to come to terms with army people and realise they were human, but at the time I was scared of their attitude and thought they were bound not to understand.

There seemed to be people around who looked as though they were ready to help if problems arose. I remember it as a very frightening occasion; I feel nervous as I think about it. Paradoxically, my few letters of support, including the one from the Dean, made me feel quite guilty. It occurred to me that Christ at his tribunal had no letter from any Dean at all.

All the conscientious objectors sat in a row and were called for questioning. We each had about ten minutes to put our case. I don't think I actually had the question about the raping of my sister, but something very near it which I coped with. On the whole it seemed to go reasonably well, and I didn't feel too badly about what they said. When I think about it, they had an impossible task. How can you judge the sincerity of a person's conscience? I recognise now how arrogant I was: I was judging them. I didn't believe they had any status at all, that they were basically wrong, and had allowed themselves to be brainwashed into an impossible situation. There was another world I was trying to create. They knew nothing about it, and didn't seem to want to know.

When I look back on this I think they were very reasonable, and did a good job. The result of all this blood, toil, tears and sweat (you see, I too quote Churchill; we all did) is that I was given exemption on the condition that I went into hospital work. I got a small card which said 'This person is a conscientious objector'. This was wonderful. It was almost like a passport, and it gave me some status in wartime society which was a great relief.

I must tell you about the man who followed me in the dock. I always picture this chap in a striped apron and straw boater because he said he was a butcher. His only statement was: 'You're all murderers. I won't do anything for you.' I'm sure I must be telescoping all this. They must have asked him some simple questions, but that's all I remember, and it struck me very forcibly. He was virtually inarticulate. His way of expressing himself was to shout and this riveted my imagination completely, because it was so dramatic. He was overt and aggressive; it appealed to me enormously. His objection was at once dismissed by the tribunal but fortunately he was swept up by the representative of the Central Board for Conscientious

75

Objectors who organised an appeal for him and presumably helped him to present a better case.

Very much later, when giving a peace concert on the Isle of Wight, I met a butcher who was a long-term pacifist. He was very active, always ringing up places, like the *Pravda* offices in Moscow, to object. He was a real eccentric who'd lived a lifetime as a practising butcher and keen pacifist. He might even have been that man. I marvel at the story of these two butchers, who slew animals for a job but stayed their hands at humans.

I was immensely glad the tribunal was over. Of course, it was an important stage in my career. I was launched into a new pattern, off to start work in hospitals. Everything was going to change.

At this time one of my pacifist friends, John Corsellis, told me about the Friends' Ambulance Unit, the FAU. This was formed in World War I to provide ambulance and medical services in Europe, to alleviate the suffering caused by war. It had been re-formed at the start of the Second World War with the same aim. Not all members were Quakers, but all shared Quaker ideas about peace, war and reconciliation – a pacifist stance.

John extolled the FAU and told me how it had training camps and offered a whole way of life. The idea of being part of a unit of like-minded people was very appealing. To actually belong, to have a name and a place – this was something quite different from being the isolated individual puzzling about the rights and wrongs of it all. If I had to be a hospital porter, it seemed a good idea to do this in the FAU. So, along with other young men and women who were also seeking non-violent ways of participating in the war efforts, I joined the FAU, and in doing so experienced a tremendous sense of relief.

The FAU had a huge concern that youngsters who felt as I did would have a role to play, and from the beginning it seemed willing to work with the army and have parallel units, but under its own aegis. The attitude was: 'We won't take orders from army officers, but will be pleased to co-operate and work in

76

designated areas, especially ambulance and relief work.' With the truly global nature of World War II, this meant service in many different countries including places like Ethiopia, China, Palestine and Greece, where, to my delight, I was to end my FAU service.

You can imagine the smiles returning to the faces of my father and many of my friends. I was in a recognisable unit; eventually, even wearing a uniform with a flash on it. Absolutists were very disapproving of this. It looked too much like collaboration with the war machine, and of course it was. But to its members, the unit was typical of that war when all sorts of apparently ill-associated people worked together because, as the war developed, civilians and the fighting services were both victims. We were there to alleviate suffering, and face the 'arduous and dangerous' alongside the rest of humanity, and it didn't matter whether those in need were civilians or servicemen. We had a real job to do. This cheered me up a great deal. I'd found a place, and a role.

I had to face an appeal tribunal in order to get a variation in conditions to join the FAU. This was held in Birmingham and what a difference! Instead of having to cope with my seething mass of emotions, a very nice person, Michael Cadbury, a commandant of the FAU camp, spoke on my behalf: 'We have spoken to Donald Swann and would like him to join the Friends' Ambulance Unit. Please may he do so?' Their acceptance was more or less a rubber stamp. It was an appeal with a smile on its face.

That was the beginning of a partnership with people who were in the war effort good and strong; and I went off to train in a camp, called Manor Farm, on the outskirts of Birmingham. We lived in converted cow sheds in very primitive conditions, and did our basic training there. For me this was a breakthrough. Suddenly I was living with a most interesting mix of people from all walks of life. After a very sheltered life at public school and university, it was like a breeze of fresh air. I also met Quakers for the first time. The whole ethos of the unit was very democratic.

77

Although we had ranks – section leader, camp commandant – there wasn't anything at all military about the unit, no barking or shouting orders and we certainly didn't salute anyone.

We had physical training, running around a nearby lake. We also went on route marches, which sounds a bit odd. I think the idea was that as we would be linked to the army as ambulance auxiliaries, the time might come when we'd have to march from point 'A' to point 'B', and when men march, they march, they don't walk. So, it would be extremely embarrassing if all these conchies shambled about and couldn't make it; so we learnt how to put the left foot before the right. We weren't all that good at it, but we did our best and marched up and down Northfield Road, Birmingham. The FAU aimed to be co-operative because that apparently was the nature of the contract the Quakers had made with the armed forces. They said: 'We'll get our members to a point where everybody's ready to do whatever you say: if they've got to fly anywhere or be pushed into a boat they'll do it. If they can't swim, they will swim. If you want ambulance workers, they will do that; if you want cooking done, somebody will know how to cook. And they can put all their belongings into a kitbag and tie it up without making too much of a mess.' So all these skills were imparted to us and we coped as best we could.

As for our medical training, at this point it didn't go much beyond home nursing and first aid, the usual splint and pressure points, all rudimentary stuff; and we passed the authorised courses in it. But it proved very helpful when I went off, after this period of training, to work as a porter and orderly in Orpington, at a branch of Guy's Hospital. I did most of the things menials do when working in hospitals and learnt all about the institutional life. We were all scared of matron. In those days matrons really were awful. Of course, we had reason to be scared because some of us were severely impractical, and suddenly having to do neat sheets and suchlike was a real challenge. This was a time when hospitals had very strong regimentation. Some of the doctors were extremely fierce and you could easily feel humiliated by them. Our attitude was to try to get on with everybody, but some consultants were repellently dictatorial. We had really rough times on the ward if we were being bullied: that part was pretty bad. I asked a nurse in St Thomas's hospital recently whether matrons were still frightening. She said: 'We've got twelve now!' What a wonderful solution.

But we learnt quickly. I was a mortuary trolley operator for a while; and then, most interesting of all, I worked in an operating theatre for about four months and saw most of the operations. I was the one who pushed the patients in, and took them back to their wards, then washed the theatre out after the operations. That experience has been extremely helpful to me whenever I've had an operation, because I can imagine it all, and have less fears.

Perhaps the thing I remember most vividly was bathing the elderly 'chronics', the ailing and sick men on Ward Nine, right up at the top of the hospital. We each had to bath about nine a week. These were very, very sick people who couldn't move; we had to lift them out of their night-shirts and put them naked on to a trolley, then take them to the bathroom and bath them. Some could hardly speak and most were incontinent. We really feared this, I think we could only do it because we were in a group and had group support. We'd tell each other things that happened to have a bit of a laugh about it – joking was a way of coping. That was my introduction to the chronically sick old people of the world. What a hard finishing to life that is, lying in beds very close to each other without privacy. I found it extremely difficult and don't know that I'd find it any easier now.

What a contrast with my former life. Imagine the change from studying Lamartine and Gogol to suddenly finding I had to shave the pubic hair of a man with an open razor! I was petrified. I was sure I would kill him. Nobody had given us lessons on how to use such an instrument, but I had to do it. I remember I rang my father and asked him how to operate this dreadful thing, and I nearly gave up altogether. I could have cut off his vital organ. The patient was a very fierce military chap but, in the end, he took pity on me and together we coped. But it was very awkward indeed and a far cry from the delights of Tolstoy.

Interestingly, when the patients found out we were conchies they weren't concerned. We experienced no hostility at all. We never minded the name conchies. In fact this is what we felt ourselves to be, it was our jokey name. A medical passport is probably one of the most wonderful things. If you just lift your finger and become involved in the nursing situation, everybody relaxes. The patients, military as well as civilian, were just glad there were people around who could produce a bed pan or have a chat. We got along with the nurses, and struck up a few friendships which helped. For me, this was the beginning of my entente with army people. I now knew I could talk to them.

Also, it was wonderful to have fourteen or so fellow pacifists – men and women – around you. If we experienced confrontation during the day, in the evening, back in our quarters, we'd have a laugh about it. This sense of unit identity was crucial; and I have since read stories of FAU members, not to mention personal friends, who say their lives were completely changed by it. I can't exaggerate the number of skills and unexpected things we learnt. I remember, in what used to be a lunatic asylum – now called a mental hospital – I learnt how to run a sort of intercom system. To an egghead, the acquisition of any practical skill is a solace. Also, it was this sense of being partners in an enormous enterprise and the fact that we'd got this conscience thing beat at last, instead of it being a nagging, worrying thing. It suddenly occurred to me that I was released from being a musician. What a relief not to have to worry about piano practice, not to have to write essays. Now everything was sorted out and nurse would tell us what to do. I am convinced that in all this there was a pattern and a purpose. Is this surely not the way things will be? If the world gets worse and worse, there may be more and more ambulance and relief units and humanitarian involvement.

But can you understand why I was aware that this was a very

comfortable place to be? I was not in prison, as I once feared I might be, but in a good position doing useful work. Yet the war was continuing, ideas were still flowing and somehow, we were outside the main conflict; not wholly, as we were still arguing and debating, but in a way cocooned. But this was another cocoon that was to burst because, when we started working abroad, sometimes our position was very vulnerable, and we had to speak up and defend it.

My opportunity for overseas service came in 1943. This meant a further training camp called Mount Waltham in Netherhall Gardens, Hampstead, where we were taught European history and International Relations. Our Quaker tutors really wanted to brief us on the people and situations we'd meet, and some very interesting people turned up as tutors. We were joined by the Friends' Relief Service (FRS), another branch of the Quaker relief work, with rather stricter limits on their activities in wartime than the FAU. Although we'd had FAU women in the hospitals there seemed to be more of them waiting to go overseas mainly as nurses and relief workers. I was delighted about this. The whole quality of our work was improved by their expertise and sensitivity. We knew that we'd be going right into the thick of contemporary history, to countries where people had lived under occupation forces. What was going to happen when they were liberated? What state would they be in? What would they need? This is where we'd come in: we were to go in after the army to help the civilian victims of war as others are doing at this very moment.

They said there was a chance of going to Greece, so I started learning modern Greek too. My tutor was a marvellous man, a Greek poet, Demetrios Kapetanakis. There were a lot of stranded intellectuals at that time, especially in Hampstead, and they were recruited by the ever-imaginative Quakers.

As well as learning Greek, I learnt how to cook for eighty people. Tucked away in my files, I still have recipes for cooking beans and soups for eighty. I've never managed to whittle it down to one, but I certainly know how to handle a large group and cope with huge tureens and cauldrons. I received more medical training so that I could handle more complex cases. We also learnt how to dig latrines, and this also came in handy. The emphasis now was on practical training and we had very little PT and no route marches at all. At this stage, I was expecting to serve as an interpreter and ambulance driver. I already knew how to drive, but was to get a much more sophisticated course when I arrived in the Middle East. When I look back on it, I remember it as a most interesting course; and perhaps the most important lesson was learning how to be a functioning member of a team of twenty, and how to work with the army.

Eventually I was told 'It's the Middle East and Greece for you' and I went through the attendant excitement of going on a huge troop-ship, one of the big liners, the *Stirling Castle*. We had no idea of our status. We certainly were not privates, nor were we officers. But we were very much with the army – fifty conchies right in the midst of a couple of thousand troops. The army was rather baffled by us and gave us the rank of NCOs. Some of the troops were getting used to the fact that they were now having to mix with people from the Red Cross, and Save the Children, but others hadn't met our like before.

I remember one extraordinary incident. One of the soldiers was a very dab hand at the guitar and started playing; of course, we pricked up our ears, but when we started listening to the words, they were the rudest songs you've ever heard. Imagine us, this bunch of conscientious objectors, listening and wondering whether we ought to laugh. The songs were so filthy, we didn't know whether it was right or wrong to listen. So we had a section meeting on the subject – good Quaker stuff. Should we laugh, or not? If we did, was this collaborating? It is hilarious to recall. Yet this problem does not go away. If you find yourself in a funny, filthy play, do you laugh or walk out? Generally we in our Quaker unit eschewed explicit language and swear words but we were not prudes. One FAU wag, Paul Townsend, paraphrased the FAU motto 'Availability, continuity and intelligent co-operation', as 'Availability, contiguity, and intelligent copulation'; and when

'Blanco', a jokey warrant officer on the *Stirling Castle*, called our Hallam Tennyson 'Oscar-fucking-Wilde' for reading *Dante's Inferno* in the original Italian on his bunk at night, I admired the word-play.

We had two weeks on board. It was pure adventure being on a troop-ship. We went through the Mediterranean and eventually arrived in Cairo. I learnt a great deal about the army, and being with them made me grateful for the FAU: for example, for our friendly leader, Lewis Waddilove, with whom we shared our thoughts. I felt that we had the better deal, and the troops were going to have a far rougher time. Some of them would even go to the front, whereas we would be kept out of a shooting area. I could see they always acted under orders. Whatever they were told to do, they had to do it. They couldn't argue or discuss the rights and wrongs of it as we did, and that seemed pretty hard too. There was a certain resentment among some of us towards the army, but towards the end of that journey it was wearing off. We were learning to make friends with people who didn't necessarily share our point of view – vital for the work ahead of us in Egypt, Palestine and Greece.

5 Across the Sinai Desert, Palestine, and Greece

We did another short stint of training at Maadi camp, just outside Cairo. Apart from the magic of being in a desert area, my main impressions of that time are seeing some dancing Dervishes, and driving at speed through the Dead City, a prohibited area where to stop was forbidden. We learnt how to drive near the pyramids. I wrote home about this. They thought I was driving *up* the pyramids, but I told them they were too steep, it was *round* the pyramids. On the top of the big pyramid of Giza I read Shakespeare's sonnets at night with the same Hallam Tennyson. We thought we heard a ghost – a strange shivering – but it was probably a slight wind.

I remember too walking in and out of mosques, and being appalled by the gruelling poverty of the people. Now that I had some awareness of disease and illness, I recognised that a great many were walking about with trachoma, dysentry, malaria and TB. This led to some very animated discussions on the theme: 'Why are we fighting a war in Europe when right here there are people around us suffering anything up to eight diseases? Why don't we get our ambulances out and take them to the villages around Cairo to help these people?' They were living in mud huts, often washed away with the floods of the Nile. But we were told: 'Oh, there's no answer to all that! You're involved in quite another predicament.' But our instinct was spot on: if the British army had managed to sort out the Egyptians, they wouldn't have experienced Suez in 1956. But we could do nothing – that was the way it was. We lived among the Arabs, but remained aloof. Look what is happening today in the Gulf, as I write in early 1991, as a result of this!

Then came the exciting moment when we went off in our three tonners across the Sinai desert to Nuseirat camp in the Gaza strip, as it's now called. Unable to speak Arabic, we each got an eight-egg omelette at Ismailiya by mistake. Our brief was to work as an ambulance and relief unit for a host of Greek refugees who had been driven off their Dodecanese Islands by Germans and by starvation. From places like Rhodes, Kos, Karpathos and Symi they arrived in Turkey and tracked their way through Turkey and Syria, eventually ending up in Palestine where the British Mandate looked after them.

Nuseirat is on the Mediterranean coast in desert-like country, with the big Arab town of Gaza a little to the north. The camp was enormous, mostly canvas, but with a few wooden huts arranged in three main sections, housing about three thousand refugees who lived in family units unless they were single people. They shared tents or huts. There was a large mess for the refugees and special places where the military and our group ate. The army was responsible for the overall administration and security. Relief workers, including the FAU, were responsible for welfare, cooking and registration. There was always so much to do to keep this huge camp going and all our training came into use. Certainly those of us who'd been taught how to dig latrines at last got their chance.

As young men and women this was a thrilling experience. I could speak a fair amount of Greek by then, and suddenly realised what a wonderful thing had happened to me. As interpreter, I could actually talk and learn from the refugees. I was also registration officer and had to find out who they were and how they came there, and their immediate needs. I would say things like: 'He is the grandfather of this family. He is called Mr Karakalbakis. He is a civil servant on his island. I think he needs extra food to build him up . . .' In this way I became a personnel officer and that was the sort of work I was eventually to do all the way through the war. It was social work in an international atmosphere. Because there were a lot of refugee women with nothing to do, I started to run sewing workshops. I went off to Gaza for needles, threads and materials and a very efficient Greek woman organised the women into making dresses and other things.

So, in time, things got more organised. I suppose in Africa and famine areas, people are still striving to do the same thing. If you're a long-term refugee, you need something useful to do. Sometimes there would be terrible rain and the tents would get washed away, then all the practical refugees would scurry around, sweeping out the mud, making the place whole again. There are always lots of sick people in refugee camps, and they would be helped by the FAU medical people.

I think I was very privileged in having the opportunity of getting to know these Greeks and hearing their fascinating stories. Why didn't I marry a Greek girl? They were so attractive, singing and dancing, teaching me songs, teaching me Greek. But some of us felt that our emotional life had been totally eaten up by the war. It was as though we became creatures of conviction rather than human love. But I did fall in love with their music, and soon it became part of my whole system. I began to know it, sing it, play it on my guitar, and it fertilised my whole experience. After a while it came to me that I was learning everything I wanted to know. I was forgetting Oxford and Russian studies. It was just as if this whole life took over. In the midst of this refugee camp there was an immense music party. I even went to Jerusalem and bought a piano. I was given a hundred Palestinian pounds to pay for it and brought it back on the truck. Here I was at the piano again, music was coming back to me: folk-music, camp music, silly ditties, songs from the troops. There was also a Greek actor who did imitations, some of them very funny. Once a one-legged shadow puppeteer came with his shadow puppets. The Greeks called him 'the devil' and he told fascinating, haunting stories with Lord Byron as a central character. This art form is called 'Karakiosis', and Karakiosis is a Greek figure who always wins out against his oppressors.

86

Add to all this the Sinai desert with camels moving in the distance, and the stars so close to the horizon. It was pure magic to me. Quakers in the unit would hold silent meetings of worship in the desert. Sometimes I'd attend: they'd last about ten or fifteen minutes, and it would be quite wonderful to sit in the quiet of such a timeless place where so many religions had been formed. I can't think of a better place for meditation and prayer. As I write there is incessant talk of desert war. I can remember desert peace.

We had a lot to do and often the responsibility seemed overwhelming. We were only lads. I had my twenty-first birthday at Nuseirat. I only mentioned it after midnight when it was over, and thus had a beautifully silent celebration. There were risks of picking up serious illnesses in those parts, and I contracted amoebic dysentry which wasn't too good. Although I love the Greeks, they're not the easiest of people to organise: every man is a leader and they're all politicians. You couldn't get them to queue. Once there was a great clothes distribution – huge bales arrived. I had the job of handing them out, and tried to do it fairly, but it was sheer chaos with everyone pulling and grabbing, with a real risk of riot. Instead of organising themselves, they left it all to us. Later I was told by colleagues who had worked with Yugoslavs in Italy, that there it was exactly the opposite: everything was worked out to a 'T' by the Yugoslavs, the people moving like a brigade. This was inconceivable to the individualistic Greeks.

As we got to know them better we'd discuss our pacifist stance with them. As Greeks, they found it pretty difficult to take in, but I think they understood dimly that we were people who were not interested in killing and violence, and they rather liked that. But the idea that somebody could say: 'I will not fight a war' is very difficult for the Greek mind to understand. On the whole, it was the case that if the opportunity arose for a bust-up, they would have one. I've had some very interesting discussions with Greeks about Quakerism, and they don't find it easy. Sometimes they made me feel that my pacifism was a bit English Protestant.

When it came to their culture, the Greek Orthodox mind is linked with the Greek nationalists, and the story of their modern history is fighting the Turks, or living resentfully under their yoke as a subject race. It wasn't surprising that the idea was alien to them.

Most of the time we got on well with the army with whom we were co-operating. But there were moments of strain. For instance, we were supposed to salute them, and we actually saluted. Can you imagine it? But some of our men just couldn't do it, or they did it so badly that they were reprimanded. There were times when we looked very raggety, and that was just not good enough for the military who were in overall charge. I recall another time when a small group refused to stand up for the National Anthem, and they were put on a charge for this terrible thing. Generally, in those days, you did stand up for the National Anthem. In army circles it would seem like an insult not to do so. For my part, I think I'd stand up without worrying too much about it.

I remember certain individual arguments. On one long journey with a staff sergeant, we went into details of the dilemma. I asked him exactly how many men he'd killed, and what he was prepared to do in battle situations. He told me, and I told him exactly what I wouldn't do. It was mutually revealing and very interesting. Essentially, he couldn't understand conscientious objection at all, and he despaired of my point of view. He believed the army was there for the right reasons; the idea of passing up an order of any sort was really unthinkable, which it is really. Once you're in the armed forces, you've got to do what they tell you. Whereas our point of view was that we had our individual responsibility to stand by our convictions at all times. There was this whole idea of living with a conscience and to go on living with it. It's a permanent partner; a quiet, second identity that goes along with you. Willing to discuss a different view, at that time I felt nevertheless two hundred percent certain of my own view. My pacifism was deeply reaffirmed. There was so much to do in a world of great need. It seemed to me there was a very big war against want that we were fighting. We had our own battle.

During my spell of working with the army, far from thinking they were all bullies, I'd learnt to respect many of them. Many questioned their position and suffered crises of conscience and deep despair. There have been times in later years when I've felt that some of the most pacific people I know are in the army. When you think of it, they are the ones who strive to keep the peace, and are ready to suffer and die for it. In many circumstances they stand between warring factions. They seek a reasoned world, where you can at least order people to do something, rather than the maniacal world of total anarchy. Indeed, paradoxically, some of them have worked very hard for the Peace Movement, especially in the nuclear age. Brigadier Michael Harbottle and the Generals For Peace movement is an example. During the Cold War years of the past decade, he drew the military from East and West together in a continuing dialogue. And how about the ex-servicemen's campaign against nuclear war?

From time to time in Palestine, we'd get leave and visit the biblical sites. This greatly expanded my experience. In a very important discussion with a Quaker from the Friends' School in Ramallah, I became aware that in this area of the world, there was always a north, an Assyria or Syria, and always a south, Egypt. Now, as before, the Jews were in the middle having forced the Canaanites out. I was fascinated by these 'invaded' peoples of old Palestine. I even heard that in the region where Goliath was slain, they'd recently found skeletons of very long men. But in their land of milk and honey, what were the Jews going to do? Their usual solution was to fight either the north or south. Christ's answer was to fight neither. Until they learnt their answer from him, they would have no peace.

It was during my first visit to Jerusalem, where I was recuperating from amoebic dysentry, that I had a vision of Christ walking behind me as though he had appeared especially to confirm my belief. I had just seen the whole of the Jericho valley from the top of the Mount of Olives during the most beautiful red sunset. Russian Orthodox music was issuing mellifluously out of the convent on the hill. I felt totally moved and uplifted. The effect of this vision lasted three months. In the camp I felt exalted as though I was living in a new dimension. I would wake up in the morning with this wonderful feeling of Christ's presence in the tent. I think I was really blessed. The more I think about this experience, the more I realise my illness was an important factor: it's often the case that extraordinary lightness comes over you as you emerge from the dark of sickness.

But why am I there in this refugee camp in Palestine? It's basically Hitler's gun. Pushed out of England by a war I'm totally against, where have I arrived? In a most extraordinary place where the dividends are piling up. The sick people of my world are no longer chronics that I have to bath, but eloquent Greeks who are teaching me a completely new language. As though that wasn't enough they were turning me into a composer. It was this great gap in my previous musical life that enabled my mind to go quiet. Listening to these rhapsodic Greek melodies, I cast off the shackles of being worried about whether I could play Mozart and Beethoven, and just let the music well up from inside me. So these Greek refugees gave me a new life. I was a relief worker, small fry, true, but my service was to them. Yet it worked out that their service to me was infinitely greater and was to change my life completely. Add to that the glowing experience of living in Palestine, I think I met one of the best of human paradoxes.

It might appear that I related much more to the Greeks than to my own unit. In a way this is true. As well as their Dodecanese songs and dancing, they were always talking about the sea and boats and of their islands. I began to dream of these islands myself. I longed for Kos and Karpathos. This wish was soon granted, as my desert magic was coming to an end. The refugees were preparing for home. The German occupation of Greece too was nearing its end – this was in late 1944. So we of the FAU got in our trucks and hurtled back across the Sinai desert; the same camels looking at us from a distance, the same old Mount Sinai with the monastery on top. Back to the pyramids and Cairo; experienced and confident young men ready for a bit of further training in Maadi camp, then the delights and dangers of Greece and its islands.

I boarded a boat in Alexandria, crowded with Greeks returning to their islands. Most of them were bound for Karpathos, one of the twelve Dodecanese Islands lying offshore from Turkey. For me it was Kasos, a much smaller island near to the southern tip of Karpathos:

> Far, far off in a distant southern sea
> There is an island on which breakers fling,
> Throwing gigantic waves against the scree,
> Encircling the island with a ring
> Of surging foam.

That's how I saw Kasos first and described it later. But a better poet, Homer, also spoke of Kasos as an island surrounded by foam. I fell in love with it and on my best nights it returns to me.

The British army had for a few months fed the entire population, and this is still remembered. Now relief workers were coming, and I was one. The main problems we dealt with on Kasos were not too dissimilar to those of the camp. As interpreter and registration officer, I'd go round with the Section Leader and explain what people were saying, or requesting. Often it was the case that several houses had collapsed, so they needed bricks and materials to prop the houses up. Sometimes it was a food question. How much had they got? What could we distribute? Who would get most of it? Were the children in special need? There are hardly any roads on Kasos so there wasn't a great need for motor transport, but ships were a different matter. Would they come? Would there be enough supplies?

Most people had suffered from the German occupation: they would tell of the murder of the mayor, or the time when the Germans shot a whole village. But, generally, the Dodecanese Islands had not been through the traumas of the mainland.

Mainly it was hunger that drove the islanders in their tiny caiques over to Turkey, perhaps only fifteen to twenty miles; then the long trek down the Middle Eastern seaboard. Also, it seemed that they didn't want to dwell on the bad times; they were trying to discover what could be salvaged and how to go forward. There was an extraordinary atmosphere of relief. People were excited and pleased to be home.

I was only on Kasos for ten days, then I was sent to Karpathos, the bigger island nearby. The first thing I did was to bury somebody. I think I was in charge of getting wood, when an undertaker was required. I remember too a clothes distribution. These would have been clothes from the West. There were all sorts of things, some useful, others not, but everything seemed welcome to people who had nothing.

After a few months in Karpathos I went to Rhodes, the biggest island with all the wonderful crusader castles. There I became hospital almoner and got the chance to meet the patients as they arrived. I would watch these beautiful people coming in. I remember one girl came in with a tiny baby, and she looked just like a madonna, the perfect image.

I loved being on the islands. The beautiful hills leading down to the sea, something to look at almost every hour of the day. People were living out in the open. I remember we took one old man back to his home in an ambulance. When we asked him where he wanted to be dropped off, he said: 'Under the tree, under the tree.' That's where he lived. Of course, with the wonderful climate in Greece, it is possible to live under a tree. It's not quite the same as sleeping rough in Stepney or Waterloo.

The people were singing folk-songs of great interest and depth: wedding-songs, work-songs and laments. Cecil Sharp and Vaughan Williams would have given their right hands to be there. Even now I have a printed book of the songs. They are incredibly complex, and you have to be erudite even to annotate them, so we're not talking about the Greek equivalent to 'Knees up Mother Brown' or 'You are My Sunshine'; although I learnt

Greek popular songs too, accompanying myself on a guitar made by an Italian prisoner-of-war out of a wooden box. The frets were made from a toothbrush. Later at Oxford I was to study modern Greek folk-song and discover the influence of Ancient and Byzantine Greece on them. One folk-song I brought back attracted the keen interest of my professor, John Mavrogordato. It is a dialogue between a villager and a dead man under the tombstone. I keep singing it now. Because of its mysterious poignancy, it is the most consoling song I know. A lot of the songs were extremely violent: they would sing anti-Turkish songs telling of how they cut Turks' heads off and stuck them on poles, in 1821. It seemed terrible to me to have war stories rejoiced and feasted over. Most of their best songs were to do with war and fighting; and they never tired of retelling dramas of sacrifice and martyrdom. I'd say to them: 'Why can't you relax? You got rid of the Turks; now you've got rid of the Germans and your job is to make friends with other nations and see if you can make peace as well as war.'

There was an extraordinary experience when I went to bring an old lady from the countryside to the town of Rhodes. She thought I was a Turk. Evidently she hadn't been into town since 1910 and there had indeed been Turks about then. Since that time, as I've said, there had been Italians, Germans and now the British. She had no idea how all this had happened; so many different occupations had bemused her. I was stunned. I had a similar experience in the village of Ramallah outside Jerusalem. I visited a Quaker school there on several different occasions: once when the children were technically British, once when they were Jordanians, and once when they were West Bank Palestinians. Each time I visited, they seemed like the same children, sitting in the same classroom. Surely there is more to the world than occupations? And if we go back to Nuseirat camp in Palestine: before our Greeks there were Poles, after the troubles in Palestine, the Arabs moved in and are there to this very day – the homeless Palestinians, really long-term refugees. One of the most extraordinary experiences I've ever had was to return to that camp for a television programme twenty-five years later and start filming the place where I had actually been a refugee worker. It was then I saw yet another lot of refugees. Ironic and pitiful.

I was still on Rhodes when the war in Europe ended, and was in a camp called Efialtis, which is the Greek for nightmare, when I heard about the atom bomb. I was as far from Nagasaki and Hiroshima mentally as I've ever been in my life. More immediate to me was the sight of my first banana for years. I took a boat out to a Turkish ship in the bay. The sailor gave me a banana. I was overawed. Our war had ended. I remember feeling that somewhere a long way off statesmen were trying to work out the peace.

In the early post-war period I moved from the Dodecanese to join another FAU unit in north Greece. I was in Igoumenitsa in Epirus near the Albanian border, still doing relief work, but now, as the FAU were beginning to pull their people out, I came under the wing of United Nations Relief and Rehabilitation, or UNRRA, as it was known. It was exactly the same work but I changed my uniform from khaki to blue and got a bit of money in the process, (whereas the FAU provided pocket money only). The sojourn in Igoumenitsa lasted a year and was enthralling. I was immersed in the language, the surrounding hills and the people.

Apart from my relief work, I had a most extraordinary time travelling through these hills making a census of the villages. They were romantic, evocative places. Ancient mosques and destroyed empty houses from which those Turks who had collaborated with the Germans had fled. Also the Turks had been landlords of the area so were often much loathed. But I would go to these empty places, listing the numbers of families there had been, getting the information from the villagers, discovering when the Turko-Albanians had left, how and why. This document must be unique, as it took me months to compile. But when I finally delivered it, it was just buried. The topic was too sensitive. But I knew in detail how the houses were burnt and who killed whom. It was a sobering experience. About forty to sixty per cent of the villages had been burnt out in Epirus, mostly at the time of the German retreat.

How did it all end? One day, as I visited the Albanian border with some people from the UN, I flung my arms wide embracing the countryside around me which had been home to so many different races – Albanian, Greeks, Turks, Bulgars, Romanians, Vlachs – and exclaimed: 'What a beautiful thing it would be if this were all one country! Surely we all are one!' This remark was taken down by a Greek soldier and sent to headquarters. A note was sent back to UNRRA saying: 'Mr Donald Swann is a corrupting influence and is making dangerous remarks and ought to be relieved of his post.' Was this the end of my war service, pitched out for believing that the world was one? I left. At this moment Albanians are crossing the same frontier, in the same place and uttering the same remarks.

I'm pausing to wonder at our FAU contribution to the Greek refugee situation. It seems to me, after the agony and misery they'd endured, we were the lucky ones who carried the news that there was a better world. As English eccentrics, very different from army personnel with our civilian talk and behaviour, we could have presented a quietening and pleasant influence reminding them of calmer years. That, I am sure, was our contribution. I hope there are still people like us working and saying: 'Yes, the world can and should be one.' In a more practical sense, along with other relief organisations, we helped to produce the welfare and other assistance they so desperately needed. Even so, I'm sure if you asked any FAU member about this, they'd stress how important and formative this experience was in their lives, and I know that many have remained in touch with Greeks they met during the war, as I have; and one of our group, obviously without emotional hang-ups, married a Greek girl.

For me, the importance and influence of this period on my life cannot be exaggerated. It was crucial. To begin with, I learnt that music comes from within. I guess it was my mother's streak of folk-song coming out. The music I was going to compose was growing inside me. It was like an inner well. The Greeks struck this for me. It was deep and going to last – to last for ever. Withdrawal from the musical culture that I'd been brought up with gave me the key. And yet, when the time came, I was ready to go home.

My journey home, now 1946, was through Italy – Brindisi, then Rome and a long train journey – the last time I was to travel on a Movement Order. On the boat from Dieppe to England I saw a queue, and it reduced me to tears. I had forgotten that people stood in an orderly line for anything instead of squeezing up in a great crowd like the Greeks, and wondered whether the British had become so well organised and mannered because of all the deprivations and the hardships. This was just one of my first impressions.

I found my father living in a new home in Richmond. He had remarried, a musical lady called Irene Bonnett, at the beginning of the war. They seemed very pleased to see me back. I had a tiny room at the top of the house, with a piano. I felt very uprooted at first. I wondered: where are the olive trees? The sheep with the bells around their necks? The ouzo – where is it? My service in the FAU was of great interest to my father. We'd had some wonderful correspondence. When you think, it was an experience in common. As a socialist, he was very happy that Attlee and company had been voted in. So was I. I'm among those who think this was one of the best times for this country. There was a great surge of hope: the introduction of the National Health Service, the New Education Act. There was so much to believe in. It was wonderful. I'm rooting for those times again.

I had been released from the war under the category 'B' release – this was for students who'd interrupted courses to enter the war. So back I went to Oxford to pick up threads of my studies. It was most uncanny returning to post-war Oxford.

Other Oxford contemporaries have written about this. There were large numbers of undergraduates, the whole place was much busier because everybody was returning together. The Oxford I'd left had been a pretty bleak, beleaguered, bereft sort of place; now it was much more of a going concern. There was a great deal of laughter. Lots of mature students, wearing their bum-freezer gowns and wandering back from breakfast with pots of marmalade in their hands. What a contrast to their war experience! Some had been in charge of battleships or bombers or in the line. We were different, yet the same people. I had grown up, and no longer worried about who was, or wasn't an aristocrat. When you think of it, the aristocracy had been working in the shelters, the WVS, Home Guard. They'd been right through the whole, huge experience. Things had changed, but they were not finished!

We soon found the same friends and started almost where we'd left off. In my case I added modern Greek to Russian studies thinking it would be a good idea to study the language I'd learnt orally. There was a lot of tension in that: to read poems and write essays for tutorials on a subject I'd previously been speaking in a demotic manner, whilst wandering around the hills and listening to folk-songs. I never resolved that. But my mind was running with a further experience; I started writing many songs of my own. Now, when I play the Greek tunes it all comes back: the islands, the sea, retsina (the marvellous Greek wine that tastes of turpentine), and the extraordinary way every Greek family treats Lord Byron as a personal relation. But at that time I started meeting new theatrical friends. There was a lot of fun now – we were all beginning to enjoy ourselves.

With all this fun, music, and university revues, how on earth did I get down to an exploration of the rightness and wrongness of my pacifism? Somewhere along the line, maybe because lots of ex-servicemen were my chums, I began to wonder whether I'd made a terrible mistake and that I had gone into the whole pacifist thing because of some sort of psychological error. Maybe, because I didn't want to clonk the next boy at school, I'd made a philosophy out of it and had given myself five years of conscientious objection. I was worried that I'd just been a coward and thought therefore I ought to recant. I remember getting really worked up about this and turned to Theo Cadoux, a friend of mine. He'd also been in the FAU and was about to become a professional philosopher. He was able to think this through for me and suggested I met his father, Dr C J Cadoux who had written a book called *Christian Pacifism*. He analysed the whole thing from A to Z.

This book is the only scientific exploration of conscientious objection I've read. All the different styles of conflicts from big wars to little skirmishes are analysed, and he lists all the different grades of reaction the individual can take in a fascinating table. Starting from the most mild, if somebody tried to burgle your house, you could say: 'Please come in; I'd like you to have a cup of tea', and then persuade the burglar of his error. This might be called the 'ultimate welcome'. The next would be barring the door and saying: 'Please go home', but to take no further action. Then on and on until you hide under the bed; then ringing up the police, bringing up the whole question of the use of police force. Then continuing up to the point where you beat him. The next stage: you might kill him, if he's attacking you, of course. Then further on, the vendetta. You say: 'Ah! because he's harmed me, I'll retaliate on his whole family.' Finally, because of the escalation the whole thing becomes a *casus belli*: there is a war, and you blow up his relations.

All this fascinated me. I began to tick off at which point I functioned. My position was, and is, that I would want the police to intervene. But I've always believed in the dream that if you don't arm yourself to the teeth, you might have more time to worry about the people who've got nothing to be burgled about, who have no food, who are dying of dysentry or something equally vile. Why not get on with their war – their war against want? So I began to feel that even if I had, in a sense, been a coward in the war, my witness and relief work was in its own way important, and that I would like others to continue

98

with it. So I eventually relaxed and joined the Fellowship of Reconciliation, the first peace body I consciously joined after the war. From that time I tried to become a useful member of this group. Eventually I wrote them some music and a valuable partnership began.

But since that time I have felt that doubt is the very corollary of faith. I remember somebody asking Bishop Neill at the Christian Mission, Oxford, at this time: 'How can I believe in God if I doubt so much?' To which the bishop answered 'I don't know of any Christian who doesn't doubt eight times a day.' I now believe doubt is an essential part of any faith.

When I compare my war experience with other conchies, I think I was clearly lucky. I'd had a good war. I met some who'd been in prison, and some who had worked down the mines and had a relatively boring time. As well, of course, many of my ex-soldier friends had some very rough times indeed. Some were wounded. But on meeting them in Oxford I never experienced any unpleasantness or hostility from anyone. People were immensely tolerant of each other.

I learnt too that many of my military friends had experienced a crisis of conscience. Others had contracted disabling diseases, including Michael Flanders, my friend from school whom I met again on the last day of my time in Oxford, sitting in a wheelchair in an audience where I was playing the guitar on stage in Ben Jonson's *Epicoene*. He'd been disabled through polio while in the navy. At the time I was wearing doublet and hose, and he said he recognised me only because of my horn-rimmed spectacles.

Although I'd filled in applications for almost every job imaginable, including the BBC and Foreign Service, I realised at Oxford the emotional upsurge in songs was so important that I would have to live that life wherever it would take me. I remember going up to Michael and saying 'Do you remember the shows we did together at school? I'm now looking for a career. I've no idea what to do but do you think you could write a few words if I wrote a few tunes?' He agreed. That was the start of my next phase, and our partnership.

6 Words and Music Take Over

By the time I approached Michael that summer's day, 1948, in Worcester College gardens I had reached a state of mild despair. I hadn't got a job and was desperate to get started in my chosen career as a composer. By then I had already accompanied three revues by the gifted Sandy Wilson and his group of aspiring actor-singers. Although I'd been gaining a good Oxford-style musical and drama experience, I hadn't discovered an actively personal lyric writer with whom I could work to order. Seeing this gifted friend from my school life sitting there as large as life in an enormous wheelchair was quite wonderful. You could say it was the answer to a prayer. Looking back there's no doubt this was an historic moment for us. For several years after this meeting he was just one among many of my musical collaborators but our partnership became increasingly important and indeed before long we were to provide each other with the rent.

It was during my time at Oxford that I met Laurier Lister, a prominent theatre director and deviser. He had great grace in that an undergraduate could write to him and say 'Dear Mr Lister, I've written ten songs for a university revue, may I come and show them to you?' He bothered to reply, gave me a lovely meal with different cutlery for each course which impressed me a lot, and introduced me to his friend Max Adrian. They went through all my little pieces treating them with utmost respect. He immediately accepted five Greek songs, saying: 'We'll make them into an intimate revue item, a little "charm" section.' Suddenly I found that the things I held most precious from my wartime life were transformed into a West End revue item and I was collaborating with famous theatre people.

Sandy Wilson's revues were being performed in Oxford during my time there. He would choose Oxford titles like: *High, Broad and Corny* (the streets) and *Ritz, Regal and Super* (the cinemas) and attracted gifted performers, many of whom became well known. Kenneth Tynan, for instance, later a theatre critic, was then a brilliant mimic and sketch writer, full of witty ideas including those of his somewhat Godless philosophy, which shocked me, I must say. We were all somewhat in awe of him. John Shlesinger and Lindsay Anderson, both now film directors were then actors. I would be at the piano and found extemporising and accompanying them easy and enjoyable – I just loved it. My problems between the classical and the folk were being curiously sorted out by driving a line through the middle. Intimate revue music is a quasi-classical, quasi-folk mix and I was developing quite a strong middlebrow style through it. So we were a lively team and even got to the Playhouse Theatre in London at the end of our time together trying to inspire our London contacts with our 'brilliance'.

To remind me of the more serious side of university life, below me was the room of Dr Armstrong where he taught strict counterpoint to his pupils. Like my uncle Alfred, I managed to get a piano in my room and often I would get carried away with my compositions and play out of hours. Dr Armstrong would patiently come up and say: 'Do you think you could possibly play a bit quieter, I'm trying to teach counterpoint below.' We had great respect for each others' idioms but they were very different.

All this was a far cry from my wartime experience and the people I was now mixing with were very different from my FAU friends. There was also the challenge of balancing the mood of intimate revue work and my quieter, more introspective task of setting poems I was given to study to music. 'Miranda' was a setting of Constantine Palamas, a Greek poet who addresses the Miranda of Shakespeare's *The Tempest*, saying: 'Give me some of Prospero's magic; root out the Caliban in me and give me something of Ariel's magic.' I was enraptured with this intellectual love lyric and set it to music. Years later, in the revue *Drop of a Hat* I sang it every night for 700 nights. It was followed by a jokey Greek song which returned us to the prevailing mood of the show.

I remember another night in Oxford, just as I was going to bed, a friend suggested another poem to be set to music. It was a poem by Gérard de Nerval 'Je suis le ténébreux' – 'I am the shadowy one'. Very beautiful and symbolic, but impenetrable. It was years after I'd set it to music that I realised second and third meanings. I loved it and got carried away with it. I set it in a jazzy style and that too got into *Drop of a Hat*. People would laugh at this unexpected French song with whoops and strange cries in the middle of the light humour. One night the Cultural Attaché at the French embassy came to see the show. She came backstage saying it was the only thing she could understand, and how grateful she was that I'd set this poem by a French poet who was famous for walking around Paris with a lobster on a string. He too had his stories!

It was during my time in Oxford that I was introduced to John Betjeman and his poems. John Betjeman was an Oxford poet of an earlier generation. To set him to music was apposite because of the verbal, humane, as well as humorous aspect of his poetry. I eventually set seven poems for him, and Laurier Lister used one for *Oranges and Lemons* in the West End. After I'd left Oxford these Betjeman songs were published. John came to see me in my home in Battersea wearing a very striking and colourful waistcoat. He identified the architect of Battersea Polytechnic, which was right behind my room. I never realised this had an architect until he walked in! He was very friendly about the published songs, although he was diffident about my setting of the famous Joan Hunter Dunn because he really loved reading this himself. In his own recording, he reads it to background music, whereas I'd vocalised it and set it in an intensely lyrical Lieder style which he found slightly over-written.

This reminds me of a remark by my Greek professor about my setting of 'Miranda'. He too loved this poem and had translated it into English. When I played it to him he said: 'I don't think poetry set to music is a very good idea. Ever since Homer things have been going downhill.' What a wonderful thought. It's interesting in terms of words and music: Homer, poor old blind man, would sit strumming away and singing the Odyssey in a sort of rhapsodic, melodic way. But if you set Homer, Goethe or any other poet floridly with piano or orchestra the words are submerged because of the ornamental setting. So Professor Mavrogordato wasn't far wrong, and the folk-songs he idolised from Greece don't have that problem: the words float above the music. This is what John Betjeman recognised, the difference between a song setting and a spoken song. But I knew I was destined to set poems in the Lieder style and have continued to do so.

With Joan Hunter Dunn, the urge to set this to music came after meeting a girl momentarily at a ball in Lyme Regis. This was my first sight of the English Rose, and I was very stirred by her. At that time England was still new to me after Palestine and Greece. This girl encapsulated the beautiful countryside, and all the English places I had visited since my return, into a very romantic picture. John Betjeman also felt this: apparently he was working in the Ministry of Information and saw a wonderful girl going down a corridor and said: 'I bet she's a doctor's daughter from Camberley.' She was, and her name was Joan Hunter Dunn. He, of course, loved the word-play and wrote his poem. I sent her a copy after I'd set it – she was then living in Singapore.

Later, I had a lot of fun writing a song with John Betjeman about a lift girl. It was for a singer called Jenny Johnson who had a range of six or eight octaves. John Betjeman wrote the lyric which I set to music incorporating all these octaves which musically illustrated the lift going up and down. I've seen this printed as a poem but it was actually written for Jenny Johnson's song.

I didn't write many songs for the Oxford revues, but they'd singled me out as an accompanist as I've mentioned. I contributed odd items. One of them was called 'My Sister Ruth'; the lyric largely written by Paul Townsend, to my tune. But we all put lines into this. Eventually it was sung at the Dartington School of Music Summer School by a number of people including the philosopher C E M Joad who happened to be there doing a bit of music scholarship of all things. There was a line 'The watercress contractor from the sewage farm', and Joad sang 'The watercreth contractor from the thewage farm' which amused everybody very much. It's funny how there always seems to be a lisp joke. I suppose it's a feature of revues that you try to get illustrious or semi-illustrious people into them so they can get a bit of a laugh for the revue at their own expense.

Now that we're talking about lines, it seems strange but after the many settings by Sandy Wilson, the only song of his I can remember verbatim is a song about Horsa sung by Hengest:

> Has anyone here seen Horsa? H O R S A?
> He can be a scourge when he's got the urge
> And he's had it all this week . . .

There's another stanza which went:

> For rape and loot and pillage
> Make our invasions fun
> But rape at home in Jutland
> It simply isn't done!
> Oh . . . has anyone here seen Horsa . . .?

It was a little bit like *1066 and All That*. There were Horsa and Hengest out of our history books and suddenly alive, with music, dressing up in tunics, and everybody falling about with laughter. In this early post-war phase we were caught up with

104

a flippant mood of peace. Suddenly we were let off. We didn't have to worry about battleships, tanks and bombers or even about consciences. Sometimes the revues harked back to the war: there were funny sketches on the theme 'I can never forget I was in the Army, Navy, and RAF' with three chaps being very humorous about their war experiences. But generally it was the case that we were responding to the changing world around us. Remember we'd voted in a Labour Government, Churchill was on the back burner, suddenly it was possible to laugh. (If you like, that's a political statement!) There were still values strongly held, but we felt we could laugh at them and with them.

As I recollect this I realise how all my Oxford experiences fed into the area of light entertainment. That is what I was beginning to grow towards, gathering fragments, with or without music, that tell an episodic epigram. That is what intimate revue is about: a mix of epigrams and little songs which, when put together by a thoughtful and dynamic presenter, make up an interesting necklace where all these little jewels of numbers are balanced out. Laurier Lister enters the theatre history books as one of the most illustrious impresarios with impeccable taste and a wonderful sense of the visual. For some reason revues are not popular in the theatre now, although there are a lot of revue style radio programmes. *That Was The Week That Was*, on television in the sixties, offered a more astringent and bitter style but still with many little songs and sketches. And the Players' Theatre club puts on Victorian revue all the time. I love it and am still a member.

That was the context Michael Flanders emerged from, with an exceptionally strong verbal sense of punning and an ability to comment humorously on all the things he could see going on around him. Sandy had the same gift. He's become famous because of *The Boy Friend*, and it's as though he wrote precursors of it all the time we knew each other. He seemed to know the twenties style inside out. He even looked as if he came from that era, but he was exceptionally brilliant in revue and people have tried to persuade him to return to that genre. Having written *The Boy Friend* he continued to write musicals, but he's just told me that he is contemplating a revue revival.

The issue of literacy is very relevant to revue humour. I would say that the English are generally very literate. Some argue they're not, and they're becoming even less so, but I'd say there are a lot of people who have gone through O- and A-level English Lit. and History, and have laughed along with Flanders and myself. I've always strongly felt that not speaking down to audiences is very important. It became one of the main talking points when the unexpected success of the two-man *Drop of a Hat* turned up. The interviewers who flocked to see us would ask: 'What is it that makes people come to see this rather than the other things they could see?' We had to find answers, one of them always went back to this thing about literacy. Michael used to boast that we were the only entertainers who made jokes in Latin – not too many, but a few. If Michael was sitting here now, he'd make the point, I know, that audiences are usually underestimated.

There's another side to this. When the Royal family came to hear us for the first time (Prince Philip liked the Greek bit I remember) all the aristocracy followed for about three months. Michael used to joke that they laughed but couldn't understand a word of it. In one of the shows he said this publicly. 'Bang goes me Peerage!' he ruefully added. I can hear him saying it. We were aiming for the literate and educated audience, we found it and it kept the show going for eleven years.

I think our approach was a direct legacy of the Oxford experience I've been talking about; very different, incidentally, from the Red Brick university of the post-war period – the Jimmy Porter experience. That was another type of astringency and another type of humour coming up in those early post-war years. The Oxford tradition was still words, music and fantasy, exuding Christianity and Humanism, Carroll,

106

C S Lewis and Tolkien. I sound as though I'm speaking from some height, but Oxford and Cambridge certainly have been very strong influences on revues and, of course, the serious theatre as well: actors like Emlyn Williams, John Gielgud and many others graduated into the theatre through the universities. The curious thing is that Michael Flanders didn't get into that era. His disablement prevented him getting back to Oxford after the war, but he was doing other interesting things including broadcasting. He continued his links with the university and this is how he entered my professional life but on the back of all these other things that were happening to me.

People often ask me how I go about setting poems and lyrics to music. The lyric stands on the piano until I begin to penetrate it to the point of fascination. It goes into my mind and takes shape. At Oxford I would take a poem from my file – it could be Pushkin, Suckling or Froissart – I'd place it up on the piano and let the poet's intensity come out. Then I'd feel: good heavens, how he loved that girl! Or that the poet was lost or betrayed; and the betrayal would turn into a tune or harmony. It goes right inside you and you begin to make it your own, and begin to think: that's me too, I've been through this. You have to feel that. It differs from instrumental music because meaning is so crucial – the vital thing. I always keep words to the fore as I work on a piece. It is essentially to do with enhancing meaning through music, providing an infrastructure and a balance to a lyric.

Lots of people puzzle about the relationship of lyric and music. They say 'Which comes first, the words or the music?' as if it's to do with the A or the B. But usually it's the merging of A and B and the *idea* of the lyric: you've internalised its essence and it haunts you, then the memory twists it and turns it into something that appears as a song in front of you. It's a most ecstatic experience. It goes to the head and is addictive: once you've done it you want to do it again and again. Ask any song-writer and I'm sure they'll tell you the same thing. Collaborating with Michael Flanders was only different in that it was much more a 'cooking' process, done around the piano which became like the kitchen stove. We sat and worked at it, words and music growing together.

I ought to remind my readers that although I've gone on about this musical life at Oxford, for most of the day I was getting quite carried away with my Russian studies which included Old Slavonic as well as Russian theology – very complicated stuff. My Russian professor, Nicholas Zernov, was a very distinguished professor of Orthodoxy. Soon after I left college, I was playing for Maria Marten in a production by Alec Clunes in the Arts Theatre, London. There I was sitting in the pit playing the piano dressed as a gypsy. Like my father, I find it very embarrassing to dress up. Suddenly I noticed my distinguished professor had come to the show and sat right behind me. I was so transfixed by this I could hardly play. There he was with all his knowledge of Orthodox Russian religion, and here was I in a completely different world. It was a traumatic moment. I pondered its meaning.

I eventually concluded that you've got to be reborn in each experience. My professor was immersed in Russian Orthodoxy. I had been in that world but I'd entered another one, and to be a revue-writer, or song-writer, or any writer, is to be lost totally in another experience for a period of time. At that time I had re-set forty Victorian songs in the style of old Victorian music hall, and I was immersed in Victorian music. I've now learned that this process of loss and rebirth is both the most beautiful and the most painful experience. You get so caught up, as I was in Greece. How I ever left it, I can hardly understand. Then suddenly it's Oxford and revues, a new phase and I've got to believe in every little lyric. As the story unfolds into my long experience with Michael Flanders, it's more than most people can understand that eventually I wanted to break away. They can't understand that I was reborn in our shows, but also died in them.

The same thing happens with an individual song. It has life and strength but then begins to fade at some point, leaving a residue. If ever you look at it again, you might feel like playing it. Sometimes its residue still has meaning and feeling, but often it has gone from you. You are absorbed in the strange, haunting new experience that is turning itself into a new song. That, I think, is what song-writing is all about. I was going to have the good fortune of working with some excellent writers of revue: Arthur Macrae, for instance, very much in the style of Noël Coward, and with Alan Melville, the brilliant Brighton wit. But now I think it is time to track the strange way in which Michael's original lyrics and my music fitted together, and how gradually this partnership began to take over my other work.

When I left Oxford and told my father that I was going to try my luck as a composer he was sympathetic but baffled. What had a degree in Russian and modern Greek to do with music? Anyway my sole experience was accompanying Oxford undergraduate revues and setting a few poems. He just couldn't see where this could lead in a career and financial sense. I returned to the beautiful house in Richmond where Father and my stepmother were living, and they immediately hoisted yet another piano up the stairs to the drawing room. I had bought this out of my UNRRA money. Although we didn't need it at home, having a perfectly good piano there, my father bought it from me which made me feel a lot better as it paid the rent for about six months. I was totally without funds and sold practically everything I possessed: the flute that I could never play; and my stamp collection which I'd collected painfully, evaluating every stamp meticulously. I calculated £500 worth of stamps, but sold it for £7.50. My books went too, bar the Oxford books of verse, Russian, German and French – I clung to the polyglot. The whole of my youth disappeared. I felt rather good about this, thinking I'd purged myself as an academic. Now I'm excited about study and begin to feel like an academic once more, but at that time I felt that I'd pulled the plug on it and could now be lyrical and develop the inner well.

The Richmond home of my father and stepmother – 'Bunny' as she was known by all her friends – had a most wonderful musical atmosphere. She had been a pupil of Gustav Holst at St Paul's Girls' School and evidently, from letters she bequeathed me, they had a close pupil-teacher relationship. She was a violinist as well as a viola player, and my father and she had a host of musical friends. So, true, I came home and sold the trappings of my youth, but look what I got in exchange! A most wonderful musical home; and I found it was perfectly easy to invite any theatrical friend to Bunny's home.

Laurier Lister was a regular visitor. I mention him so many times, a gentle, devout man, member of the Bible Reading Fellowship. Not only was he courteous and helpful to young composers but to all actors and theatre people. At his lovely home in Sanderstead, Surrey, which he shared with Max Adrian, there was a stupendous garden. Laurier was a keen gardener and would laughingly tolerate my inability to tell one flower from another. As a producer and director he was meticulous and somewhat precious. Often in rehearsals he wore white gloves. Michael and I wrote a rhyme about him:

> Laurier Lister
> Is always called Mister,
> The man who produced Penny Plain.
> It's tasteful and clean
> And the staff of Roedean
> Have seen it again and again.
> I'd trust my sister
> To Laurier Lister,
> He'd never be caught in the bar.
> Producer, deviser, he'd not compromise her,
> L A U R I E R,
> That old L I S T E R.

(Tune to match)

Max Adrian and Joyce Grenfell often came with Laurier. Michael seldom came because it was easier for me to drift over to Hampstead Garden suburb where he lived, to write songs in the orbit of his mother. At this time I went out a great deal, taking in as much as I could of the theatre. But certainly in Bunny's home I was most wonderfully cared for and the Gerhard Adam piano which entered my life in the Elephant and Castle, and on which so many of my songs were written, was still there when she died in 1990. Funnily enough, when *Drop of a Hat* took off, I was so fond of the model that I chose a Gerhard Adam for the show. It was like having a friend on the stage. It's important to me to have familiar things around when I perform. This enables me to relax and feel at home. That's the mood of all the revues I've ever done: I'm at the piano and the music just grows out of it.

In that early post-Oxford stage I realised I could set virtually anything to music – the telephone directory, if anybody thought that would be interesting. The whole business, I was discovering, is something like tailoring, making suits. The most prosaic material can be set. Eventually I even set the Lord Chamberlain's theatre regulations to music and they turned out to be very funny. More of that later . . . The thing was that I was feeling confident. I could set anything and my job was to go on doing it.

Theatre people would ring up with requests or suggestions. There was Rose Hill, a beautiful soprano from Sadler's Wells. Laurier wanted to use her in a revue, could I write a song for a soprano? I rang Michael and we talked about it, all the possibilities, and he came up with a lyric about a soprano who was tone deaf but nobody knew because her accompanist fed her with a key when she got lost. The idea seemed good so we got working on it writing little sections. Then Rose would come along and say she liked this, but couldn't we change that. Laurier would come in to encourage us saying it was going to be marvellous. Then, in the style of the time, when the song was worked out, incredible attention would be given to it: a wonderful costume, props if needed, and its position in the revue. Rose would rehearse it for weeks and when everything was ready, she would do that item and a few others.

For us this meant we had a song in a West End Revue. When the royalties came in, six to eight per cent was divided between the authors. On a point system, if the show included one three-minute song, it became a section of your percentage – six per cent in the first period of a show, then if the show lasted, eight per cent. In those days it might be one to three pounds a week on any one song; so if you had five or six you had twenty pounds, which in the fifties meant I could cover all my expenses and pay rent to my father. I was also beginning to pay my own little bits of income tax. The first time I met my accountant he said: 'I expect you spend about £1300 annually on entertainment.' He assumed that theatre people spent nearly all their time drinking champagne out of slippers, and the rest of it walking around the park getting inspiration, which meant claims for shoe leather. I wish it could have stayed so simple. Later I was to get muddled by my finances – the more I earned, the more worried I became. An awful confession, but true. But in those early days it was rather more blissful. Just a little coming in, but enough. I think I was enormously lucky. Thanks to Laurier Lister and another fine revue producer called William Chappell, I was given a good start.

I'd like to put in a word for all free-lancers. Although I recognise the inherent insecurity, it's a glorious freedom being at the beckoning of your inward mind rather than some employer. Whatever comes into your mind, providing there is an opportunity to fulfil it, you can do so because you are free. That is the world I have always relished. I like to feel fresh and ready to start on the next idea as it comes through the door, which is why the long runs of the 'Hat' shows were rather disturbing for me.

What else? I would ring up distinguished artists to try to place my work. I remember a long talk with Hermione Gingold, telling her I had a lot of things she might care to use. Like all theatre people she was very helpful, and told me to send her a few to look at. She was then playing in a series of revues called *Sweet and Low, Sweeter and Lower* – all very popular. She never actually did anything about my material but I was gradually getting to know people like her and some of them used my songs. I set some of Joyce Grenfell's lyrics, mostly in the style of musical parody, and she performed them for many years. All this was very enjoyable and profitable too in a mild but pleasant way.

Having produced songs, Laurier Lister would ask me to demonstrate them. I would visit the artists to play and sing the items through at the piano. So I was getting a lot of performing experience, and it has never left me: the feeling that the song become real if I can churn it out in some way; even if I can't sing it well, I can put it over. That was becoming my genre. I still do it, and love it. In this period of the early fifties, before *Drop of a Hat*, I wrote about 200 songs with Michael and most of these were demonstrated in the way I've described. In the next few years, in any one revue there might be seven or eight. In *Airs on a Shoestring* at the Royal Court, which ran for nearly two years, we had about thirteen songs. Gradually our stock was increased. We had them filed in alphabetical order and we were always ready to pull them out of the hat, as it were. 'Always ready to perform at the drop of a hat' was our motto, even in those days before we ever thought of putting on our own show.

We never considered publication of these songs because, essentially, they were written for live theatrical use. But very soon we met Ian Wallace. A friend of mine introduced us; he was then getting known as an entertainer as well as an opera singer. He lived not far away in north London and asked if we could write him something for a Glyndebourne Green Room Rag. We had a chorus about a Hippopotamus on the file. I say 'we' but actually it was entirely Michael's piece at that stage. He was driving down to Brighton one day and found himself whistling this song – words and music, the lot. That rather annoyed me because I liked to write all the music, but every so often he had a good tune. 'Mud, mud, glorious mud!' it went, based on 'Beer, beer, glorious beer!' Not a song everybody is singing in the street now, but was generally known at the time. The tune is like a vamp, very simple and easy to remember.

We played this chorus to Ian Wallace and he liked it and felt the heavy animal suited him. So we purpose-wrote the verse which I put to music. It unexpectedly took off. He sang it to his Glyndebourne friends and they loved it. Suddenly we realised we'd got a very good audience among classical musicians. It was strange, because we were real middlebrow people, perhaps with highbrow taste. But the classical musicians became very good friends of ours and we often mingled in that set.

That song was immediately published by Chappells. We then proceeded to do the Warthog, the Whale and the Rhinoceros. We had this little bunch of animal songs coming out which were taken up by bass baritones like Ian Wallace who never failed to be a protagonist of our material, and still continues to be. Although I'm jumping ahead a bit, I must mention the song 'The Income Tax Inspector', one of the last songs we wrote for Ian which he has made entirely his own. Actually, it won an Ivor Novello award. I don't remember much about the award as I've never been one for such things, but I vividly recall one of the lines:

My stalwart pen is never lax

In the manuscript in my illegible script, two words were elided, so it read:

My stalwart penis never lax . . .

When confronted with this Ian was somewhat taken back. (Sorry, but my schoolboy humour never fades!) I think this and the bus conductor song are the only non-animal songs that Ian took from us then, but of course he knows them all. He gives his

114

autobiographical books titles like *Pardon Me If I Sing Mud*, or *Nothing Quite Like It*, all from the song with which he became wholly identified. On the opening night of *Drop of a Hat* in the West End he turned up in full costume from the Drury Lane show *Fanny*, next door, in order to lead the audience in our last song, the Hippo. That was the most marvellous tribute.

So the Hippopotamus song meant we started a connection with song publishing, but this was nowhere as important as the live, theatrical side which seemed much more real and interesting than sending things through the post to publishers. Michael came to write about twenty animal songs. Intriguing, because he wasn't a great animal lover. He never craved animals in his own home, but he would go to the zoo to see the gnus and reflect on them. I think this was more in the manner of Aesop or La Fontaine and others who treat animals in an anthropomorphic way, hinting at human foibles.

I'm a little shy of talking about my musicals but I always thought that I was going to write the next *Oklahoma*. It's the challenge of managing a consecutive piece from end to end and developing a story line. Whenever the chance came up, I would grab it. At the time of the Festival of Britain in 1951, I knew a lyric writer, Maurice Browning, from the Players' Theatre and for months we constructed a musical play, *The Bright Arcade*, about the 1851 Great Exhibition, Prince Albert's masterpiece. It was romantic and historical. There were lots of lyrics about the Great Glass Hive, as the palace of glass was called. *The Bright Arcade* was not put on then, but twenty years later it appeared as a beautiful television film in which Kenneth Corden used the actual exhibition sets taken from the Victoria and Albert Museum.

Sydney Carter, poet and folk-singer, was at that time in the Grays Inn Road, London, happily extolling in verse the dust-carts that rattled past at midnight, the discarded telephone kiosks and Coram's Fields. The Liverpool Spinners would sleep on his floor. Later were to come 'Lord of the Dance' and the miraculous songs of religious insight. Now both up to the hilt in song-writing, in the same Festival of Britain year, Sydney and I plunged into a romantic yet earthy musical, *Lucy and the Hunter*, set in Brighton 1843. Lucy, a dreamy sixteen-year-old, is guided into three dreams by Daniel Boone the Hunter, and she learns about the maturing of love through pain. In the dream she grows up. It is a New Year musical. One of the dreams takes place in Greece, where Lucy sees Lord Byron; one in medieval France and one on a Crimean battlefield, that is, a dream of the future. Was it a musical of the fifties? I believe yes, but not only. I've continued to perform its songs since then, very often with Bill Blezard, composer, arranger and pianist who is specially identified with this piece.

I am sure I have never written anything so tuneful or melodic, nor so near to folk-song. Sydney himself wrote several of his own tunes. The part of Lucy is for a modern Judy Garland. I projected myself into this young girl Lucy, as composers do, looking for inspiration in her half-formed dreams. I found it. At the first performance at the YWCA in London, Sydney played the role of the dancing bear in a skin. Another half-formed dream?

Laurier Lister helped me present a musical in the West End. Joyce and Reggie Grenfell put up the funds. This was *Wild Thyme*, with words by Philip Guard. But although it had a marvellous director, Wendy Toye, and none other than Ronald Searle for designer; and Denis Quilley, now a well-known actor, made one of his first appearances in this musical, it didn't run. It was all about one very hot summer's day during a wet English summer and how a beautiful romance develops out of this. Well, it came on in August 1955, during a tremendous heat wave: one summer that everyone was longing to end! So the climate killed it. Yet to this day I recall the total dedication of the cast. I have a stunning recording (on an old Soundmirror paper tape) of the last night at the Duke of York's Theatre. It sounds like a panegyric.

116

It was on the fifth Sunday of the seven-week run of *Wild Thyme*, that I was married to Janet Oxborrow whom I'd met at Dartington Summer School a year back. The whole cast came to our wedding reception in Battersea and Joyce Grenfell did the washing up.

Writing musicals is an exciting process. The vital thing is their dramatic structure, a story-line over and above the three-minute sequence; and room for the lyrical, humorous and all sorts of moods – a world in which you can bathe opposed to the quick splash of a song. Michael Flanders and I were besieged by those who thought we could write musicals, and I was certainly very keen. Somebody even gave us a title called 'The Wompom' about a strange plant or fruit that could make practically everything you needed. We spent hours working on the theme song, but this was the only item we produced and we sang it ourselves. Once I had an exciting idea for a musical about the navy, and after I'd spoken about my ideas to Michael for a couple of hours he wrote a rather rude song called 'Oh England, Trust Your Semen'. It was the only thing to come out of this huge conversation about the Royal Navy. He had a way of aphoristically encapsulating grand ideas into a few lines, and I think under his influence and that of being a personal performer, my development in musicals was deflected.

But maybe my time will come. It could be with *Mamahuhu*, the Chinese for 'could be', a musical conceived not so long ago in the heart of the Ohio countryside with my Quaker friends Mary and Evelyn about the 'could be' of love relationships. Yes, there is still *Mamahuhu*.

馬 馬 虎 虎

Not far up the road from Michael Flanders in Hampstead lived Gerard Hoffnung. How did I come to meet him? The revues had a pictorial side to them. Along with the words, music and actors there were backcloths. They're not too common today but you have to imagine someone singing on the stage with a huge ornamental backcloth behind illustrating the subject matter of the song. This would be changed for each song. When we wrote 'The Last of the Line', a song about the last tram, who would be the designer? Of course it had to be Rowland Emett who was wonderfully gifted in the Heath Robinson mechanical tradition; so his tramcloth was right behind the singers.

Ronald Searle was also well known then, and his grotesque schoolgirls were becoming famous. When a song was needed about St Trinians for *Airs on a Shoestring*, Michael and I wrote the song and Ronald produced a magnificent backcloth of the school. So the visual side was developing and, not being able to draw myself, I was enthralled at the sight of the words and music visualised. Because of this I came to know the Emett family well and they told me about Gerard Hoffnung who was making a name as a young cartoonist. I visited his exhibition at Piccadilly; he was wandering around and I introduced myself and we started talking about music, one of his side interests then, soon to become a major one alongside his cartoons. He met Michael and a very amusing side of our lives developed through our friendship. On one occasion Gerard was departing for a long trip abroad and, for some reason, had to spend the night in Mrs Flanders's home. He spent the night in a huge four-poster bed which was hardly ever used. She put in a stone hot-water bottle. Exactly at midnight the bed collapsed. Both the ends sort of folded over each other squashing Gerard and the stone hot-water bottle which broke. He made for his plane rather earlier than expected! Everything that happened to him was a strange sort of visual joke.

I got to know Gerard very well because I could exemplify some of his humorous ideas in music. On 10th November 1956, just before *Drop of a Hat*, he gave his first major concert at the Royal Festival Hall – the first ever Hoffnung Festival Concert. This was outstandingly successful: every ticket was sold within twenty minutes of it being advertised. I remember newspaper headlines outside: 'Rockets promised by Khrushchev!' It was the time of

Suez, the Hungarian uprising and the birth of my first child, Rachel: a dramatic time alongside which we were witnessing, in Gerard's show, something unique and very funny.

Hoffnung worked with a great many composers. He'd inspire them to work for him and we certainly enjoyed producing anything we thought would suit his eccentric musical form. At that time musicians hadn't laughed at each other very much. They did so privately, but not in public. He triggered the idea that if the best orchestras and musical performers got together to have a musical romp with specially prepared music, it could be a very special and enthralling night off for the musical public. The idea succeeded in his lifetime and continues to enthrall because his widow, Annetta, puts on Hoffnung concerts all over the world, and new music is being created in that genre by people not acquainted with Gerard.

In the original concert they played the only purely orchestral piece I've ever written, another version of Haydn's 'Surprise' Symphony. I simply put in a few extra surprises. It's still being played, and now they add even further surprises – pianos have children popping out of them, celestas are dropped from the roof – all sorts of jokes. As Haydn is dead, I get most of the royalties. Two of these concerts were put on in 1988 at the Festival Hall. In the first was Malcolm Arnold's wonderful Grand, Grand Overture in which his joke was to include vacuum cleaners. The nature of the promotion is that they get reasonably well-known people to participate. I got roped in for this one and played the Hoover along with Esther Rantzen, who turned out to have met Gerard as a schoolgirl. It was a strange experience, with memories from another time, but enjoyable. The second concert was particularly good, as it had quite a lot of new works written by some excellent composers including Wilfred Josephs. Not everybody approves of the musical clowning. Uncle Alfred came to the first concert in 1956 and was heard to say in the middle of it: 'Is this really necessary?' The fact that classical music was being ragged didn't appeal to him. In a way I think it's rather English: we like to see the funny side of any institution

119

– church, monarchy, you name it. Gerard's contribution was to do it outstandingly, in the visual as well as musical sense. His influence has continued right through my life.

It's time I mentioned my work with Henry Reed. He's known to many as a poet, particularly a very fine war poet – many will remember 'Naming Of Parts', and 'Unarmed Combat', I'm sure. As well as being a fine poet, he had a true gift for radio. He was commissioned by Douglas Cleverdon in the mid fifties to write a series of features for the Third Programme.

It is important to say something about Douglas, a gentlemanly, witty and extremely literate book publisher and radio producer, to whom respects and tributes have recently been pouring in after his death. Having published David Jones, and commissioned Dylan Thomas to write *Under Milk Wood* for radio, he had a similar galvanising effect on the poet Henry Reed and on all of us who worked for him. For many, he enshrined the very epitome of the Third Programme, now Radio 3.

The series of seven features Henry and Douglas collaborated on arose from a putative biography of a man called Richard Shewin, which included a cast of some fifteen characters connected with his life. Each feature presented a new development of this satirical and often very erudite story. One of the characters was a 'composeress' called Hilda Tablet. She was a bit of a send-up of Elizabeth Lutyens and, although a female character, of Benjamin Britten. Mary O'Farrell played Hilda Tablet and I was given the chance of 'realising' Hilda's music. Eventually, she nearly hijacked the whole series. She was an eccentric character who always wore tails for her main concerts. Henry got very keen on her and wrote another feature called *The Private Life of Hilda Tablet*.

I wrote and played songs and piano music for the radio series, but when Hilda Tablet composed an all-woman opera at Covent Garden called *Emily Butter*, I actually chalked up about twenty minutes of an operatic score. I did have a few problems with the music: Hilda Tablet wrote largely twelve-tone music, and I experienced some difficulty writing an atonal and twelve-tone

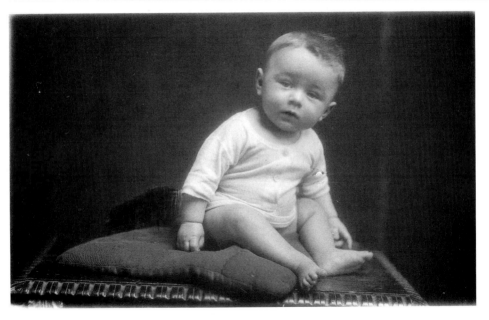

Little Dutzik in Llanelli, 1924.

First performance on any stage.
Anglo-Russian Club in Baron's Court, 1926.
I am front centre, sister Marion on my left.

Uncle Mohammed in action.

King's Scholars of Westminster School, 1938.
I am second left standing, no glasses.

My parents,
Herbert and
Naguimé Swann, 1930.

Three sisters,
(my mother's)
à la Chekhov.

Father and three uncles, young.

In later life, Freddie, Alfred, Herbert, Edgar.

Sunning myself on top of a hill in Corfu, 1945.

Middle-East Friends' Ambulance Unit 1944.
I am first on left in front row.

Top left: Going up to Christ Church, Oxford, with my father, 1941.
Top right: With Janet, Rachel and Natasha, 1960.
Below: More at home in the establishment.
With Archbishop Coggan in the early seventies.

Michael Flanders.

Posed pondering
with Michael.

Sydney
Carter
in his
'den'.

Donald
Swann
and the
Singers
in the
seventies.

Shall
I make
it into
serious
music?

score. Henry was most obliging and altered the story so that in the middle of this purported Covent Garden opera, the Consolidated Musicians' Union goes on strike, therefore leaving nothing but one piano. This suited me fine and the actors began to sing very melodic music because they couldn't stand Hilda Tablet anyway. He arranged it so that I could get back to my comfortable middlebrow style. This was a very fruitful episode for me and it has been a lasting experience. We were treated with the greatest respect by the BBC and there were constant repeats of the series. Humphrey Carpenter has revived it at a recent Cheltenham Literary Festival.

I used to beseech Henry to stop writing for radio and write a really good libretto for a musical. If anyone could do it, it would be him. But he loved broadcasting and I can understand this because there is something about radio which is quite different from the theatre. I'm just incredibly pleased that I had such a good collaboration. As well as the pleasure of working with such an outstanding cast of actors, it brought me through to the point where I had explored all that I could do with that imitative style.

So in these years 1948–56, Michael was but one among many other artists I collaborated with, although I was becoming increasingly aware that whenever we completed a song together it was always snapped up. My old school friend had become a very professional, viable partner. By the time the revue *Airs on a Shoestring* turned up we were getting more and more requests to write songs. It could be that our two-man show was inevitable.

7 The Birth of *At the Drop of a Hat*

The revue *Airs on a Shoestring*, in 1953, proved quite a milestone for our partnership. It was put on by Laurier Lister, starring Max Adrian, and was an outstanding success, running for two years at the Royal Court just before it became a modern-play theatre. *Penny Plain* and *Oranges and Lemons* were Laurier's earlier shows which Michael and I had written numbers for, but now we were asked to do far more. One was a parody of Benjamin Britten called 'Guide to Britten' which received very good notices and became widely quoted. One stanza went:

> A rising young composer, he published every spring
> An Olde English Folk Song for Peter Pears to sing.
> The judges at each festival
> Admired his *sinfonietta*,
> And voted it the best of all,
> They'd never heard a better.
> 'Twas applauded by the masses,
> The middle classes too,
> And even by the Harewoods and the County Set,
> Yes, even by the Doggy Doggy Few!

Max Adrian's acting wit was brilliant. He acted as conductor and there were four other dinner-jacketed singers performing this song. Britten was invited to the show but he never came. It was during this show that 'Last of the Line', our lament for the end of London trams, came in:

> Diving down the Kingsway Tunnel like the gaping jaws
> of hell
> To the river, where you'd give her all you'd got!

122

> Oh, the sight of sparks a-flying! Oh! the jangling of the
>   bell!
> Oh, the scent of wooden brake-blocks running hot!
>
> From Woolwich Park to Camberwell, from Highgate Hill
>   to Bow,
> On to Wapping, only stopping by request,
> Down a hill or round a bend we would drive at either end
> And we never knew which end we loved the best!
>
> L P T B
> Has signed your R I P,
> And here we mourn your passing down the line,
> Until some day
> We drive you through the Milky Way:
> Good-bye old Tram!
> They won't get us
> To drive their ruddy trolley-bus!
> Goodbye old Tram!

We also had another about a Sherpa who didn't want to go up
Everest: 'Everybody up Everest! Last one up's a Sherpa!' We
had a lot of laughs out of that show and I certainly derived a
lot of satisfaction from the large amount of composing I did for
it. At this stage Michael too would appear at the play-through
sessions for performers. For the first time we were presenting
our songs together.

A key point in our collaboration was when we performed in
Whistler's Ballroom in Cheyne Walk, in 1950. Michael wanted
to explore with me some new songs we'd written at the piano,
and it seemed a good idea to invite some friends along to listen.
Ian Wallace, Rose Hill and Peter Ustinov came too. John Amis
was helping us with the organisation, as he often did. There is a
lovely story of when he approached the very Chelsea gentleman
who ran the ballroom. 'How much do we have to pay for the hire
of the ballroom?' 'Ten guins.' the gentleman replied, meaning
ten guineas. John Amis's aside to me was, 'We always abrev.
It's a hab.'

So there I was with Michael for this one night. Those who
are still around remember it. He was exemplary in performing

his own stuff and the hundred or so audience seem to have loved it. But nobody thought that he was going to do it later, no one imagined that a chap in a wheelchair would go on stage. But he began to believe in himself again as a performer. It continued to be the case that our material was fed into revues. But this one-off performance increased our reputation as good chums who could present their material at the piano. We were beginning to get a name.

As a young bachelor, before my marriage to Janet, I had moved with Michael into a studio flat in Scarsdale Villas, Kensington. This was flat 1A where George Benson had once taught acting and singing. It was ideal for Michael because it was enormous, all on one floor, and devoid of furniture which meant he could whizz around on his wheelchair very happily. For a time I lived there, sleeping on a sort of parapet which I would climb up on at night. There was a precipitous drop of about twenty feet just by my bed. Having asked Michael to produce a huge, expensive blind to cover the vast window, I left after about three months, and moved next door. Michael needed assistance in the home and even had a real live butler for a few weeks. This butler left in a huff. His parting words were: 'This is the first position I have had where I am not delivered my own *Times*.'

We had another break when Laurier put on a complex revue, *Pay the Piper*, with elaborate sets and an orchestra, which toured for eighteen weeks and included a large number of artists. I remember the Warthog song was enacted in this revue: there were about twenty animals dancing about in the most amazing costumes – enormously expensive. I went to the dress rehearsal and I laughed at every line, but when the curtain went up nobody laughed at anything, and it ran for only two weeks in London to a severe lack of audiences. That is one of the reasons why eventually we began to sing the songs ourselves. It turned out that two men at a piano singing the same Warthog song could get a whole lot of laughs and amusement. Whereas twenty actor-animals prancing about distracted minds from the word-play and it didn't seem funny.

124

Somebody like Noël Coward, who was then flourishing, was functioning on two levels. He could do songs in a dinner jacket, but at the same time was exemplary at writing plays in which songs featured. We were much more song-writers at the piano, and were beginning to realise we could reach a maximum effect through sitting and playing. Nowadays you see composer-singers all the time, especially in the Pop scene, but then we seemed to be starting a new genre of being author-performers. Actors were looking askance at this new genre wondering what was going to happen to their jobs.

Certainly, I was getting the urge to perform my own material. Partly this was economic. Laurier went to live in America for a time and I began to feel out of a job. I remember writing a lengthy letter – illegible as usual – to Michael, then in Italy, outlining about twenty things we might do in the future. Item Seventeen was personal performance. At this point, Dartington Hall Summer School of Music comes into the story. I used to go down there with a trunkful of tunes and would persuade anyone who would listen to do something. Now these classical musicians liked to laugh. The Amadeus Quartet was there; John Amis, Alfred Deller the counter tenor; Anthony Hopkins, the composer and musicologist who too would do humorous as well as serious things. We had three weeks of this every year and I would help move chairs around, push the piano – that sort of thing.

Came 1956, and I thought surely Michael, wheelchair and all, could come down? Maybe we could play some of our recently created songs for the entertainment of the musicians. There's a long, low theatre in Dartington School, and we were billed as 'An evening with Michael Flanders and Donald Swann'. I remember we put underneath 'Eggheads of the world unite' – one of Adlai Stevenson's great lines. At that time we were writing prolifically. In Michael's studio flat in Kensington we'd begun to have big parties when we would play the songs to our guests. People would look forward to these. So by the time we went to Dartington together we had a useful list of items that we could perform as a duo. 'Have Some Madeira M'dear' was one, 'Misalliance' another. This was about two climbing plants and was written for one of Laurier's revues, but the actors felt diffident about being a honeysuckle and a bindweed. So we said 'All right, we'll do it ourselves':

> Said the anti-clockwise Bindweed
> To the clockwise Honeysuckle:
> 'We'd better start saving,
> Many a mickle makes a muckle,
> Then run away for a honeymoon
> And hope that our luck'll
> Take a turn for the better,'
> Said the Bindweed to the Honeysuckle.
>
> A Bee who was passing remarked to them then:
> 'I've said it before, and I'll say it again;
> Consider your off-shoots, if off-shoots there be,
> They'll never receive any blessing from me!

We considered excising the line about the Bee when Princess Margaret was almost affianced to Group Captain Peter Townsend, as it might be thought that the Bee advising them not to marry was the Arch 'B', the Archbishop of Canterbury, i.e. *lèse-majesté*.

When we performed it we got a very warm response. In fact the Dartington feedback to our act was very appreciative, and there's no doubt the classical musicians did wonders for our morale; the fact that we considered them such a discriminating audience gave us enormous confidence. This was particularly important for Michael who, despite his love and knowledge of the music hall, if anything was more classical than I was. Later we were to learn that the most discriminating audience is the general public rather than musicians, who tend to laugh at anything slightly musical. Because of the holiness with which music is normally regarded, they fall about when it is sent up. But the Dartington musicians were special, and when we started *At the Drop of a Hat*, it was their mailing list that provided us with our first audience.

126

To end that little chapter, Laurier had returned from America and had been asked to lecture on how to write and devise a revue for the West End. He asked us to go along and play examples for his lecture. So off we went all over the south-west. There were always problems getting Michael into his car with the wheelchair, but we made it, and the examples were going marvellously. That was when Michael began introducing songs with a witty preamble. When Laurier Lister became unavailable people who had heard the lectures would say: 'Why don't you come along and just do the songs as they are; forget the lecture.'

Michael started to write a script linking the songs, and soon realised that he was getting more laughs from this than from the songs themselves. I think the real triggering thing was that he knew he was being listened to, that his own lines projected from his wheelchair to any audience were beginning to command a good response. I was also being carried away by this new experience. I'd always enjoyed playing, but to have an audience of anything between one and two hundred, and be reasonably paid for an evening's entertainment was really quite unexpected. Suddenly it seemed that Item Seventeen in my letter about personal performance was the one!

Near the studio flat in Scarsdale Villas there was a little theatre called the New Lindsey. It has since been knocked down and is now part of a road. Freddie Piffard was the manager. (Later he got savaged by a lion in Africa, but somehow he survived and came back.) We said we'd like to hire the theatre for a week, maybe two, and if he'd care to come to the studio, we'd play our material for him. Round he came. We had all our songs together and performed for about half an hour singing and playing. 'Very nice material,' he said. 'Who's in it?' I looked at Michael and he looked at me and we said: 'It's *us*!' Freddie Piffard said: 'Well, the rent's forty pounds a week, and if you can find your own audience, take it.'

So we hired the theatre. Michael had a lady friend at that time who was quite a publicist. Our Dartington supporters provided our first audience. A standard lamp was produced from Michael's old home. An attractive young lady from Dartington Hall called Judith Jackson, who is now a motoring correspondent, came on stage with the one prop, which was the hat Michael was going to wear in the Madeira song. Somebody else put the lights on. That was it. All very simple. This was 31st December 1956 and, rather like *Go To It* in the early days of the war, there was no other opening night in the West End, so quite a number of critics turned up on spec. The show was unexpectedly well received. It was quite extraordinary.

The New Lindsey took about 150 people, and although it wasn't full every night, we had an exceptionally good response. People were talking about us and we had lots of good notices in the different papers. Michael couldn't believe they were watching him in a wheelchair. He thought there was something wrong with them. I couldn't believe I was out there at all. I just didn't know where I was. I kept the music in a music stool which surprised everybody because I'd lift this up and take the music out from time to time. I used to drop the music book, and would laugh in all the wrong places, and worried all the time what they would think of a particular number. I remember we did a song about bed – a clean song about being tired. But this put the audience to sleep so we had to get rid of it.

Joyce Grenfell came and said: 'Oh, you must go on tour, get lots and lots of practice', and it seemed a good idea. Others said: 'Don't go on tour, we want to see more, the audiences are beginning to clamour.' Two weeks into the run we took the third week – another forty pounds. We thought: 'Goodness, we can't but fail!' but they still flocked in. Then Jack Minster and E P Clift came to see us, saying they'd got the lease on the Fortune Theatre and we had to go there at once. We thought they'd gone out of their minds. True, we were keen to do personal performances but wasn't this too extreme? Wouldn't it interrupt our other work? I was working with Henry Reed and there were all sorts of lyrical things I wanted to write. What was the point of being stuck in the same place every night? Michael said that he was a broadcaster, well in with the World Service; it just wasn't on because it would totally interfere with his career. Yet it was quite an offer. We had a very bad forty-eight hours and I remember being sleepless and worried about it. I don't recall exactly what changed our minds, but we decided we ought to take this opportunity, albeit with trepidation and some reluctance.

We'd put on the first simple programme at the New Lindsey: 'We'll play our songs at the drop of a hat regardless.' The idea was that if you put two song-writers at the piano, they never stopped. Freddie Piffard said: 'I can't put all that on a ticket. Just give me a part of it.' So we gave him *At the Drop of a Hat*, with a drawing of a little hat. That was the beginning of the title which we then took to the Fortune, but there gave it a subtitle: 'An After Dinner Farrago'. A theatrical farrago is not very common, and we coined the word really. It means a medley; in our case a cabaret act at the piano. The word caught on, as it seemed to appeal to people and went with our quirky humour.

The Fortune Theatre is next to Drury Lane, not quite in the West End. It is small, seating about 350, and was not too clean at the start although it was tidied up in time. When we arrived the seats were so rickety that some collapsed during one of our early shows. A whole row of people just faded out, which we attributed to our humour. Our run started on 24th January 1957. We didn't expect it would last more than a week, but it lasted for over two years, uninterrupted except for one month when Michael had pneumonia.

There were three stage hands with practically nothing to do. Their only job was to lift Michael down the stairs backstage and up again. Once they dropped him and he nearly had concussion. It was all very primitive: he couldn't get into a dressing room so he had a rudimentary curtained cubicle just off-stage with a simple mirror. I think he was always nervous of being wheeled in and out. Everything was measured down to the last detail to map where he could go. Most theatres are raked, that is to say they slope down slightly to the footlights. That's not so good if you're playing in a wheelchair. So we had a platform made to make the stage flat and prevent Michael falling over into the footlights. This was covered with black cloth and wouldn't be noticeable, and when we started travelling we took the platform with us, or else others would be made on the spot. There was enormous attention to this sort of practicality. The ironic thing was that in those days disabled people couldn't come to the Fortune, as there were lots of rules and regulations and no provision whatsoever for the disabled. What a ludicrous thing: he could play but others couldn't watch him! This is when Michael began his campaigning for access for disabled people to theatres. His wife, Claudia, has continued this cause and was recently awarded an OBE for her work: she is outstanding in that field, running an organisation called Tripscope. Thank heavens that nowadays the disabled have a much greater voice.

Gradually, from the good notices we were getting, we discovered there was something interesting about author-performers. It was a new genre and people were loving it. As Michael said in one of his opening lines, it was done on the principle that the less you had to do with actors, the better! The satire had great appeal and this was balanced with a very fine lyrical quality Michael possessed. Here am I going on about my lyrical settings of French and Russian poets, but Michael had his own gift for it, in 'Misalliance', for instance; even in the Warthog song there's a real tenderness which he masks in his own code style. There is also the pathos of an armadillo singing to a chunk of military coded hardware on Salisbury Plain, for instance:

> Then I saw them, in a hollow, by a yellow muddy bank –
> One Armadillo singing . . . to an armour-plated Tank!
> Should I tell him?
> Gaunt and rusting, with the willow tree above,
> This – abandoned on manoeuvres – is the object of your
>   love!
>
> I left him to his singing,
> Cycled home without a pause.
> Never tell a man the truth
> About the one that he adores!

130

I got in my setting of Gérard de Nerval and 'Miranda' from the Greek. Then to break the mood, Michael would say: 'Let's do a funny song in Greek', so I would do my Greek version of 'Old MacDonald Had a Farm' with all the animals in the farmyard – cockerels, pigs, donkeys – making funny animal sounds in Greek. It goes on forever, and that's the joke because he would keep trying to interrupt me, swooping backwards and forwards in his wheelchair. 'Oh no, not *another verse!*' he'd exclaim. It turned out that not only were we song-writers at the piano, but I was playing a sort of fool, an idiot who couldn't stop. Michael, being a very theatrical person, realised this was a good and funny on-stage gimmick. I pretended I never knew what the jokes were about: I thought the Madeira song was about cake, that sort of thing. He would feed lines to the audience across me and I had the presence of mind to react accordingly. I soon learned the art of playing along with him: acting, of course, which I'd never done before.

We discovered that various things were happening that we hadn't bargained for. The musical audience which came in force from Dartington was soon replaced by the ordinary public, and the show was acquiring a considerable renown very early in its run. From the managers' point of view it was a gift, because there was literally nothing to pay except just to get us in and out. So we found we were riding a hit. We never conceived it could run in London for over two years. That was outside our wildest dreams.

Because a lot of our material was so topical we were always responding to events around us. Sometimes, there were strikes. There was a very long bus strike during our time at the Fortune and for a time we couldn't sing the Omnibus – 'Transport of Delight'.

> We don't ask much for wages,
> We only want fair shares,
> So cut down all the stages,
> And stick up all the fares.
> If tickets cost a pound apiece

Why should you make a fuss?
It's worth it just to ride inside
That thirty-foot-long by ten-foot-wide,
Inside that monarch of the road,
Observer of the Highway Code,
That big six-wheeler
Scarlet painted
London Transport
Diesel-engined
Ninety-seven horse-power
Omnibus.

There was also an air crash, which meant our sketch about travelling by air was temporarily in bad taste, but most of the time we were able to do the same material.

No two shows were ever exactly the same because in the script part Michael would invent all sorts of strange funny lines. He delighted in introducing something new to me because I'd laugh uproariously about one second before the audience. I was developing still further the theatrical tricks that were required by an on-stage actor in a two-man show. When he'd exclaim in exasperation 'It's like acting with Lassie!', I would respond by looking shocked. Or 'The Enid Blyton of English light music' he would say of me, and I would react in keeping with the mood.

All this was spontaneous and genuine, and it seemed quite natural to me. It was the sort of thing you would do at a party if a friend or relative was telling a really good joke on you. Somehow, he managed to keep this up and change it just enough to make it seem sparkling. So, although the songs were often the same, it was really a new experience every night, and when people asked us 'How can you do it night after night?' our first answer was that it differed every night because it had an idiom, a rehearsed spontaneity. That was its genre. I once saw Spike Milligan in one of his shows. At the end of an hour an alarm clock went off on stage when he was in full flow: it was the 'end of the first half'. He ignored it. It was uproarious, a lovely, funny idea. I remarked to Jeremy Taylor, co-performer

132

with Spike, what a marvellous spontaneous device it was, and he said: 'Oh, but he knows exactly when it will go off. It's all worked out most carefully.' Michael too had that gift. I could sit at the piano quite naturally playing whatever chords I wanted, but he seemed to know the timing in relation to himself and the audience in an uncanny and exact way.

Michael's friend, Michael Meyer, wrote in an obituary for Michael that had he not been disabled and pursued a career as an actor, he might have been among the top five or six performers. As it happened this thwarted actor, constrained by disablement, was devising a purpose-built script whilst lying immobile in Stoke Mandeville hospital, and was culling jokes like 'Piles for Pears' from his nautical experience derived from making piers in war circumstances.

> Of the first *Beggar's Opera* they used to say
> That it made Gay rich, and it made Rich gay:
> Revived by our hero after all these years,
> It made Bundles for Britten and Piles for Pears.

He created little jokes from every source imaginable and these were collected, anthologised, sifted and musicalised.

Although in many ways I became the legs of the partnership, because I was mainly seated at the piano, I became as static as he was. There were two of us seated before the audience instead of standing, but it seemed perfectly natural. I saw Richard Stilgoe and Peter Skellern in a double act recently. In a way it resembled what I did with Michael, but I couldn't get over the fact that they stood up. What a peculiar thing! Michael reached a point where he had total command of the seated position. He used to say that at a party he was the only relaxed person present because all the others had to walk around him. He also had a theatrical producer's mind with his great attention for detail. He worked out to a fine art how he could function on stage. He knew exactly how his wheels looked to the audience, whether he'd turned half left or quarter left, whether he was smiling, when he looked glum, when he'd put the hat on. Then he would wheel himself under the lampshade so that its fringe fell over his forehead.

The audience thought it was all completely spontaneous – that the whole thing was invented on the night. But some of the critics knew what he was doing and would ask us how it was planned.

With this immediate success, people might think we had a right royal time. This wasn't so; we both clung to our simple lives. A lot of people would come backstage to congratulate and thank us. Lots of them were very grand people like Sir Malcolm Sargent and Laurence Olivier, but we never kept drink backstage, and we must have seemed very puritanical. Michael would take his special car which he had been given by the Ministry of Pensions and go home. Janet and I were living in Battersea with our small daughter. I wanted to retain my nice, quiet family life, and the idea of going back in a car or taxi seemed distressing. I didn't have a car of my own. So after all our backstage visitors had gone, I would go and wait for my 170 bus at Kingsway and ride back along Nine Elms Road. Whenever I ate near the theatre between shows, I would always go to the local egg and chips place where I could get a nice poached egg on toast. The disconcerting thing was my dinner jacket, but I got over this by imagining I was a waiter. The grand part of the West End didn't rub off greatly on either of us. Michael came from a theatrical family: his father was a theatre manager, and his mother a violinist and song-writer, but he still had a strong urge to maintain a simple style. He never liked drink and never wanted to live it up backstage.

Gradually, we were discovering there was no end to the audience, that we'd reached a point where we could run as long as *The Mousetrap* at the Ambassadors. So a completely new question arose as to how long we would continue. After three months I was almost rebellious. It seemed to me that I wasn't writing any music and wasn't taking anything in except the applause of the audience. Michael spent a long time persuading me to stay put: he told me what a God-given chance it was, that if I wasn't there I would be in the pit accompanying some revue. He reminded me that Sandy Wilson had written *The Boy Friend* and wasn't going to need me for a bit, and that my lyrical material was not exactly flourishing. 'Don't you think this is your chance to give pleasure to others? You've always wanted to earn a bit of money, and whereas others are earning fifty pounds a week, you're earning five hundred. Isn't that something?' As I was a socialist he eased my conscience by reminding me that most of it would go on tax, which of course it did – 19/6 in the pound for great chunks of it. Claiming income tax relief on worn-out shoe leather was no longer relevant. It took me a long time to adjust to it. I say this with some shame because it seems an ungrateful attitude to being suddenly well off. But let me put it this way: we encountered enormous responsibilities and I took the financial one very much to heart.

There were other pressures, because virtually everyone wanted us to play in cabaret. We must have had about 200 offers in a year and took on about ten. These would have been for after the show, or on a Sunday. Broadcasting offers, too, poured in. The most interesting aspect was the interviewers, many of whom asked searching questions and allowed us to discover what we were all about. In every interview Michael said: 'I am an actor and I happen to be in this show.' I would say: 'I am a composer, and for various school, college and West End revue reasons we've joined together in this show and we enjoy relating to each other.'

8 Crafting the Songs

Before proceeding with this chapter I simply must show you the path of the 'Hat': *At the Drop of a Hat*; and its sequel *At the Drop of Another Hat*, which started its run in 1963. So far the first show has been born at the New Lindsey Theatre in Notting Hill Gate and has arrived at the Fortune Theatre in Drury Lane. The second show would play at the grand Haymarket Theatre and later at the Globe Theatre in Shaftesbury Avenue. Both shows were taken on tour, in the UK and abroad – all part of a pilgrimage. Here is the pilgrimage in full. Don't let it muddle your eyes, but you may want to look back on it as you read on.

The Route of the Hat

New Year's Eve 1956	New Lindsey Club, London
1956–57–58	Fortune Theatre, London
August 1959	Edinburgh Festival, Scotland
1959–60	Nine O'Clock Theatre, New York
1960–61	Princeton
	Wilmington
	Pittsburgh
	Cincinnati
	Des Moines
	Denver
	Los Angeles
	San Francisco
	St Paul
	St Louis
	Chicago

	Detroit
Spring 1961	Toronto, Canada
	Geneva, Switzerland
	Vevey
	Lausanne
1962	Canterbury
	Oxford
	Leeds
	Newcastle-upon-Tyne
	Aberdeen
	Edinburgh
	Liverpool
	Manchester
	Birmingham
	Toronto, Canada
1963	Richmond, England
	Brighton
	Cambridge
	Coventry
	Dublin
	Oxford
	Cambridge
	Coventry
	Bristol
October 1963	Haymarket Theatre, London
Fall 1964	Melbourne, Australia
	Auckland
	Hamilton
	Palmerston North
	Wellington, New Zealand
	Christchurch
	Adelaide
	Brisbane
	Sydney
1965	Hong Kong
	Guildford, England

	Oxford
	Brighton
October 1965	Globe Theatre, London
Fall 1966	Boston
	Indianapolis
	Louisville
	Detroit
	Cincinnati
	New Haven
	Philadelphia
	Washington
	Toronto
	Cleveland
New Year's Eve 1966	New York

My involvement is in the 'how' rather than the 'when'. This ensuing chapter is about how the songs were created. Their genesis and their life is all one to me. How could it be otherwise? Similarly the 'Hat' shows had two American tours, both of which have merged into one story, and will be the subject of the next chapter. The subsequent chapter, relating to my partnership with Michael concerns the various sequels, a trip to the Antipodes and the gradual unwinding, all of which has assumed its own mood as I wrote this book. But some of you may suddenly become 'linear'. Wherever are we now, you might say? If so, please look at The Route of the Hat. Yet somehow I feel my mood may catch you. After all, this book is not a check-list of my activities; it is a soliloquy, an enquiry.

After two and a half years of *Drop of a Hat* we pulled the plug on the Fortune Theatre, much to the annoyance of Mr Minster and Mr Clift who were beginning to retire on the proceeds. We had three months off, then in the summer of 1959 went to the Edinburgh Festival where we played for the first time to an audience of about 1300. We'd never believed this possible but it turned out that the number of people in the audience means nothing at all. We discovered something else. Michael's way of

139

saying it, was that you played to the person in the front row and they passed on the laugh through the back of their necks – like a process of osmosis. If the first five or ten rows are with you all's well. This could be part of the answer to the huge rock concerts at Wembley Stadium: as long as the response in the first few rows is enthusiastic, the artists are visible, and the sound is good, then the thing works however many people there are. We always spent an enormous amount of time to get the sound just right so that nobody doubted they were hearing anything but the live sound, at speech level.

What were they listening to? The anthropomorphised animals have already been mentioned. I remember a letter from a relative saying what a funny thing it would be if a warthog bought some scent in order to quell the awful smell it produces. This set Michael scribbling and he produced a touching song about a lady warthog going to the forest ball trying to disguise her own true smelly nature with lashings of scent and make-up and a frilly frock, hoping the other animals will ask her to dance. But:

> No one ever wants to court a Warthog,
> Though a Warthog does her best;
> Her accessories are dazzling for a Warthog,
> She is perfumed and daringly dressed.
> We know her these and those
> Are like Brigitte Bardot's,
> (originally Marilyn Monroe's. Nice how the rhymes fit,
>   isn't it?)
> Her gown is just a scintillating sheath,
> But she somehow fails to please
> 'Cause everybody sees
> That she's a Warthog,
> Just a Warthog,
> She's a Warthog underneath!

But when the gentleman warthog appears he recognises 'The sweetest little, neatest little, dearest and completest little Warthog . . .' and loves her for herself. This is just the sort of moral tale that appealed to Michael.

The whale 'Mopy Dick' was a song inspired by Vaughan

Williams, no less, about a bottle-nosed whale lured into the Antarctic where he's frozen and miserable:

> If ever I catch that school of porpoises
> They won't get no Habeas Corpuses.
> I'm lost and alone in a frozen zone
> And I'm almost frozen too,
> A shivering, quivering, bottle-nosed whale,
> The bottle-nosed whale with the flu.

Then he'd tell the story about how Kensington Borough council dug a section of the pavement and curb out so that he could manoeuvre his wheelchair from the car into his studio apartment. The idea was fine but there was always a great car stuck where Michael wanted to park. 'I would stick pins into a wax model of his big end', he'd say, and the story got funnier and funnier every night. Well, he happens to look at its number plate one day and discovers it begins GNU. So this song about the frustrations of parking in London brings us to a song about a Gnu. Rather like the shaggy dog stories of Muir and Norden which come to a peculiar end. We went to the zoo and there was a Gnu looking at us. Then, it was pronounced 'Nuu', and the Oxford dictionary still supports this. I believe Michael changed the language because so many people think it is 'G-nu'. Of late, I've met somebody in a 'Gnu' publishing house who said they sound the 'Gn' and bless Michael every day for it.

> I'm a G-nu, I'm a G-nu,
> The g-nicest work of g-nature at the zoo!
> I'm a G-nu, how do you do?
> You really ought to k-now w-ho's w-ho.
> I'm a G-nu, spelt G N U,
> I'm g-not a Camel or a Kangaroo,
> So let me introduce,
> I'm g-neither Man nor Moose,
> Oh, g-no, g-no, g-no, I'm a G-nu!

Looking at the programme of our second 'Hat' show: 'Flying by Air' is Michael's very funny story of the complicated way he used to go into aeroplanes. He was hoisted up by fork-lifts and pulled around in various ways, which was really very difficult for everyone. But in his sketch it was hilarious. He'd tell them all the funny things at great length and then, because everybody else would be expecting a song about the air, he'd sing one about a train:

> I'll travel no more from Littleton Badsey to Openshaw.
> At Long Stanton I'll stand well clear of the doors no
> more.
> No whitewashed pebbles, no Up and no Down
> From Formby Four Crosses to Dunstable Town.
> I won't be going again
> On the Slow Train.

Many of the stations are from a disused Derbyshire line. Once, a lady came up to me and said: 'A line in your song sums up my life. I was born in Littleton Badsey and am now married to a man in Openshaw.'

'Sea Fever', from Show One, was based on our knowledge of Stanford's sea songs and the fact that Michael had served in the Royal Navy. It is a big sea ballad, and Michael gets sick in the middle of it as he rolls and rocks around. 'Greensleeves' was a marvellous skit about the English theatre, full of wonderful jokes about pre-Shakespearian dramatists. He was, of course, working on his knowledge of the period. This is how he introduced it after a couple of bars of the tune:

> Do you know that tune? Yes – *Greensleeves*. You know
> it Donald, don't you? He knows it. And he doesn't like
> it. Says it always reminds him of an afternoon in Christ
> Church Meadow. It was Swan-Upping Sunday . . .
> It's interesting how *Greensleeves* came to be written;
> actually 1546. A bad year for the Theatre. Gorboduc was
> doing poor business at the Globe. *Gammer Gurton* was still
> giving everyone the needle. And apart from a revival of
> *Everyman* that's about all there was on. Not even *The Boy
> Friend* and *Salad Days* of course.
> All the dramatists seemed to have stopped writing.
> *Shakespeare* hadn't even started. *Dekker* had amalgamated
> with H M V. *Beaumont* had quarrelled with *Fletcher* and

joined Tennants. And the Master of the King's Revels was getting a bit worried as he had to have a new revel on for Candlemas. So he said to a playwright friend: 'Look *Kydd*', (that was his name – K Y D D) 'couldn't you write another *Spanish Tragedy* or something?' And Kydd said: 'Well, it's not so easy you know – I mean all the best plots have been used. And the public's only interested in bear baiting anyway. They don't care a fig for the Live Theatre.' He was a very Angry Young Man . . .

Here is 'All Gall', about the career of General de Gaulle:

This ole man he played *One*,
He played knick-knack at Verdun.
Cognac, Armagnac, Burgundy and Beaune,
This old man came rolling home.

This old man – World War *Two* –
He told Churchill what to do.
Free French General – Crosses of Lorraine;
He came rolling home again . . .

One of our circular songs.

We would ask Sydney Carter for songs. 'Youth of the Heart' was an Irish song he'd written with me in the style of an Irish ballad. This gave me a chance to sing a reflective ballad in the middle of all this hilarity.

Oh, the youth of the heart
And the dew in the morning,
You wake and they've left you
Without any warning.

Michael knew I'd been a conscientious objector. Although he'd been in the navy, he was very interested in the rights and wrongs of fighting. He translated, from the French, a very strong anti-war song, 'Lovely War', by Georges Brassens:

War has had its apologians
Ever since history began
From the time of the Greeks and Trojans
When they sang of 'Arms and the Man';
But if you ask me to name the best, sir,

143

I'll tell you the one I mean –
Head and shoulders above the rest, sir,
Was the War of Fourteen-Eighteen.
Head and shoulders above the rest, sir,
Stands the War of Fourteen-Eighteen.

Every war has its own attraction
From Total war to Border raid
Call it Rebellion, Police Action,
War of Containment or Crusade;
I don't underrate the late war
We see so often on the screen
But that wasn't a really Great War
Like the War of Fourteen-Eighteen
No, the late war wasn't a Great War
Like the War of Fourteen-Eighteen.

At this time the Aldermaston marches had begun. I remember
wheeling Michael for about fifty yards along the Gloucester Road
in one of the marches; not far but significant for us both. Later
he made a very strong statement in a song called 'Twenty Tons
of TNT'. It's utterly chilling. Here is a verse:

Father, Mother, Son and Daughter,
Twenty tons of TNT.
Give us land and seed and water,
Twenty tons of TNT.
Children have no need of sharing;
At each new nativity
Come the ghostly Magi bearing
Twenty tons of TNT.

We got this into *Drop of Another Hat* along with 'Lovely War'
with enormous difficulty. The order was so structured on humour
and audience reaction so that to introduce an anti-nuclear song,
however trenchant, meant we had to be sure to hold our audience
who may not have come to see a show at the Haymarket to be
riveted by the number of tons of TNT there is per person in
the world. We did it.

There was also 'The Reluctant Cannibal': somewhere along
the line he devised this idea of a cannibal who conscientiously

objects to eating people: 'Eating people is wrong.' He was the father cannibal and me the youngster. It was the sort of thing that helped the show along immensely because it was antiphonic and dramatic; it had some extremely good lines. The father tries to persuade the young reluctant cannibal:

> . . . But people have always eaten people!
> What else is there to eat?
> If the Ju-Ju had meant us not to eat people,
> He wouldn't have made us of meat!

'I won't let another man pass my lips!' the young cannibal retorts.

The song is quite clearly about fighting and war because in the end the father cannibal says in exasperation: 'Why, you might just as well say, "Don't fight people",' and the two cannibals fall about laughing at such a ridiculous idea.

Somebody wrote to us saying: 'Please don't do that song, it's insulting to the local population.' We wondered how many cannibals were living in the region of the Fortune Theatre! The correspondent obviously misunderstood and thought we were laughing about 'natives'. It was a parable about hypocrisy, and when I started doing peace concerts, it was much admired by the peace movement.

In the second show our 'antiphonic' item was 'The First and Second Law of Thermodynamics' accurately defined in lyric form, and now used by university professors for teaching the basic laws. On that occasion I was the moron student:

> *Tutor*:
> Heat is work and work's a curse
> And all the heat in the Universe
> Is gonna cool down cos it can't increase
> Then they'll be no more work and there'll be perfect
>   peace!
> *Student*:
> Really?
> *Tutor*:
> That's entropy man. And all because of the Second Law
> of Thermodynamics, which lays down that . . .

Both:
You can't pass the heat from a cooler to a hotter
You can try it if you like but you'd far better notta
Cos the cold in the cooler will get hotter as a rule-a
Cos the hotter body's heat will pass to the cooler
You can try it if you wanta but you'll only look a
    fool-a . . .

Michael had attended an evening class on Thermodynamics. This illustrates his methodical and scientific approach: it was always important for him to know the exact details. He wrote a very funny sketch about Stonehenge, having studied Professor Hawkins's erudite book on the subject; even working out the relationship between every stone. But Neolithic Man, watching it being built, can't see all the subtleties: 'Is that all there is to it, just two up and one across all the way round? If that's modern architecture, roll on the Ice Age I say.'

'Have Some Madeira, M'dear' was Michael's song about a roué and seduction. I'd heard of zeugma in school, and here was Michael wallowing in it:

    He had slyly inveigled her up to his flat
    To see his collection of stamps,
    And he said as he hastened to put out the cat,
    The wine, his cigar and the lamps:
    'Have some Madeira, m'dear! . . .

A later line goes:

    I don't care for Sherry, one cannot drink Stout,
    And Port is a wine I can well do without . . .

A chap wrote from one of the main wine dealers and said: 'Please don't go on with that line about Port, it's affecting our trade.' Michael replied: 'I'm really not responsible for the characters in my pieces.' He always had his way out. But it is a slightly libidinous piece, though. People would ask what we were going on about giving a sweet seventeen-year-old Madeira wine. Michael would reply: 'Well, I'm portraying a roué. What can I do about it? It's the way it came off my pen!'

146

Michael's sister worked for *House and Garden* magazine. He had dozens of magazines sent to his apartment, and gradually built up suitable lines for a song called 'Design for Living', about floors made of bottle tops nailed upside down to the floor and the type of social climbers who think that way:

> We're fearfully *Maison Jardin*
> At Number Seven B,
> We've rediscovered the Chandelier –
> Ever so very Contemporary!
> We're terribly *House and Garden*.
> Now at last we've got the chance,
> The garden's full of furniture
> And the house is full of plants!

It's interesting and poignant too that Michael wrote about many of the things that might have frustrated him: the bus he couldn't get on, the train where he could only travel in the luggage compartment. He could hardly get his hand up to post a letter; somebody had to do it for him, yet he wrote a very tender song about a pillar box:

> A solitary figure
> In a little coat of red,
> He always does his duty,
> Holding high his weary head.
> He never tries to run away
> Or bite the Postman's hand
> And so I feed him sandwiches
> To show I understand.
>
> Pity the poor little Pillar Box
> Standing in the rain all day,
> Gazing out in each direction
> Hoping for the next collection . . .

There was a real affection for many of the things we wrote and sang about – objects and places of all sorts. At the time people would come up to us and tell us we had a strong feeling for the domestic. There was one song about cookery gadgets we didn't use very much, that had a choice line: 'That thing on the shelf's been whipping itself for the best part of a week . . .'

147

Looking at the songs now, I think the derivations are interesting, but the thing that seems to endure is the very high level of verbal fantasy. Broadly speaking, this has not been analysed. I wonder how many have examined the lyrics. One song about a tennis umpire appears in a book of light verse. However the performance value was so strong, there was more to it than 'light verse'. For a start, Michael's 'mouth' imitation, the aural effect of a tennis ball being struck, was funny and riveting:

> Bonk, Bink – Wimbledon – June – Ladies Singles, Third
>   Round.
> Groundsmen are asked 'How's the state of the ground?'
> Players are photographed jumping the net
> But here sits a figure they always forget –
> The Umpire Upon Whom The Sun Never Sets . . . Bonk,
>   Bink . . .

I'd like to draw attention to the felicitousness of his puns. Some people, when faced with a pun, shrink or turn their nose up. In Michael's case they were so apt. Introducing 'The Seven Ages of Woman', he'd say: 'It has struck me that Shakespeare had perhaps been a little remiss in only writing the Seven Ages of Man. Nowadays that would certainly be called a bit of male chauvinist Bacon.'

It's interesting how people crave social commentary: everybody wants to hear a joke about a politician, or somebody in public life. We had such lines – 'yes, we have no Guiana!' – just about the time Guiana was disappearing from the British Empire. Anthony Eden was being pushed out of politics at the time the show started, and he went off to Jamaica. We went on television one night with a song:

> We want to winter in Jamaica,
> Ja'make us fit to muck things up again . . .

Two days later he resigned. If only Michael were here today! His couplets might dislodge a few more.

The Americans reached the moon sometime during our run. Michael said, 'We went out to look at the moon, and there it was:

Coca Cola written all over the top of it!' He would always find the right line. It would seem that as an author, if you can find a few really good apposite lines, your revue is right up to the minute. If our work is examined, I think most of it was like 'Misalliance' or 'The Gnu', but we knew we couldn't get by without reference to things happening around us. When the Profumo scandal was on, Michael managed to think of a verbal juxtaposition: 'Nil combustibus pro fumo' – no smoke without fire.

The Bishop of Woolwich became very popular because of his quasi-agnostic views. A line was found for him: 'It's like the Bishop of Woolwich. He doesn't exist; just an idea in the mind of God.' There was always just enough social commentary for the audience to go home thinking it was immediate entertainment reflecting the time we were in.

All our material had to be passed by the Lord Chamberlain who was the Theatre Censor. We set his Regulations to music and sent him the lyric to vet:

> Smoking is permitted in the auditorium
> So if you want to have a smoke and you've got the price
> Just light it up and puff away to Paradise
> Because smoking is permitted in the auditorium . . .

'I like it!' came the reply from St James's Palace.

Here is a conversation between the Prime Minister and the Chancellor of the Exchequer, which we altered for each successive government:

> There's a hole in my Budget, dear Harold, dear Harold
> There's a hole in my Budget, dear PM my dear.
>
> Then mend it dear Peter, dear Peter, dear Peter
> Then mend it dear Peter, dear Peter, my dear . . .

Harold Macmillan came twice to the show and was delighted with it. He came backstage on both occasions. The newspapers turned up snapping him laughing and joking with us, all good stuff for the *Evening Standard*. Little gobbets would emerge: 'Another celebrity visits *Drop of a Hat*.' So after a bit, what with the Lord Chamberlain liking his lines set to music, we were invited to his drinks party in St James's Palace. I turned up wearing a blue shirt. Everyone else was in morning dress. Michael was the only one seated, hardly anyone could see him. It was one of the parties where he didn't feel more relaxed than anyone else. Somebody said: 'Have you been to the Garden Party?' When we replied no, we hadn't, they saved our face by saying: 'You must be on the *other* list.' Macmillan came up to Michael and said: 'I can't understand how you go on doing that night after night. All those songs! You manage to hold the audience for two hours! I can only manage twenty minutes.' Michael suggested: 'Why don't you try singing it instead?'

So we survived that event all right. We never wanted to imitate the high and the mighty, we both loved our homes and the simple life. Despite the fact we were in main-line theatre, things continued for us in almost a humble way. Sometimes we called ourselves 'A two-man monastery': there were no chorus girls dancing around, just the hat lady. Mostly we worked only with the stage manager, the stage hands, and the man who took care of the sound, so we had a fairly austere life. It's as though we resembled a sort of church service with the introductory hymn, the Introit, the sermon, the little bits in between and the Dismissal – another of the Lord Chamberlain's regulations:

> The public may leave at the end of each performance
> By all the exit doors . . .

The 'blue' joke didn't fit our style at all. In fact we laughed at the new outspokeness. Here's a song we had to bring up to date almost every week:

> Ma's out, Pa's out – let's talk rude:
> Pee – Po – Belly – Bum – Drawers!
> Dance in the garden in the nude:
> Pee – Po – Belly – Bum – Drawers!
> Let's write rude words all down our street,
> Stick out our tongues at the people we meet,
> Let's have an intellectual treat:
> Pee – Po – Belly – Bum – Drawers!

Ken Russell's filming in Regent's Park
Pee – Po – Belly – Bum – Drawers,
Full Frontal Composers, Bach to Bach
Pee – Po – Belly – Bum – Drawers,
From the folk-song scene to the world of Pop
They get their words from the Porno shop –
Things seem to start where they used to stop
With Pee – Po – Belly – Bum – Drawers!

It seemed to us that we were genuinely cheering people up. In a way this could be related to the generally more euphoric 'you've never had it so good' time, but there were many people even then who were grateful for being enlivened. My sixth-form Latin teacher came to see the show. He later said he'd never laughed like that in the whole of his life, and he particularly relished the line in 'The Reluctant Cannibal': 'And he used to be a regular Anthropophaguy'.

Yet for all the humour, there was bite. Michael felt very deeply about issues: the anti-war songs were just one example. I think people recognised that we weren't just skating on the surface. One of our original fans was the Left cartoonist Vicky. Michael was a keen Labour supporter and was pushing out some quite strong ideas through his songs. A social conscience runs very strongly through everything he did and this gave the show a certain edge. But in all I think we gave people an affable evening with some caustic moments – it was never anodyne or feeble and totally without cruelty. Were we sculpting in an euphoric age?

As for crafting the songs: I've mentioned the cooking process that went on with Michael in the early part of our collaboration. An essential part of this was that we would always spend the morning talking about Life. If I was being brave I'd say we were philosophising: they were really deep discussions. To me, collaborations are always inseminated by thoughts: you need to feel good about everything you're doing and to laugh at the funny things you've seen together, then out of that might come a single line or tune. That is how we had built up the songs in the immediate post-Oxford time. Sitting around for days on end in Hampstead Garden Suburb, we would quietly and happily cook up these songs line by line. At the end of every day we'd play them through to Mrs Flanders. Philosophy in the morning, song-writing in the afternoon, supper, then performing to Michael's mother.

How did I find my tunes? I think it began in many cases with imitative music. Having orginally started with a skit on Arthur Sullivan, I grew expert in identifying and copying certain styles. Take the Britten skit: I would go through the Britten scores and produce little gobbets from this so that the song would relate to his music. I had a fair understanding of English song-writing: Peter Warlock, Roger Quilter; most of the Lieder styles were familiar to me. So my first feeling was how could I find a way of making it work? With any tune there has to be a development – a beginning, a middle and an end – but compared with the music of Sydney Carter that I know so well, mine is more complicated; it is not folk-music. A song like 'January Brings the Snow' is almost imitating a folk-song; in 'The Gasman Cometh', I took the tune from 'Dashing Away with a Smoothing Iron', and simply changed it a little bit, just enough to make it copyright Donald Swann! But it is really based on a folk-song. I was also drawing on music hall and ballads. Then when performing, I would add my little touches: the very business of ending and changing key, or somehow floating things at the keyboard which is really the idiom I find most spontaneous and comfortable. Michael seldom touched the keys but in *At the Drop of Another Hat*, we had a duet where he played just two notes. Even that was very funny. 'Oh dear!' he'd say. 'The writing's been rubbed off!'

I did have a spot of trouble with a song called 'Ill Wind', also in the second show. Michael had a faulty record player that played much faster than it should. Listening to Dennis Brain playing Mozart's Horn Concerto in E Flat at this galloping speed, Michael was inspired to set a lyric about a horn that went missing, to the famous Rondo section. '. . . lost my Horn, lost my Horn, found my Horn . . . gorn.' So I was presented with a bit of too-fast Mozart to play. It was quite terrifying. I've mentioned how classical music foxed me, and there were lots of jokes concerning this on stage: 'At last you've got some good music to play' – that sort of thing. I took this challenge very seriously and tried to play the orchestral accompaniment of the Horn Concerto. At last I tipped my cap to a great composer and took it seriously; I tried to get it right, overdid it and got writer's cramp which lasted nearly nine months. It was excruciating. I could hardly play. My father would come with a syringe before performances and inject me to try to stop the pain. What I did in order to get over this terrible thing was to rewrite the orchestral accompaniment taking out some of the more difficult notes to make it more Swannish. Simple! You could hardly tell the difference. I actually recovered from writer's cramp when my father advised me to start writing with a biro on a slate under water when I had a bath. A brilliant idea, very soothing and it worked for me. But it was bad while it lasted – so bad at times that I couldn't even sign a cheque.

Michael's health was generally good, but he had chest problems from time to time. Once he caught pneumonia and had to take a month off. Before he retired to his sick-bed, he went on stage with a very high temperature and a bottle of red medicine which he needed to drink throughout the show to keep him going. Holding it up to the audience he said: 'This is not, as you may think, sparkling Madeira.' They all laughed. Then, after a long pause he said: 'It is Ajax, the foaming cleanser.' All his work was done on one lung and singing apparently did it good. He just longed to sing and was terrified for his health when the show came off. He used to say: 'While I'm singing it expands my diaphragm and I feel fitter.'

As well as bringing his syringe my father brought his friends along to the shows. He liked Michael very much and even contributed German and Russian translations for the Hippopotamus song:

Schlamm, Schlamm, herrlicher Schlamm
Das ist der Ursprung, die Quelle, der Stam . . .

Грязь, грязь, чудная грязь,
Лучшее средство как кожная мазь!

The chorus was eventually translated into twenty different languages by friends, with two versions in Latin. With the second show we found there was pressure to keep coming back to the old numbers. People would wait for the Hippo song:

A bold Hippopotamus was standing one day
On the banks of the cool Shalimar.
He gazed at the bottom as it peacefully lay
By the light of the evening star.
Away on a hilltop sat combing her hair
His fair Hippopotamine maid;
The Hippopotamus was no ignoramus
And sang her this sweet serenade . . .

So we wrote a new version, a second edition:

The amorous Hippopotamus whose love song we know
Is now married and father of ten;
He murmurs – 'God rot 'em!' as he watches them grow
And he longs to be single again.
He'll gambol no more on the banks of the Nile
Which Nasser diverted last spring
With Hippo-potàmas in silken pyjamas
No more will he teach them to sing:

Mud, mud, glorious mud,
Nothing quite like it for cooling the blood!
So follow me, follow,
Down to the hollow
And there let us wallow
In glorious mud!

We had many requests for the Omnibus song too. To keep it topical Michael produced a marvellous accent for a West Indian bus conductor – very funny. So several of the old favourites crept back with little changes.

As well as Father, my uncles would come along too: uncle Freddie, the Mayfair socialite, turned up for some of the earlier performances and enjoyed the celebrity, fun part of it. He liked to think I'd made it into the realm of the people he knew so well, the upper crust, and I think he enjoyed the material. Uncle Edgar had died just before the start of the two-man partnership although he heard, and enjoyed the earlier revue songs. Uncle Alfred was largely in America. I visited him there and he came to the show and enjoyed himself.

We also had a tremendous amount of support from the church. So many vicars came backstage that we devised a system: we awarded one point for any vicar who came to see either of us, two for a Canon, three for a Bishop and four for an Archbishop. The scoring depended on whom the ecclesiastical visitor knew – me or Michael. We were going very evenly and then one day Archbishop Joost de Blank, who was both Archbishop of Cape Town and a Canon of Westminster Abbey at the same time, turned up, and Michael got so many points that he won flat out.

Because I met so many vicars, I joined the Actors' Church Union. It is an interesting organisation whose representatives come round the various theatres, often in the middle of the show, to convert, or ask if there is anything else they can do for you, like get you baptised or confirmed. They realise that actors are rather freaky people, drifting around from dig to dig as they work. There is an ACU rep in every city. They try to cater for emotional and spiritual needs, recognising that actors can get warped by being made up to look and act like a character other than what they really are. I remember one representative in particular, a very laconic chap, who always appeared at the Haymarket and would sit with us in the interval, just at the time when we wanted to have a bit of peace and a quiet cup of tea. We never said a single word, just sat in total silence; we looked at him, he looked at us then, having done his religious duty, he went away again. Most peculiar.

By 1963 the satire boom had begun and there were one or

two rasping critics who said we were too sweet, too benign; that there wasn't enough that was hard hitting in the David Frost genre, which was then becoming popular. One of Michael's opening lines countered this: 'The purpose of satire is to strip off the veneer of comforting illusion and cosy half-truths; and our job, as I see it, is to put it back again.' He was able to find a joke about everything. But apart from these carping critics, mostly it was going as well as ever and the new songs were much admired. I was still sitting at the piano 'playing Hamlet to Michael's Falstaff'. (Another critic.)

People sometimes ask me whether I ever resented making a fool of myself. No, I didn't. I was just pleased that the pattern which we'd devised had given me a comedic role. There is no way I could play a comedian, so I think I realised that I'd been handed a part on a plate: a sort of Laurel to a Hardy part, or Wise to a Morecambe sort of thing. I was fully aware that my role was getting a lot of response and laughter, not so much for me but for the very situation producing it. So I was grateful. But it's probable that somewhere along the line it contributed to my feeling that I was only partly there, because I was the Fall Guy and less the composer inventing extemporised music, or thinking out something original at the time. I was less fully functioning than Michael was. He had opportunity to embroider his script, nightly polishing it up, producing new barbs, possibly at my expense; whereas in my role there was no way I could do this. So maybe it made me feel somewhat put down, but not because of the way he spoke about me. I would ascribe it to playing any one part for a very long time. Say you were a tramp in *Waiting for Godot* for thousands of peformances: you'd begin to think you were just one of the tramps, not the person you are as you leave the stage. And even though I had my egg on toast at the Golden Egg outside, it didn't totally restore me.

This raises some very interesting questions about what actors are in any case. Some say they haven't got a soul, no real life, that they are only what they portray. Michael used to come out with that theory; he rather enjoyed it. He had a joke about an

actor coming for audition saying: 'I only play scornful parts.'
Michael wondered a lot about actors and their emotional life
and whether they really could function off-stage. I think by the
time he got married and had his family he realised that an actor
could be both successful and fulfilled. But talking of Michael's
marriage reminds me of America. Broadway, here we come!

9 The American Experience

Great excitement! An impresario, Alexander Cohen, sent a telegram in spring, 1959: 'Please come and appear on Broadway.' We thought this was another escalator on which we could climb – too good to refuse. Most London actors dream of appearing in New York, and for us it was a great opportunity. So a new phase in our partnership was the touring life abroad, which was interspersed with spells back in Britain, playing in the London theatres I've mentioned, as well as touring the provinces.

Negotiations were going ahead with Alex Cohen throughout the summer of 1959. He was to have a major influence on our lives from that time onwards. There was a contract rather like the Old Testament – with innumerable riders, subsidiary clauses and controversial questions. This must have been a very unusual experience for Alex: he was booking two men, a standard lamp and a hat, compared with a play or musical which had lists of actors and a plethora of props. I remember the lighting expert coming over to assess lighting requirements; he looked at the show, decided it didn't need anything special and went back.

We didn't need costumes: we always wore dinner jackets and to that extent we harked back to the old partnerships. I'd heard of Layton and Johnstone although I'd never seen them; Flanagan and Allen I saw at the Victoria Palace when they were part of the Crazy Gang. This was one of their opening couplets (with each leading a greyhound): 'Oh what a pity, there's only White City to walk the dogs around'. A Flanders line, I thought. The Western brothers were about during my early youth: 'wearing the old school tie'. We too were in this idiom. I can't remember whether the performers in *Beyond the Fringe* – the next show to emerge from the universities – wore dinner jackets, but we were still locked into that style. I wore a very heavy suit which eventually gave me asthma. I wasn't sharp enough to realise you could get a lightweight suit. In America I actually hired one with a curious stiff, starched shirt, from a waiters' shop. I seemed to retreat into old-fashioned habits because I also wore pointed patent shoes which gave me a sore foot. I eventually had to have half a toe off – not an occupational hazard one usually associates with a pianist! Looking back, I don't know what came over us. I'm sure we could have performed in lounge suits and ties, or even open neck shirts, but we kept to our dinner jackets. We never questioned it. I recall that, in an attempt to be theatrical, I had a music stool made – a rather large one with a red cover, which I still have. I insisted on having a box made for it, at great expense, and this stool travelled with us all over the place.

Most of all, from the time the Broadway offer came up, we began to re-script; this was probably the biggest thing we did to the show. Going to America was a theatrical and verbal experiment – as the whole show had to be re-thought in terms of American culture and languages. Like all theatrical people we knew a lot about American theatre. The British are brought up on American culture in any case, but we became particularly involved with the linguistic side of it. We were lucky in that Alex Cohen was an Anglophile who had put on many English shows; he even had a home in England. I was very impressed with his story about his son being stuck in a lift in Knightsbridge and dialling his father, Alex, in New York, on the emergency phone in the lift.

When we first arrived in the States, Michael had jokingly remarked during a radio show that he was looking for a bride. Within twenty days he re-met Claudia Davis, the daughter of an American professor whom he had known in England. Claudia was very experienced with language; sitting poring over the script, reverbalising it, Michael and Claudia found they were talking not only about pavements and sidewalks but about the rest of their lives together, so they married very quickly. As a linguist I was also involved in working out verbal nuances and punning. The assonance structure was important to get right because it is this aspect of the lyrics that determines the music. So I was a constant partner to all the discussions and involved with all the changes. This was quite a challenge but great fun.

To give an example of the sort of thing we were working on, here is a snippet of Michael's introduction to the Bus song. At that time British buses had a driver and a conductor, but the American buses only one man:

> Next we have what is rather an English song; really it's about a bus. Buses I know you have over here, and until quite recently I believe you had these double decker buses, which are still very much part of the London scene. The big six-wheeler, scarlet painted, London transport, diesel engined ninety-seven horse-power om-ni-bus. Omnibus is just long for bus, of course . . . we have more time, and so on . . . Comes from the Latin word, omnibus, meaning to or for by with or from everybody . . . which is a very good description. This song is a tribute to that gallant band of London Transport Workers, who day in, day out, year after year, in all kinds of weather, negotiate for higher wages . . . We have twice as many of these as you do because instead of just having a driver who does everything in a wonderfully ambidextrous and sweet-tempered manner – except for the cross-town ones, of course – we have a driver at one end, who just concentrates on driving, and a conductor at the other end, who conducts . . . and he decides who gets on and off and so on. Very old principle of the English common law, known as the division of powers . . . the executive must be separate from the judiciary. I commend it to you. This song is called 'A Transport of Delight', which is rather witty when you come to think of it.
>
> If you'd imagine this great bus here, rather wider than this (points to the piano) has stairs going up the end. The conductor has a gadget strapped around him in the morning by his wife or a close friend . . . whereby when it goes 'ting ting' it prints your ticket, which is rather up to date really, and then he gives you change, which is rather old fashioned . . . Engine up this end . . . and oh, this bus has rubber mudguards, so that if it hits you, you can't prove it.

160

The sound, unlike the lighting, caused enormous problems, not only in New York but in every American town we visited. We seldom rehearsed the script, but we would rehearse the sound for hours on end. In the Golden Theatre, New York, this became critical. There were four different sound systems for the four previews with technicians being sacked left right and centre for not providing the right sound. It was vital to get it perfect because our English voices were not getting through. The English accent is adorable to the American ear but there is a vast difference in inflexion: the sound goes up at the end of a sentence for Americans, but it deflects at the end of an English sentence. So we were learning to go up at the end of each phrase, but often they wouldn't catch the end of a sentence and this is what the sound engineers were trying to cope with. In the end we had radio mikes, which were quite new then, and I wore a sort of gun holster underneath my waistcoat which housed all the technology.

I also experienced great anxiety about my pianos. I am always touchy and worried about them. Steinways I connect with concert pianists – the Great. Towards the end of the Fortune run, I had a Blüthner and loved it very much. This is what I wanted. The Americans found it impossible to find one for me, so they offered me a Knabe and I wrote to my musicologist uncle Alfred in America asking him what he thought of a Knabe. He replied 'Tchaikovsky wouldn't touch it!' so I turned it down. Eventually, at enormous expense and much to the annoyance of everybody, I settled for a Steinway which I was then stuck with. It was far too bright and bravura for my style and I don't know why they couldn't have found the quieter Blüthner. But I did have my stool, my little piece of home which gave me comfort. The notices read: 'Two Men and a Lamp.' This must have been very strange for Americans: all they could see was a man in a wheelchair, a chap at the piano, the lamp and the, now American, hat girl who would bring on our other prop.

We were in America for about three weeks before the opening, meeting innumerable press people who wanted to know our story. As we drove into New York from the airport we witnessed a bank being robbed. We assumed this was America just as we knew it from films. We were taking in the New York experience: how it felt, how it looked; what it was like ordering English muffins in a café when the man yelled down the hatch 'Burn the British!' That, of course, crept into the show. 'Donald was about to leap out of the café, he was so frightened', Michael would say.

I must say something about Alex Cohen, a most flamboyant character. In one of the programmes he likens himself to Barnum and Louis XIV. He loved extravagant gestures and in the transposition of an English show for American ears he went the whole way. The first night was an amazing event with fish and chips being served in the theatre, and tea and biscuits in the interval. He flew over The Happy Wanderers, a busking group from Leicester Square that he'd met in the London streets. They were performing on top of the Golden Theatre facade which had been blanketed with posters of current London hits. There was a man dressed like a British Bobby outside and the *Daily Express* was flown over for that night. To give the right atmosphere, he also arranged for a London fog to be projected into 44th Street. It was completely effective and the police arrived asking him to disperse it, as nobody could move. Reporters were buzzing around sending in headlines like: 'Traffic stops on Broadway as new show from Britain opens.'

He changed the start time from 8.30 to 9 pm: a huge theatrical experiment, which meant you had dinner and came to the theatre to enjoy an entertaining evening. Yves Montand had just done a wonderful nine o'clock theatre opening which we were early enough to see; Victor Borge and Marlene Dietrich had both recently appeared; later it was to be *Beyond the Fringe* and Elaine May and Mike Nichols, who were just stupendous. So we were involved with the high-powered creative thinking of this Anglophile producer. He's still there doing the same thing and by now he's one of the two or three leading American producers.

162

At that time he was groping for his new role, and we were lucky to be part of it.

It was essential to Alex that we had seven good notices. At that time there were seven reviews to cull from the first night. There was a first-night party and we were waiting for the reviews until 3 am. There were six rave reviews but *The New York Times* was not as wonderful as it could have been: only half was in rave terms. This meant we had only six and a half rave reviews. Immediately, Alex put a full-page advert in *The New York Times* saying 'You've read your own notice, here are the other six!' Well, you can't imagine a more glowing way of countering a marginal possibility that it wouldn't succeed totally. And it did. It found its own audience and ran for eight months. In its way it was a good British import. But with all Alex's expenses, he did not in fact recoup his investment until we had started touring; and it was somewhere on the move like Pittsburgh, when we were touring six months later, that the show broke even and the investment gradually came back for those who put money up for him. He told us that because the Golden Theatre was called a music theatre he had to employ musicians for the orchestra even though they played cards all the time. Michael just couldn't resist this:

> Shocking lot, musicians. Not a solitary moral value among them. I should know. We have five musicians in this show . . . we have to, it's a Union thing. I don't understand it but there it is . . . Good luck to them I say. They count Swann as one – which is nice – and then we have to have four more. They live down here in the band-room. They're all cellists – and they smuggle women in cello cases . . . And the women fit!

We found our New York audience extremely literate. Of course it's only a minority who go to live theatres and those who came had largely been in England. There was an enormous backcloth by Al Hirschfeld who portrayed Piccadilly through American eyes. Big Ben struck nine o'clock as the show started, and just prior to the second act the audience was titillated by coloured slides of London's products and services. On the whole the audiences were ahead of the jokes. They knew London as well as we did, and now they were re-tracking their memories of it. 'The English sent the wrong boys in 1775 and lost a colony', one critic wrote. 'If George III had sent these boys over, things might have been different!' We felt very warmed.

I was finding my way around New York; Niew Amsterdam, as Michael insisted on calling it. I would go in my waiter's suit in the underground – the subway. Some people find this forbidding but I loved it: it reminded me of the Elephant and Castle. I had maps and knew exactly when to get on the express or the slow train, and I still know the routes very well. It has become a little more dangerous with muggings, but millions of people pass through it every day, and I found it quite something. Then I would wheel Michael from his apartment to the theatre. I know the flagstones on Sixth and Seventh Avenue and could draw them for you; many years later I returned and discovered that I still knew each little change of gradient intimately. There were other helpers besides me. Then, when we had this exciting drama of Michael's marriage to Claudia, she began to wheel him too.

It was disorientating in some ways: two men with their lamp and hat in Notting Hill Gate, or up round the back of Drury Lane still fitted our lifestyle. I could hop on a bus and Michael had his disablement car. Suddenly we had a Cadillac the length of a block. Apparently this was the car to take us to the theatre. It was a bit of a shock until we made our own, more modest arrangements.

By now my second daughter, Natasha, was born. It had been decided that Janet would bring the family over if the show settled down to a long run. Where should we live? Should it be in or out of town? For a time we lived in the legendary literary and theatrical hotel, The Algonquin. There, uniquely, we had a pram with two very young children going up and down the lifts, which were slowed down so that it should feel old fashioned – that's prestigious, you see. We had a family life, but Janet found it hard. She had been horrified, arriving at the airport, when an enormous limousine (which she described as being miles long) came to pick them up. She'd never seen anything like it before, let alone rattled around in its vast spaces. She was quite dismayed and couldn't take it in. And New York has a sort of success feel to it. Everybody feels they've got to rise to the top in the most stunning and majestic way possible. So it was difficult keeping the modest life together.

There were other curious aspects: Broadway, we discovered, is twenty-three miles of the Edgware Road. It bends a little, which is unusual for a New York street, but apart from that it resembles the Edgware Road from end to end. Then the theatre: the very name – Golden – sums up its glamour. Would you believe, in this wonderful Broadway theatre I had a really terrible dressing room, if you could even call it that? At the Fortune, the furniture was ancient, rickety stuff picked up from a junk shop in about 1912, but at least it was something. The dressing room in the Golden had nothing in it at all. It was antidiluvian. Times Square is not dissimilar to Piccadilly Circus: it attracts the poor and dispossessed, so going to the theatre means pushing your way through beggars, which is distressing. It was not all pure pleasure.

The best part of all was the two hours nightly on the stage. When we were actually in the theatre and the curtain went up, all the little edits and carefully wrought introductions worked – it was marvellous. Most of the songs survived intact in America. In the later show, *Drop of Another Hat*, we spent a few weeks on Cape Cod writing a song about diet especially for the Americans, but that was an exception; mostly we didn't write special numbers. The main thing was to make good the songs we had. The challenge and excitement was of introducing them: how can you succinctly explain our slow trains to Americans and still keep it relevant and poignant? When I did my Greek song in England, the introduction depended on people being fairly near Greece. In America, the point was how far away they were, and the strangeness of it. So Michael merely increased the surrealism of the introductory chat:

> I have a request here. It's in a rather illegible, not to speak illiterate hand, but it comes all the way from *Greece* which is exciting isn't it? – *Greece, Europe* – and I'll read it to you. It says:
>
>   *Dear Sir* – look how he spells sir, look at that, C U R. Dear Sir . . . I arrive *New York Thursday* on a reverse Fullbright, whatever that is – one of these foreign cars I suppose . . . Kindly demand of your partner, Donaldopolous, to sang again the sung – oh blimey here we go – to sing again the sung he song – me – all those years ago outside the *Temple of Pallas Athene* . . . ! *Youth Hostel* . . . (Turns to Donald.) Remember this chap? No name at the bottom. It's just *signed: An Exile, one who through no fault of his own has incurred the hatred of The World Telegram and Sun.* Well I know Donaldopolous will be delighted to give us a taste of that song – so everybody out of the pool for *Don Swann.*

There was the Wompom song I've mentioned earlier – the funny, universal plant that could make clothes and bricks – 'nothing that a wompom cannot do'. When it got to America in close proximity to Madison Avenue, it began to take on overtones of advertising. Alex was quick to spot this and said we must do it because they'd see it as a commercial or a spoof advert:

> You can shape it, you can square it,
> You can drape it, you can wear it,
> You can ice it, you can dice it,
> You can pare it, you can slice it . . .
> Oh, there's nothing that a Wompom cannot do!

Lines like these acquired a new significance there.

Take 'Misalliance', already quoted, the song about the honey-suckle and the bindweed, about a right-handed and left-handed plant trying to get together and finding they were not allowed to join up. We liked the sentiment of it, and it ended up:

> Together they found them the very next day.
> They had pulled up their roots and just shrivelled away,

166

Deprived of that freedom for which we must fight –
To veer to the left or to veer to the right!

There was a strong statement going through this song, but the idea of two plants talking to each other and forming relationships was a bit too strange and fey for American tastes, although they liked the last line. I think it's the case that Americans like concrete jokes, things that make explicit points. When people asked us about the differences in humour between a British and American audience, we'd say it's something to do with the concretisation of humour. (I wonder what others think about this?)

I do believe more people understood and appreciated 'Green-sleeves' there than in England. It was probably something to do with so many Americans 'majoring' in English. They spotted all the puns and jokes and found it very funny; we were rather pleased about that. I think the Hippopotamus song was less interesting although they enjoyed the rollicking chorus at the end and would always join in. Once again, the idea of a Hippo wallowing around in mud is unfamiliar. It's more an African thing; it belongs to the British Empire.

Michael was reaching a very high point in theatrical skill. He had now coped with three solid years of performing, felt better because of the exercise to his lungs, had found his American bride, and was beginning to enjoy enormously the challenge of working out how he would deal his cards each night. I was finding the celebrity part of it worrisome up to a point. Although we had our ups and downs, I realise how lucky we were to have somebody like Alex managing us: he probably understood the script and us better than any other manager we'd met. I know Michael believed this. But had we gone to a smaller theatre, a calmer sort of place, off-Broadway, and put out the idea 'here we are, a couple of chaps who like to mess about at the piano, come and find us', it might have been less of a strain. Because we were in this high bracket, having to draw in very good money and earn successful reviews, and all that goes with it, I think it made us to some extent not quite the people we were underneath. Michael, by becoming Anglo-Americanised, found that it suited him that little bit better; and the fact that New York is flat meant that he could wheel himself around easily. Janet found it more difficult, the huge tall buildings daunting and claustrophobic. She came from the peace of Suffolk and I think she was missing that terribly. (We later bought a cottage there.) Some of the theatricality she could take, while at other times it was a real struggle for us both.

Underlying that, I was crying out to write the other music welling up inside me. I'd write a few poetic settings in hotel bedrooms, or sometimes I'd find a piano in the hotel bar, or a little corner where I could work alone. But the show took up most of my efforts and I was trying also to keep family life going, walking out in the parks in the cold snow with my little daughters. New York is a fascinating place and I've had the good fortune to know it on a completely different level since then; living in less affluent parts of it and tasting its experimental aspects – the way-out churches, for instance.

The eight months came to an end. By now our lives were controlled by this popular show. It almost surprises me that I've been able to give so much material about two war stories – my father's and mine – in this book. All this had been put into the background; my composing ambitions were muted; I was caught up in this enormously successful story. We then had six months back in England in the spring and summer of 1960.

Meanwhile Alex was preparing a Theatre Guild tour for thirteen American cities, over three months. This was a huge hurdle for Janet and me: we couldn't decide whether the family should come or not. Eventually, there was a compromise. Janet and the children came to Los Angeles and San Francisco over Christmas, and we had some good family days with lots of swimming. So we found a way round it, but again, it was more than a bit of a strain and problem.

But the American cities tour! This meant going back and getting into yet another Cadillac. By this time Michael had insisted on not having a monster car but something more convenient so that he could get out of his wheelchair into the back seat. The car had all mod cons. Once I fed peanuts into the air conditioner and messed it up. I'd never seen one in a car before and thought it was the ashtray. We had our own driver, Bob Fribley, with whom I would eat Wheaties and shoot pool after the show, and mostly we drove from city to city, although we flew across the Rockies to the West coast. There were some lovely places to see – an endless continent to explore. The trip had enormous excitements, and was a wonderful cumulative experience. Michael seemed at his peak. We'd go into a new town and he'd say: 'What's going on here? What are we going to say about Boston? We've got Harvard and Cambridge nearby, can we find a new line?' Usually he did, and there would be two or three gilt-edged lines belonging to the town. This gave a journalistic edge to the show which was fascinating.

We would perform for two weeks at a time in the big cities, and one week in smaller places. Sometimes there was just one night. I remember we had one night in Des Moines, a large meat-producing area. In the restaurant there were three types of steak on offer: Monster, Jumbo and Ladies' Portion. It was a Monday night in a theatre large enough for a big baseball match. There we were, just two chaps from London. Unbelievably the Anglophiles from the Des Moines area turned up in strength. They all hopped into their Dodges and Packards and drove across the huge prairies to the theatre, and we got away with it. But it was very strange performing in such a large place.

When we reached Louisville we were on the Mason-Dixon line which is where the south joins the north; it's also where the accent becomes southern and our audiences were beginning not to understand us. It was in nearby Cincinnati where someone sitting in the circle asked for his money back. Seymour, our manager, invited him down to the front of the stalls where he could follow the London accent a little better – just at the very moment I was doing my camel song in Russian: 'Odín verblyúd idyét . . .' He yelled: 'I *still* can't understand a word of it!'

Generally speaking, we slowed down our speech even more than usual. I say 'we' but Michael did most of the talking. I must speak up for Michael's skills here. It was a *tour de force* to persuade the Midwest and southern audiences that London literary humour was funny, but he did it. There were some visual jokes, and what with the apt remarks about the places we visited, he delighted them. The music survived in its own form in every case. It's amazing how little I changed and how much he did. We played in Cincinnati twice on two different tours. On the first occasion, it was at the time of John Kennedy's nomination, so you can imagine how many came to the theatre that night! The second time was fall, 1966, and there was a strangler in the town; not the Boston strangler of greater fame, but a similar type. Nobody would leave their homes at night, let alone go to the theatre. So there were some hazards.

I really enjoyed the travelling: it's enthralling to cross a huge plain and see the tumbleweed or the Rockies coming up after driving a thousand miles – romantic and thrilling. I loved visiting all the different cities, and having lived in America since then, I realise what a unique experience this was. We met and made many friends. When travelling in America there are always people's aunts or friends of friends who are dying to meet you and take you out, and sometimes we were entertained munificently by all sorts of people. We visited many of the art galleries. It's very strange how most of European art is dotted around American cities. If you wish to take a dive into old Europe, just go to America. If ever I had a Sunday morning free I would go to the Episcopal church and have a quiet time before travelling on, and I met one or two new people in this way.

Here and there we met the university audiences, as in Princeton. My uncle Alfred turned up in Wilmington; and uncle Freddie who was touring America with his friend Charles Heidsieck of the Champagne family, met us in Chicago and told Michael a few more of his marvellous anecdotes, including this one about 'Teach Yourself Bridge'. He was one of the team playing bridge for Britain against the Swiss. Meeting up at Victoria station on the first leg of their journey, the British team discovered that it didn't know which convention to use for bidding, so a book 'Teach Yourself Bridge' was quickly purchased from the station bookshop. Arriving in Switzerland, the Swiss team asked which convention they used. 'Well,' they replied 'we're thinking about it, and we've got this book to advise us . . .' This appealed to Michael enormously. He got on very well with uncle Freddie who had something of his theatricality.

In St Paul, Minnesota we entered an hotel to see a sign: 'Patrons are warned that the electric current is liable to change from AC to DC without warning'. Whilst in Chicago we drove through Al Capone's gangster area, much to the annoyance of the taxi-driver. He was foul mouthed and complained that Chicago had so much to offer: the most marvellous skyline, a beautiful lake and some of the greatest modern buildings in the world . . . 'And what do you wanna see? Al Capone!' This terrible, horrible gangster had riveted our attention and he was disgusted. Most people think Los Angeles is too big. It resembles London and there's twenty miles of freeway. It looks nearly as vile as the suburbs of London, but I loved it; I almost felt I'd found the Elephant and Castle again! And the sun – it was America with the warmth of Greece put in. But when we opened in Hollywood we were really in trouble. As Michael recognised, the people there were so used to films and loud amplification that however high we put the sound, they still thought it weak. The trouble was that it was a film and not a theatre city. But he circumvented this too, and we had good notices and eventually the whole thing worked there. But such problems sometimes got me down.

One night we'd driven into a small motel on the banks of the Missouri river. (This would have been the second or third week of the tour.) Michael had his wife there, I was alone. I felt really harrowed and had a very bad night. I just couldn't sleep. There seemed to be something very weird about what we were doing. I remember thinking: what's the point of cracking a new city? I was in despair, it seemed all wrong. It could have been a bout of depression or maybe it *was* wrong. Of late I've thought that I don't know of a single actor who'd done a 1700-performance run: not Laurence Olivier, not John Gielgud, none. They bow out after the third month and go off to do their films or next play, or run a theatre or something and manage in this way to retain their freshness. I'm not an actor at all. I can't remember a line, yet I was suddenly yanked into this strange position. Now and then, and increasingly, I questioned it.

It was in a mood of that sort during the first American run, walking in Times Square to the cafeteria where I had my supper between the matinée and evening performance, that I went into a stationers and bought a huge postcard with a Statue of Liberty on it and wrote to my old Oxford friend David Marsh: 'What about *Perelandra* as an opera?' He replied 'Yes', and this led to my work on the allegorical, theological story by C S Lewis during my later sabbatical year in 1961 where, in the heart of Suffolk, I was restored with only birds listening to my music. But all through the runs of the 'Hat' shows I was going through a quiet struggle wondering how I could keep my serious composing going. I don't think Michael was ever in that position, but he had his low moments. There was one such moment during *The Ed Sullivan Show*. This was then the most popular television progamme in America, and was very prestigious. We waited for about eight hours in a miserable dressing room to do two numbers as opposed to our usual flow. We both decided that very afternoon to give up the theatre: it was too much. Michael was wrong footed. He never liked television, and always maintained we should perform to a live audience.

TV shows were comparatively infrequent. It was very important to be on Jack Parr, a very prominent chat-man, and Ed Sullivan more so; and there was always a long wait in a dressing room to be called to do your turn as part of a big bill. But it was essential to our genre to spend at least half an hour chatting up our own audience to create mutual empathy. So ten minutes on a TV show with an entertainer chat-man who perhaps we didn't want to talk to, was virtually impossible. However, we had some interesting radio shows where, because of the charming indulgence of American FM networks, you could talk as long as you wanted. 'Well Donald,' they'd say 'tell us how you feel', and they would give you four hours to answer. Now this might appear self-indulgent, but it's more than that: they allow you to talk about your artistic life, or how you love peace or politics. That is very much a part of American broadcasting. *The New York Times* has a lovely station where not so long ago I did another hour. They just said 'Gee, tell us all about it', and I really could. That's good.

There were some bizarre moments: I remember once I was all keyed up about South Africa and met a man on a programme who was in favour of apartheid. There were not many about, but there he was. He was a comedian, and we got quite animated about South Africa and the rights and wrongs of Verwoerd. Then, as the station break came up the interviewer said: 'You've been talking to two of the funniest men in America.' Two minutes later we continued heatedly discussing the blacks and the whites.

I mention this to show the freedom of the broadcasting there. It's very liberating. On the BBC and LBC you'd be lucky to get more than two or three minutes, unless you were a very famous person when you might get half an hour. The same is true of subsidiary newspaper reviewers in America. Every newspaper came up with a review, and after this had been printed they would send a second theatre critic who would come and talk to us in the hotel for perhaps two hours. Now this does give a fair chance to tell your story and indicate what you're about. Walter Kerr in the *New York Herald Tribune* gave us points for remaining English:

> One of the extraordinary things about *At the Drop of a Hat* (which is what this nonsense is called) is that its two quietly alarming zanies have not felt compelled to drop anything British, nor, for that matter, to scale down their persistently literary fantasies for the presumably less

rarefied tastes of the American audience. By some curious chance everything that is most conspicuously British is most explosively funny; and everything that is most literary – such as a worried discussion about the sour state of the Elizabethan theatre – lands hardest. It is good that no one talked them into making 'sea-changes' in their material, except for such impertinences as may have occurred to them since docking. The fun of the Nine O'Clock stage is as firmly, and as delightfully, Piccadilly as the bustling, jolly act-curtain Al Hirschfeld has designed for them.

I might add that we crossed the United States singing our song of Patriotic Prejudice:

> And crossing the Channel one cannot say much
> For the French or the Spanish, the Danish or Dutch;
> The Germans are Germans, the Russians are Red
> And the Greeks and Italians eat garlic in bed.
> The English are moral, the English are good
> And clever and modest and misunderstood.
>
> And all over the world over each nation's the same –
> They've simply no notion of Playing the Game;
> They argue with Umpires, they cheer when they've won,
> And they practise beforehand, which ruins the fun!
> The English, the English, the English are best!
> So up with the English and down with the rest!
>
> It's not that they're wicked or naturally bad:
> It's knowing they're *foreign* that makes them so mad!

Talking about touring, Toronto has to be mentioned because, geographically, it's on the American touring circuit. We played at the O'Keefe Centre built by the beer business. Michael's opening line was: 'See what you can do if you return the empties!' The audience fell about; they just loved it. The O'Keefe is the most handsome theatre I've ever played in. It could be the best in the world. Forget about sleazy backstage Broadway. You could *live* in the backstage of the O'Keefe: it was like a palatial suite, all modern, bathrooms, every comfort. I never wanted to leave it.

A little boy approached me in Toronto. He was working on a school project whereby he'd been asked to discover what he wanted to do when he grew up. He wanted to be me. 'What do I have to do to be you?' he asked. I said: 'Well, you've to write a few songs and mess around at the piano.' He began to make notes, then he asked what happened after I'd written them, so I told him that I would play and sing them myself. 'How much do you earn?' was his next question which embarrassed me a bit, but I told him it depended on how many people came to the performance which is true; everything I've ever earned is a percentage of the gross. 'Well, you are in a huge theatre which seats 3000. What need I do to reach this particular point?' 'You've got to meet somebody in a wheelchair who's funny.' That sums it up. The whole story is so eccentric; it remained as much a fairy story mid-term as it did the first day.

It was in Toronto that Marshall McLuhan came into our lives. He wrote *The Medium Is the Message*: the idea that any media technology, especially television, *is* the age, not just the adjunct of the age; and how television makes us part of the Vietnamese, the Azerbaijanis, the Australians because we are linked through technology into the global village. Rather like how the invention of printing bound people together whereas before, books had belonged just to a few monks. Layers of understanding, that's what he was interested in. He came to *Drop of a Hat* and requested to see Michael. He was with him for about an hour. He said Michael's many-layered humour appealed to him very much and related greatly to his own ideas. I was very pleased about this because he is one of the few people who has admired, intuited and got deep into Michael's style. The general consensus seems to be that Michael is the author of clever, funny songs like 'The Gasman Cometh' and 'The Warthog', and children find him terribly funny; then there's the sort of lascivious aspect of 'Madeira M'dear', and so on. It took someone like Marshall McLuhan to spot the content of the script part. I do hope in years to come someone might do a deeper analysis of Michael's scripts and his associative humour, how one idea travels to another. Many comedians have the gift. They start talking without really knowing where they're going, one idea sparks another and another. Certainly this was marked in Michael and is what made it so very funny and fresh: you never knew where he was going. As his partner it was delightful.

Studs Terkel, the famous American interviewer and writer was another interested in us. He interviewed us at very great length together. He is the best oral historian in America, working on many levels of American society, and he drew out of us what it was to try to understand another culture, and what it was to sit on stage and try to interpret and communicate ideas. Among many searching questions, he asked us how the show remained fresh and immediate; which turned out to be a mixture of journalistic instinct and theatrical skills, mostly Michael's. I was able to talk, as I'm doing now through Lyn to you, about what it was like to be a musician and to have a character written round me. Studs Terkel made us understand ourselves more, as a result of his interview, and it's right to remember him at the time I'm having a similar experience. I would love to listen to that tape if it could be found.

Toronto, Michael used to say, was like the final trip. The reason was the Canadians. They are, of course, half British and half American. That's not what they would call themselves, but Britain and America runs through the internal part of them. We were on stage to 3000, with other people still clamouring to get tickets every night. All the American asides were laughed at, and all the British roots. When we did 'The Slow Train' song, the British Canadians were thinking about Littleton Badsey and Openshaw with affectionate familiarity; and the American Canadians were thinking of all Michael had done to make it real and living for them. So it was outstandingly satisfying. Michael said at the time he thought this was the best, that we'd reached a peak. Zen and mysticism was not a language he used a lot, but he said he didn't think he could go wrong if he tried. He'd reached such a point that whatever he said was interpreted just ahead of time. Toronto theatre critics asked: 'How do you do it? Why is this huge audience enjoying it so much?' That's when we spoke about our theory of playing to the people in the front row and how they, by some contiguity, pass it back.

So there were strands of understanding and intelligibility in Toronto, and satisfaction too. But if this was the peak for Michael, it wasn't the same for me. In the sense that I loved the backstage, I've never been so comfortable – I even had a bath! But I was pining. It was rather a shame really. Tragic? No, it wasn't tragic, it was inevitable. In that week I met Boyd Neel, the best string-orchestra conductor before Neville Marriner, who had founded his own orchestra. Over lunch in Toronto he said: 'I think you could play in this Benjamin Britten opera I'm going to do.' I replied that I couldn't play that kind of music, only my own; he was very surprised. Be that as it may he was talking to me about my composing and I bored him for a whole lunch talking about *Perelandra*, the opera I so much wanted to complete and perform. But more of that later . . . He was very puzzled about my attitude, and I remember him saying: 'You ought to be thrilled. Everyone is screaming for more of your act. They simply love it.' I confessed to him that I was in some kind of torment. If Michael's shade is listening to this, he knows all about it and later, when the show vanished, he was understanding. He wanted to see this thing harmonised for me – the Donald he knew so well, happy.

10 Round the World . . . to the Gradual Coda

Our travels eventually took us outside America and whisked us around the world. In 1964, we set off for Australia and New Zealand. This had quite a different feel to it: the family were coming with me, Michael had one child then and he too saw it as a family event with real breaks built into the tour – a week off in Melbourne, another week somewhere else. It was a dovetail of domestic and professional life. I have very warm feelings about that tour. Being about eight years from the start of *Drop of a Hat*, we were able to relax. It's a very thrilling thing to see the world and I certainly have as many memories of Maoris and geysers in New Zealand, as of anything that happened in the theatre. Michael was up to his usual tricks. He had a marvellous new line in Melbourne: 'Here we are where everything is completely different: *Perry Mason*'s on a Tuesday!'

A lot of the cities reminded us of our American tour. At other times we were in the Bush with kangaroos, wallabies and all the strange foliage; so we had a chance to have a good look at Australia. At that time Australia and New Zealand relied on theatrical imports from England and America, and they were rather grateful to see any show from abroad. Now they're exporting artists and shows to us. Again, the ability of the show to survive in any English-speaking country was becoming clear: memories of the old country were reawakened when they heard us. The language problem was not so big; dialect and inflection were far less of a problem.

The humour was greatly appreciated. Some entertainers in our style had been very well received. Joyce Grenfell, when she went in the latter part of her life, really fell for Australia. When she wrote her book *Joyce Grenfell Requests The Pleasure* she kept returning to Australia to talk about it. She loved Australians and they her. There's also something of John Betjeman in Australia – the Victorian railings and the strange old houses. Echoes of old England but with an indigenous vitality. So there was much we could be in tune with.

Talking of Joyce Grenfell reminds me of an illuminating little incident in New Zealand. We went to a very remote place called Palmerston North, right in the midst of geyser and volcano country. There was a nice smoking volcano outside the town, and inadvertently I told someone how thrilled we were to be there: 'This is almost like the end of the world', I said. He told me he could hardly afford to come and see us, because earlier in the week they had Victor Borge and at the end of the week Joyce Grenfell, so it was difficult to afford all these English shows! Maybe that proves that however far you go and however remote the place, there is always a small percentage of theatre people.

We did have some very good moments. I remember sitting in Wellington on the beach where a man was playing the musical saw. The sound was drifting into the Pacific – beautiful and haunting.

Everybody loves New Zealand because it is nice and parochial. Khrushchev was deposed during our stay. The New Zealand newspaper headline that day was 'School Donates Flag-pole'! We appreciated the quiet and the unexpected snow on the hills yet warmth and green in the valleys. We spent some lovely days just driving through the countryside when we had time to spare. It was harmonious in every way.

Australians have a very strong and independent style of their own that we tried to play to. The New Zealanders were more English in all sorts of ways. They had the charming habit of refusing all tips. Very delightful if you've been travelling a great deal. I liked the tea-drinking habit and remember a beautiful brass letterbox in Christchurch Post Office with such a vast opening you could put a loaf of bread in it.

After four months our performing tour ended in Hong Kong, in January 1965. In the Civic Theatre where we played, there were thirteen Chinese stage managers. There was nothing for them to do: Michael was wheeled in every day and there was no rehearsal. We took pity on them and, searching for something to make them feel wanted, Michael asked one: 'Do you think I could have a glass of water half-way through the show, please?' But the water didn't materialise. When we asked about it one of them said: 'Glass of water fellow not come.'

After our theatrical commitments were finished I took my family to Japan. We then took off for Teheran and Abadan in Iran where, as I've explained, we sought uncle Mohammed. Then to Jerusalem – my second visit.

There was a song in our show which went:

> Oh it's hard to say 'Hoolima Kittiluca Cheecheechee',
> But in Tonga that means 'No'.
> If I ever have the money
> 'Tis to Tonga I shall go.

Tonga was on our route and I *had* the money in the sense that the around-the-world ticket took me there free. So we actually spent a few days in Tonga and found it very exciting, as everybody does who sees the South Seas for the first time. Natasha, my daughter, had a little child named after her: Nata'afa, as they don't sound the 'sh'. I remember too the Royal tortoise, Prince Tu'imalila, in the palace grounds, and hearing a choir singing the Queen of Tonga's songs, which was rather charming. Somehow throughout this world tour there seemed to be room to enjoy a whole life unconnected with the show. Much more of the world was coming into my life. I remember it as a very good time, and never stop feeding on some of the memories.

But we had to return to London for the second run of *Drop of Another Hat*; a UK tour; then go off in late 1966 for another spin around America, and our second appearance on Broadway – where the show ended.

Back in America the show was going as well as ever. In fact it seemed to get even funnier on what proved to be our last run.

There was so much love, affection and laughter pouring out of it, and had we not had this caesura in our lives in 1967 when we arbitrarily closed it down, I think it would have continued in America. We had grown to love tripping from town to town over that vast continent. Michael, with his American family was very much at home. I just finished up with a lasting affection for it. There are three countries outside Britain where I have put down roots: Greece, South Africa and America. My experience in America went very deep. I've spoken about being Anglo-Russian by birth. I often feel Anglo-American by adoption.

In the late sixties Alex Cohen tried to persuade us to stay on and continue our partnership. But I rejected it. Janet was back in England – American life had little appeal for her. The children were growing up and going to school. In some more fecund part of my imagination I wouldn't have minded them living out of theatrical trunks and having a wild non-English education of life; just learning what it is to be nomads like a circus family, with Donald at the piano and education on the trot. I don't think one has necessarily to be educated through the system – the O and A level bit. But it was not to be. It wasn't just family loyalties that drew me home. There was also the desire, which had been growing for some time, urging me to start again: to let me rethink, re-root myself, to let myself become English again. Yet much later, long after the partnership had ended and I was immersed in other things, I was again tempted to live there. America has a style of blessing people, which it had done for Michael and me. It has a way of saying: 'It's a new world, we start today.' Whereas in England we started yesterday. All along I've loved America for this.

I cannot pin-point an actual moment of decision that 'the show must end'. There was nothing definite or final. But during the last days of the USA tour, in December 1966, as we were approaching what was to be our last run on Broadway in the spring of 1967, there was a gradual, rather painful revelation that it was time to stop. At that time we had no definite plans what to do next. It seemed that we had just run out of major incentives. We were also writing less. It became very unusual for us to sit for hours to discuss Life or to write; that was a great diminution. We realised, even if we didn't voice it, that the water had trickled through the sand and we hadn't got so much material: the jokes from school and college, the wonderful creamy relationship when everything seemed so hilarious had declined. That was one of the main reasons, I think, for the ending of the show and of our partnership. Some thought it resembled a marriage heading for a major divorce. People around us were writing: 'Please don't break up, don't stop, you're giving pleasure to millions . . . don't look a gift horse in the mouth.' And so on . . . It looked as though it was time for a change. I began to dream of new possibilities.

I wish Michael was sitting here to have his say. I'd like to hear his version. I think his attitude would be: 'I was keen to continue had Donald been willing and had he not been so concerned with his other music and things he longed to get on with.' And then he'd add: 'I too had other horizons.' Yet he missed the show until the end of his days. It had become an essential part of him.

Alex Cohen was very sorry our partnership broke up and couldn't understand what had come over me, and this made me feel I was being recalcitrant rather than doing the natural thing. But I can't minimise the shock of the break. There were headlines such as the *Daily Mail*'s 'Breakup of Partnership!' It was seen as a tragedy, a mistake, or a couple of friends falling out. We had scores of letters and telephone calls from people who were genuinely dismayed that we could possibly end such a successful act. I remember my father's sadness about it. He found it difficult to understand how we drew the threads to a close, and would say we had other things to do together. He wrote to me saying 'You're giving so many people pleasure. You'll never do anything like it again', which, of course, is quite true. We would give interviews and try to explain how we felt, that we'd had a great thing together, that we'd done as much as we could for the moment, and that after 1700 performances over eleven years, we needed a change. It's sad, but I would say twenty years after it occurred, there is still no forgiveness for a successful partnership that doesn't continue. It isn't possible for people to take that in. If I wrote seventeen symphonies of Shostakovich's standard, they would still say: 'Sorry old boy, but could you please give us one more belting of the Hippo?'

There was a play featuring Sir Edward Elgar on the air recently. The character of Elgar said the public always grabs a section of what they like, that there is no mercy. With him it was *Pomp and Circumstance* and some of his salon pieces, and he was hurt in his lifetime that he wasn't understood in the entirety of his work. I'm not making a direct comparison of his and my music. I was understood, and was about to be given a good reception with my other music from quite different quarters. But there's a very strong affection for the 'Hat' songs. Particularly, as our LPs are taken from live shows, there is still an immediacy about the material. If someone's gasman has just come and put a spanner in the works and they're left with a cold boiler and no lights; it's there, live in the song: 'Oh, it all makes work for the working man to do!' and they're distressed that they can't hear it on stage.

Sometimes I've been in an hotel, for example, and heard people say: 'There's Donald Swann. How much he must be missing his partner!' Now that's twenty years after the end of the show and some fifteen years after Michael's death. From what little I've understood of Morecambe and Wise, Ernie Wise has experienced something like this. There was an extraordinary moment when they did a revival of the Flanagan and Allen show and Ches Allen came on and sang 'Underneath the Arches' with Roy Hudd. I was at one with everyone wallowing in the nostalgia and feeling enormous relief that he had returned to the stage for this moment when he could still sing. I would go so far as to say that British people have a love affair with two-man stage duos; they adore the form. Two-man partnerships performing now are likely to succeed, expecially if they rib each other and there's a bit of by-play.

I'm not a Gilbert and Sullivan aficionado, but there's no doubt there were parallels. The number of times we were compared with them! Often when I wrote a hymn or carol I was given, not the red-carpet treatment, but the 'Sullivan carpet' treatment – as if somewhere along the line I'd quarrelled with Michael Flanders about a carpet, and I'd gone my own way and got religion. This had to be because the mould dictates there is a Gilbert and there is a Sullivan. Is it any wonder that I have a Sullivan complex? Can my individual music ever be estimated on its own? The issue can best be viewed, I think, as one feature of the history of British entertainment. Give us the cliché and we'll finish the job.

This might be the right moment to say that there was a very peculiar moment in New York when Michael wasn't well, which meant that I had to handle an event on my own. This was a performance to the New York Ladies' Guild in the Hotel Astor in Times Square (where I later learned that Chenkin, the writer of the Camel song, had played in 1925). This was about the only occasion then that I performed solo and I just about crept through it. Everyone was petrified: there was only one man instead of two! Later, long after *At the Drop of a Hat* had faded from my life, I was going to do hundreds of shows alone. Perhaps that occasion was prophetic. It was when I realised that the material had got a validity even without the two of us sparking each other off – the songs existed in their own right. But on that first occasion it felt odd, as if only half of me was there.

When I think of our partnership it was generally very harmonious. In his mind Michael was both actor and director and I was pleased, even relieved to take direction from him, because I was neither of those things – just a jokey pianist. So I was very happy to be told 'laugh a little bit earlier' or 'let's go off together after this one', and some of his best lines were when he treated me as the joker. In all, the idea of being his professional partner was very pleasing.

After the break we never collaborated on stage again. It was as clean a break as anyone could imagine. But we did go out in style, because at the very end of the run in New York we were at last espoused to television. We had done a black and white hour in 1961, but now, in 1967, we selected the best songs and performed for two hours in a New York theatre where we really felt at home with a live audience. It was very well filmed with all stops pulled out. Michael had always refused to do television. It would have to be the end, he said, and it turned out to be so – but a good end. For most theatrical people, television is the beginning as it spreads their names before large numbers of people, but this was our *coup de grâce* – we watched ourselves fade away on that day. We nearly faded altogether: only recently have I tracked down part of the show. One hour is still missing, so I have a one-hour pictorialisation of what we did for eleven years.

It was interesting looking at this one-hour tape after twenty years. What impresses me so much are the circumlocutory introductions. I have the greatest respect and admiration for the serpentine way it was created, the way Michael gets from one end to the other through strange, winding paths. You get some idea of this on the LPs but there was far more speech in the shows, which people might have forgotten, because their minds are taken up with the songs. I still find it very funny. I was impressed with the amount of action, which I don't think I realised at the time in my position at the piano: the way Michael would move the chair around, his relationship with me, the intimacy he created by placing his hand on my stool. There were many ways in which he linked us together into a real pair and not two separate individuals. His use of the wheelchair was most theatrical: the effective use of the wheels, the angles he presented to the audience, the action when he wanted to indicate frustration with me, the stooge; it was all so professional.

And watching myself after twenty years? I look like a twit. I can't understand how anybody could sit and watch me! It's probably the case that most performers have a shock when they see themselves on film and realise just what their audiences have lived with. At the time it seemed so right that I should be the daft curate type grubbing away at the piano. All the same, I think I exaggerated the flakey, strange, daffy odd-ball. But I can see that it's very visual. The sight of myself being so very . . . loopy – yes, that's the word – was in a way interesting because, with the frugality of our set, it was something else to watch. I've since realised that watching piano-playing is something to do with watching a man digging a hole in a road: the actual physical activity is as important as the sound. Once I went to a lady who taught the Alexander technique, the-keep-your-body-straight idea. She told me that had she known me earlier, she would have taught me how to play keeping my body still and straight. 'If only . . .!' I thought. There isn't any need to jump about the way I do. It must be some sort of bodily malfunction which is now part of me. But sitting in a room watching myself, I find it peculiar and feel uncomfortable. Friends tell me that in the show it was different: in the context of the jokes, the fun, Michael's ribbing and, of course, the songs themselves, it went naturally with the structure of the show. I'm still pretty jumpy, but less so. I think I've learnt to relax and speak from the heart rather than from set lines. In *At the Drop of a Hat* I hardly spoke at all. I had to make my presence felt with my playing, which became theatrical. My clowning in the Mozart Horn piece brought this home to me when I saw it on the video. That's what I had forgotten, all the odd visual sides to the show and it was good, if uncomfortable in places, to be reminded.

I think it must be clear to my readers by now that I had, and still have ambivalent feelings about this period of my life. When I look back on these years, as well as recognising what a gift I'd been given, I return to these points of considerable tension. It's as though some part of my life was being eroded. I was 'in the middle brow', while members of my family and many friends were 'in the high brow', and sometimes I would think: 'When am I going to get back to it? Has it all gone by default? When will I change key?' I was writing and playing nice little melodies – beginnings, middles, ends – all very apposite, but this music was doing nothing for my new emotions. The main hazard was repetitive performance: every night, year after year. It seemed to go on forever. We were in a very strange situation in which there was no other form to go into. Together, we achieved a sort of plateau and the only thing that seemed right was to go on and to do it again.

In my case there was a sense of loss. True, I had always kept my hand in with other compositions, and even taken a year off to write *Perelandra* and another little opera with Colin Wilson, but it seemed that I could only do these other things on the side, in the sabbatical time I could give to them. It was rather like playing tennis only on holiday, and this when my emotions were getting deeply involved and I desperately wanted to express myself. So I've come away believing that I was given an incredible gift with this extraordinary show that went so well, but I exchanged it for some of my young creative lifetime. Maybe my other compositions, even if they had been unprofitable, would have been growing and maturing and I would have felt more and more at home with the poets I love setting. Much of the individual music I wrote during these eleven years was done early in the morning, but it was the theatre that took my main energy. People might say 'What a pity Donald Swann never wrote anything but *At the Drop of a Hat.* I wish he would have gone on playing with Michael Flanders as long as he could.' What they don't realise is the process of rebirth in the theatre.

Probing even deeper, I can only express how I felt by likening myself to a violin that the audience and the success of the show were playing. I walk on stage, I'm used, and I walk out again – a funny feeling. I think I'm talking about the loss of identity. I felt less myself. My wife noticed it, and realised the sort of strain I was living under. As time has continued I've come to realise the enormous tension existing between the performer and the writer in any one person. I would never presume to compare myself with Benjamin Britten, but I feel a sense of kinship with him in the sense that he was both a pianist as well as composer.

Apart from his great bursts of performing with Peter Pears and others, not to mention his conducting, somewhere along the line he realised that it was the composing path he would take. I was destined in that period to take the other path, that of performer. I can't say I'm sorry, because apart from anything else the *Drop of a Hat* royalties have continued to pay the rent, given enjoyment to many, and provided some sort of social service that even pleased Archbishops! It was doing people good. Once a couple of children got stranded at Land's End, and they kept going by singing the Hippo song until a boat came to rescue them. Michael and I read about it in the paper and thought: 'There's something important going on here: it's worth it.'

After the show ended in 1967 various agents would come and ask us to go to the Festival Hall for a reunion. We never did. As Michael said: 'You don't understand it takes me three months to build up a script. You think I go on and from the top of my mind say: "Good evening, here is Donald Swann, here is the Omnibus song." Nothing could be further from the truth: I've honed this script to the point where it's worthy of attention only after months of preparation.' I remember he used to say that the opening night was nothing, but it was the tenth performance where it started to be good.

Although we didn't collaborate again, we kept in touch but not nearly as much as before. I was getting immersed in lots of new things. For a time I lived in Suffolk; another time I toured around performing with new artists. If anything, I became more theatrically involved than Michael as he was beginning to live a slightly quieter life: he worked in radio and television, and wrote a very good comic oratorio with Joseph Horovitz called *Captain Noah and His Floating Zoo*. I think we were a bit sad when we met, ruminating on old times and what might have been; sometimes there was more than a fleeting sense of loss. I used to go and see him in Rustington-on-Sea, quoted in the Gnu song: 'I had taken furnished lodgings down at Rustington-on-Sea.' There he was in his flat looking at the sea which, as a mariner, he loved. During these talks we worked out a new title, *Hat Trick*, for the third show. We had a bag of fragments which we would occasionally delve into, thinking they might grow into full-length songs. There was a poem about mental health, that never acquired a tune:

> I and me are together again
> Thanks to professor McGumm.
> All hail Meadowlees Nursing Home and Sanatorium.
> We're having a grand reunion,
> We're sorting out our glands.
> I am simply thrilled with me
> And we can't stop shaking hands.

We had odd ideas for revue turns which never matured. One was for a costume trio: Beau Brummell, Beau Nash; not forgetting Bow Legs.

I wanted Michael to find words for three actors dressed as pencils: H, HB, and B. But he never did so, though he thought it intriguing. We started *The Seven Deadly Sins*, but never got further than Gluttony where we wrote a bit on cheeses; and Avarice which included the following (with a music-hall waltz tune). You can tell the date of the lyric by the refrain L S D:

> I like Money, Money, Money
> It's your pal when things are rough,
> Can't get enough of that crinkly stuff.
> I like Money
> Happiness here's the key,
> I'll take the wages and you take the sin
> In L S D.
>
> I like Money, Money, Money
> Lots and lots of lovely mun
> Raking it in is such innocent fun.
> And we all like money
> Everyone must agree
> If you're wealthy, you can't go wrong
> Give me a wallet as broad as it's long
> Why do you think I am singing this song,
> It's for L S D.
> Cash in the bank for me!

189

I still sing this song. In Thatcherite Britain it has come to sound like the National Anthem.

We had one or two songs like *Singing in the Lifeboat*. It was meant to be a song about the world changing all around us, but somehow we never managed to improve on it, or finish it. Earlier, we thought of doing a musical about the Odyssey but the only thing we ever got out were a few titles. There was a song for Cerberus, the three-headed dog:

> It's a dog's life living in hell,
> Not an interesting smell;
> And as I said to my other two heads
> It's a dog's life living in hell.

There was another one for Circe:

> Circe, Circe, please have mercy, de-piggify my crew!

As I speak of fragments I recall Michael's mnemonic for my telephone number which was MACaulay 4281: 'I bought mackerel for two and ate one.'

Twenty years earlier, I would have brought the file out on the Odyssey and said: 'Somebody's going to ask for it, let's do it. Let's do it at the Coliseum!' Everything then had enormous life. Now these fragments didn't look so prophetic.

I'd like to say something about our LPs. There were two on-stage recordings done with great care by George Martin, the most excellent recording manager; then there was *The Bestiary of Flanders and Swann*, a studio recording. Two more were issued from 'overheard' material. This was a more primitive method whereby a tape recorder was placed backstage, recording our performances. Later these fragments, recorded from our shows abroad as well as in the UK, were filtered and knitted together to form an LP called *Tried by the Centre Court*. Another selection culled from the songs we wrote for Laurier Lister's revues were grouped under the title *And Then We Wrote*. The three main LPs have been on sale ever since, all over the English-speaking world. Never runaway hits that sold millions, but very steady sales going on through the generations; as much, I think, because of the immediacy – you can hear the audience reactions as though it was yesterday. I am delighted to say that as I write three CDs are being prepared to comprise all the 'Hat' LP material and will reincorporate all the deleted songs and sketches.

Michael, rather more than me, was against the printed publication of our material. At various times he had been very fierce about it. He thought the stops and starts, the little jokes in between with the audience coming in, were vital. Actors have a real love of the actual night of the show. True theatre is unrepeatable and Michael said to write the songs down would be death to them; that when the curtain goes down we were finished. It was a living art. It didn't matter how well the Gnu song was written down: it would have no comparison to our presentation of it. He would argue that with music it didn't matter, the next pianist could play as well as Mozart himself, but with comedy you need to do something else. By the same token, with a few exceptions, he did not welcome anyone else using our material. Our old chum, John Amis, was singing the songs he liked most from time to time; Ian Wallace continued to proselytise our work as he'd done from the start of his career; and The Spinners and King's Singers made their own arrangements. But most of them we considered personal to ourselves.

I was used to bits of printed music lying about at home and pushed Michael to the publication of ten songs with Chappell & Co. Later, after his death, the main corpus of our songs was published by Elm Tree Books and St George's Press, and very handsomely illustrated by distinguished artists and cartoonists. I was to have a hand in its production, but I didn't know the strength of my own reaction against publication, and when this book was being produced, I was in great mental turmoil and just couldn't complete it. It was finished by associates. I wrote an introduction and I'm very thrilled with the book now, but I had then a built-in resistance. It seemed as though I was betraying Michael; I was writing down what belonged to the two-man show. I suppose Michael would have conceded that years after the show had ended, why shouldn't people play and enjoy 'Have Some Madeira M'dear'? But when you hear the record you realise the immediacy of his approach, which is so much more entertaining than the look of the music. I think if Michael could be sitting here with us today he'd probably say: 'Look Donald, I know you went through a lot of trouble and anguish, but up there in my eyrie I thought you had the most difficult task. I accept it and I'm glad the book is there.'

There was a strange sequel to it. In my introduction to the book I mentioned that here and there we'd got rid of the more difficult bits of my improvisation. Somebody wrote: 'Would you please send me the more difficult bits. I can't understand why they're not included and I want to know what you did when you were giving your all.' I'd like to put this in for any publisher who might read this because it reminded me of our joint attitude throughout our collaboration; that you must never underestimate your audiences. There are people who want the most abstract, peculiar and complicated thought you've got. This chap writing about my simplified music put me right.

Now that the song-book is out I feel content that people should sing our songs. Claudia and I, up until now, have been very diffident about the rewriting of Michael's lines for advertisements, often refusing large sums from people such as kitchen fitment and chocolate mousse manufacturers. We feel he was essentially writing about human foibles, not products. I think it's true that his verbal felicitousness comes very close to advertising styles and he once contributed a rewrite of the Gnu song for Typhoo: 'T-t-typhoo . . .' This reminds me of an anti-advert song we once wrote that seems much to the point. You'll have to use your imagination regarding the name!

192

Don't buy * *
It makes your woolies shrink
It gives you nasty dishpan hands
And rots away your sink
There are dozens of detergents
The choice is up to you
But don't buy * *
Whatever else you do.

Disembodied voice: 'This programme comes to you by courtesy of the makers of *.'

It's very strange when I watch other people performing our material. My usual feeling is that the speeds are wrong. Timing is so crucial: a bit faster or a bit slower and I feel something congealing inside me. Obviously, I miss the tactile thing too: the fact that I'm at the piano appears to be half the song. But another part of me, the musicological part, says that Chopin too must have felt curious when anyone tried one of his mazurkas; but I'm sure it wasn't long before someone did it at least as well as he did. Perhaps it's the case that anyone would feel edgy when others try their compositions. Michael was much stronger than that. He just didn't want it and wouldn't allow it. The consequence is that it's made us much richer. Because we published very little, the royalties go through something called Mechanical Copyright Protection Society and Performing Rights Society, direct to us and not through any publisher taking his eighty per cent of the whole thing. So the jealousy of our rights, certainly not motivated for financial gain, turned out to be a useful decision.

In the last years various people have wanted to 'play' us – someone play him, someone play me. There are many look-alike performances now – Dickens, Dylan Thomas, Oscar Wilde – and I should think that accomplished actors could achieve it, wheelchair and all. The idea has been mooted but only with initial efforts. When Michael died, Laurier Lister was dreadfully upset and devised a show called *Hats Off!* which ran at the Guildford Theatre, with a group of actors using all our material. For some reason it didn't run long. Perhaps it

193

was too early. I sat in the audience and watched the Gnu song and thought it very funny. My good friend Bill Blezard played my music immaculately. Here and there, out of the blue, there have been outstanding performances and I can watch without any sense of embarrassment. Certainly the songs seem to rekindle in people's imaginations; they seem to have an immediate life. I've mentioned the ubiquitous gasman, but there are lots of others that come up good and strong.

As for the animal songs, it seems that a lot of parents put these before their children quite early, and they're enthralled when the child starts trilling 'The Gnu' in the back of the car. I suppose they relive their youth with them. This transfer to a younger generation has given the songs a durability, and part of the appeal is that the child is learning language, and from the age of four anything to do with verbal assonances and parodies appeals. Maybe the light, tripping music has something to do with it, maybe the fact the verbal things are humorous instead of serious. Whatever the reasons, the songs do have a life in this second and third reception which is less connected with theatre, and more to do with records. But I suppose this is connected with theatre in that people who saw the show want to talk about it. They tell their children about where they went and what they saw when they were courting. 'My mum and dad got engaged during your show', they come and tell me. Very romantic.

When Michael died I was on tour, in Ayr. Our agent phoned and gave me the news. I just couldn't get out of this tour; it couldn't be done without putting lots of people to great inconvenience. I badly wanted to go to North Wales, where he had died, and even tried to commission a small plane, but it wasn't practicable and Claudia told me not to push it, and so my wife went up. So I was on the move again when he died. Ironic, isn't it, considering my earlier reluctance to go touring?

Michael died in an isolated guest house in North Wales where he was taking a holiday with Claudia. I gather he was relaxed and very peaceful. He always had to exert himself tremendously to get in and out of bed, and the car; and the business of lifting himself up by pulleys put an enormous strain on him. To his doctors his early death was not unexpected. But I didn't expect it and it came as a great shock. He always seemed so strong. Now, I understand that polio victims apparently have extra strength in the years they flourish. They seem to have more stamina, grit and ambition. They are able to hurl olympic javelins from a wheelchair. Michael had this sort of strength. People when watching him forgot he was in a wheelchair from the time the curtain went up, he was so full of vigour and vitality. But the actual struggle and strain to lead an independent life eventually proved too much for him.

A musical friend of mine knew the family with whom Michael was staying at that time. They were sheep farmers who did bed and breakfast. A few years after Michael's death my friend was in touch with this family. They told her that an entertainer, a man in a wheelchair, had died in their farmhouse. They knew nothing about her connection with me, but she realised at once it must have been Michael. They told her that he spoke mostly about sheep – asking about all their different habits, their weights, the business of sheep shearing and so on. Perhaps he was thinking of another animal song. Evidently he said to them: 'This is the first place I've ever stayed where nobody knows what I do.' He had reached anonymity and died. I was touched by that, touched very deeply. I have myself craved for anonymity, thinking it a beautiful concept. It could be that some of the fame and fortune that I have certainly enjoyed, and given good report of, had produced a strain, not only on me, but on him too. Perhaps we'd lost the pure pleasure of being just ourselves. Then, in the end, he was granted a moment like that. A blessing.

About three months after Michael died, I received a letter from a Medium. She said, 'I don't know who you are, but I've been told that you are an entertainer and a friend of somebody called Michael Flanders who appeared to me and spoke from the other side. He said he was now walking and was very happy.' I'm sorry if I appear cynical but I just didn't believe it. I thought Michael would never say anything so prosaic. That's not the way he'd put it: he would make some very silly remark to make me laugh. I hope he is happy and is walking but it was the language and style that was unconvincing. Since that time I have found out that Mediums pick up all sorts of interesting things; that there's a virtual library dictated by people like Gandhi and Martin Luther King to earthly readers, and that the material is quite good, often in the same genre. Liszt also dictates music to somebody down here frequently. But the trouble with spirits is they seem to be slightly lacking in theatricality. They never have the same sparkle as their worldly counterparts. This message was unique. Michael doesn't keep talking to her. There was a certain amount of fortuitousness in that she had no idea who we were. How it trickled back to me, I'm still unclear. It was probably from some ethereal source.

Now we're in the realm of the supernatural I'd like to tell the story of Mr Buckstone, the Haymarket ghost. It was on the stage of this remarkable theatre that a costumed gentleman appeared behind the piano during one of our shows. The assistant manager asked the stage director during the interval 'Who was that man standing behind Michael in the first half, not quite in the vision of the audience, but on stage?' The stage director asked what he looked like and when he heard about the costume he said it must be the Haymarket ghost, Mr Buckstone, a former manager who visits them from time to time. Our stage director rang up the *Evening Standard* and by the following evening it was widely advertised: 'Ghost visits *Drop of Another Hat* . . . Visitation on stage.' If you ask the Haymarket they'll give the ghost's CV; and our event is recorded in the Ghost Records where all appearances are noted. I'm rather sceptical about spiritual occurrences, but that is what happened and it did seem a bit strange. The assistant stage manager was not a fey or whimsical person, and she was quite surprised. Her first thought was that it was some actor looking in – maybe the Actors' Church Union priest dressed up in costume! But the apparition was there. Nobody but her saw it that night. If you go to the Haymarket there's nothing to fear. He's always very friendly.

That ghost has set me reflecting. When I think of the time when Michael and I parted and I set out alone, it felt like a huge thing – awesome. But if someone saw the ghost of old Buckstone at the Haymarket behind Michael, I've always had the ghost of Michael Flanders behind me in the shows I've played alone. Not breathing down my neck, but there in some way. The whole idea of speaking and then singing came from Michael. Prior to an oratorio, I will get up to say 'hello' and have a few words because I'm so used to narrative with music. The idea of being juxtaposed with a piano and music stool is typical *Drop of a Hat* style which I still follow in the midst of any other style of music; the idea of interpreting Life in a two-hour show. Sometimes I have missed Michael intensely because of his great professionalism. Although he sat in a wheelchair, I could lean on him. There was so much energy and vitality emanating from him; he could fend for himself in any situation. The moment he was not there I had to work considerably harder.

So I've had this sort of ghostly partner who tries to talk to me all the time. We were in the theatre for hours on end; living our lives within the context of flies up in the roof, battens, floodlights and backstage props, with people coming round to meet or convert us or to get their autographs signed. I can see this ghost representing all this, and I find myself giving a Report to Greco, saying: 'This I did and this I didn't.' If that ghost means anything to me at the moment, it is that after the *Drop of a Hat* experience, for all the music that I've written and am writing, and whatever the performing I've done without him, there was a major theatricality about the Flanders and Swann era which forever haunts me.

11 Into the World of Fantasy

I would like to invite you now into the phase of my life where my music reached out to new and deeper dimensions and where I have gained my greatest satisfaction and fulfilment. I would hazard a guess that only a very small fraction of Flanders and Swann fans are familiar with the music I've written and performed since the end of our partnership in 1967: who has heard of *A Crack In Time*? *Requiem for the Living*? or *The Visitors*? Yet since Michael and I parted I've been working continuously for twenty-four years – longer than the period of writing and performing that I covered with Michael.

Let me start with *Perelandra* which for me, symbolically, changed my career more than anything else. This did not follow our partnership. Rather, it sprang from it because, as I've explained, it was on the move between a matinée and evening performance on Broadway that the idea was born.

Perelandra is a story written by C S Lewis in 1941, and reflects his lyric and romantic side. Lewis's descriptions of new planets in his space fiction stories are intensely romantic and bound up with a dream world, and this is what attracted me so deeply. The fantasy world was a place I wanted to live in. It was my first incursion into such a world – the first time I tried to express fantasy in music.

The story is an allegorical re-think of the Garden of Eden story. *Perelandra* contains one of Lewis's searching portrayals of paradise, of the true world that he felt in his bones was ours but from which we had been disinherited, not only mythically through Adam, but daily through each one of us. The planet

Perelandra, which is really Venus, is an idyllic place of primeval beauty and innocence, and the story is concerned with the risk that it will fall from grace. The central character on Perelandra is the Green Lady. All the islands on Perelandra are shifting and moving in great seas. They are covered with the most exquisite trees and flowers and the apple of temptation, in the Green Lady's case, is the land that is fixed: if she goes there – and she well knows she must not – chaos and corruption will ensue.

There is a hero from the earth world, a professor called Ransom, who is taken up to Perelandra in a coffin-like spacecraft made of crystal by an eldil, or angel. Ransom is entranced with the Green Lady and her beautiful planet, its wealth of exotic vegetation, heaving seas, weird and wonderful animals and fish; and the tastiest, juciest fruit growing profusely all over the place. But another spaceship lands containing the evil professor Weston who represents science and technology. The big question is: will she listen to one, or to the other: to good or to evil? Weston tries to entice the Green Lady to the fixed land and his eventual aim is to rape and desecrate the planet.

The story reflects Lewis's feelings and fear about science and technology: he was frightened of what he would call the satanic possibilities of materialism. He loved the countryside and had this vision of a pristine, virgin world in Perelandra. The fact that the Green Lady was naked meant she had no need of the appurtenances of civilisation. There is a whole series of temptations dramatised in the story. As Weston is the devil, he assumes satanic powers: unlike Ransom he doesn't need sleep, for instance, and he takes on all the majesty of an evil archangel. To cut a very long story short, Ransom kills Weston in a very dramatic scene and the planet is saved.

Lewis wrote Perelandra in 1941, during the war, when he felt that a battle for civilisation was going on all around him. You might ask what I, as a pacifist, was doing writing music to such a death struggle, but it seemed to me that it was not too bad a thing to kill the devil.

The impact of it was that while composing it I was able to live, not with all the razzmatazz of Broadway, but in a dream world. I could live in places where eldila were walking around singing and talking. I worked on it in a little cottage in Suffolk where I lived with my piano in a quiet, secret world. I think this was the beginning of my release from showbiz. It was a very ambitious project and the opera lasted for about three hours in the end. It was essential for me to bite off my big lyrical apple. It was an important moment.

I worked on the libretto with David Marsh, with whom I had written songs and carols and who shared a great love of this book. Together we approached Lewis's agents and asked for permission to have a go at setting it to music. Lewis was very keen and from then on, over a couple of years, we'd go up to Oxford to see him with little pieces of it – a rare and rich experience. Lewis had been at Oxford during my time there. I vividly remember the one occasion I heard him lecture. He was asked whether God had a sense of humour. 'Surely this is impossible because he knows everything that is going to happen all the time', a student said. Lewis thought for a moment, then replied: 'I think that would make it even funnier.' That impressed me: I was amused by his presence of mind as well as by his own sense of humour.

People often describe Lewis as looking very much like a farmer, with a red face and a love of a pipe and a beer; an apt description. We would go to the Oxford pubs and sit and talk about our ideas and hum little snatches of what we had done. We had some fascinating discussions about details of Perelandra, a world before the Fall. I remember David had a line about spiders eating prey. Would they be eating prey in a world before the Fall? Lewis decided that we had to leave the line out because as far as he could see in this pure world spiders wouldn't be preying on helpless creatures. Then David asked why, in the whole of Perelandra, there was just the Green Lady and the King. Why were there no children; weren't they having sexual relations? Lewis was noncommittal on this. He assumed they were but said that wasn't the point. The point was that when the satanic Weston was destroyed ten thousand years of joy and fruitfulness would come to the planet.

At one point Lewis turned up with his own lyric, but we couldn't fit it in. I couldn't get used to his style: it was too awkward. He was rather fed up with that. In fact I think he would have liked to write his own libretto. A recent biography by A N Wilson suggests that he was a frustrated poet. I would agree that he was a poet, but his theology and fantasy stories are more trenchant.

It was a terrible loss when he died in 1963. I still feel bereaved of his presence. He became a good friend to us and collaborated enthusiastically with the opera. He loved it when he heard it. The first performance took place in a beautiful country house in Cirencester. He came with his friend Dr Havard, the doctor character in the book who packs Ransom into the spacecraft when he sets off for Perelandra. It was sung by myself at the piano together with a team of singers who exemplified parts of it. Later he wrote that it moved him to tears and I know it would have been the most wonderful collaboration if we could have reached the point where he fed his ideas to producers and directors.

The music is very different from what I had been doing with Michael – much deeper and wider in scope. As with everything I have ever done, it was written at the piano and the lyrical excitement and belief in it carried me through for a long time. When it was finished I commissioned a good friend, Max Saunders, to score it professionally for a symphony orchestra. So it exists both in a piano score and in an orchestral version. In a way you would expect electronic instruments making out-in-space sounds instead of a single piano, but then we each have to work with our own instrument. I was limited but also liberated by the piano where I could hear all these curious cosmic sounds. There is no doubt this was an epic experience for me, and there is a vast torrent of people who read Lewis who share this desire to be in a fairy tale: they want to go through the wardrobe and exist in Narnia. For me, the appeal lay in the more adult stories: *Out of the Silent Planet*, *That Hideous Strength* as well as *Perelandra*.

There is a song of Michael Flanders's called 'The Song of Reproduction'. Some of the lines I used to sing endlessly were:

> I've an opera here you shan't escape
> On miles and miles of recording tape. . .

This has come true! Here I am still regaling people with my opera. It *is* on recording tape, and I play it to people. I remember sitting with a music critic one day and played him the whole thing, three hours long. He went to sleep! He couldn't take it at all. I'm sure he thought 'What is he playing at? Why doesn't he give us a funny song? He is carried away on this strange thing.'

But in the period that followed the writing, David and I cut it down to a two-hour opera in two acts. Some parts were put into speech, whereas originally it was only singing and music without speech. Eventually in another great effort, I anthologised the choicest passages into a choral suite.

I think of *Perelandra* with a great sense of yearning. There is a feeling of loss to be involved in such a huge drama and then find it not being performed all the time. Michael and I were to feel this sense of loss when our partnership began to go over the hill and our new lives were being born; and I never cease to feel that my other works are lost as they are created. Paradise lost as well as regained: strange how Milton's 'lost' part is more successful than the regained. Yet with *Perelandra* I can't help feeling that I have written a lyrical opera which may take its place among English works of this form. It's only now that I realise what a 'Green' opera I wrote and I think it will find its place in the new Green awareness. These lines are sung by the chorus as Ransom and Weston face up to their epic fight for the planet:

> Now is all Perelandra cast in sleep,
> But what shall greet its waking?
> Shall its opening eyes
> See paradise still undefiled, unravished, uncorrupt?

> Or shall they see
> Foul imperfection, sullied beauty, innocence destroyed,
> And life made subject to the prince of death?

We all want to see people back in their pristine surroundings with clear waters and green forests. It's possible that Lewis anticipated the rape of our planet; he had a passionate feeling that technology would destroy the world. At the time of writing, the world he loved was being destroyed by the Second World War of this century; now the third world war – the rape of the planet – is in everybody's mind. So I am confident that *Perelandra* will find its place among the Lewis aficionados: those who love fantasy and the cosmic and whose imaginations are Green.

Lewis is enormously loved in America. Uncle Alfred and Aunt Jane became great supporters and persuaded Haverford and Brynmawr colleges to perform the opera. I remember once asking uncle Alfred whether he agreed it sounded rather like a Russian opera. He retorted that all operas sound like other operas. He was a great champion of derived music and felt there is no such thing as original music, and it annoyed him that anyone should think so. The opera's director, Robert Butman, Professor of Drama at Haverford, who had been Christopher Fry's secretary in England, spent a couple of terms working on it. I mentioned the fight to the death – the great battle of wills between Ransom and Weston. When it was performed at Haverford they found two all-in wrestlers who were also singers. When they got to the fight it was the real thing. They actually had a great fight on stage, yelling to each other the different wrestling movements: 'number three, number five!' and so on.

It was taken to New York for a single performance where it attracted a couple of rave notices from the *New Yorker* and the *Wall Street Journal*: 'We're going to hear this for the rest of our days!' So I've had some fulfilment with the piece, but not as much as I want. What I need now is a couple of productions to see whether these critics were right or whether all I've said about it is rubbish. But I believe in it. My new literary agent, Geoffrey Barlow, is conversant with American colleges, like Wheaton and

UCLA in California, which house Lewis memorabilia. He has contacted them saying: 'Do you realise there is an opera that Dr Lewis himself collaborated on and gave a lot of personal approbation?' He is confident that *Perelandra* will soon be performed there, so I'm very hopeful. It seems right that it should have its life along with his other works.

I thank C S Lewis for drawing me into the fantasy world. There is one episode I shall always remember. This was during one of our occasional meetings when David and I were starting on *Perelandra*. It was a quiet morning and we went to Lewis's home in Oxford for breakfast. We strolled around his lovely garden with him, talking about the opera. After about an hour he said: 'I hope you will excuse me. I must go now because my wife died last night.' He left us. I was very moved. Quite overcome. It is just another story of this very gracious gentleman who always looked after his guests. I mean, at a time like that! What did *we* matter? She was Joy Davidman, and he later wrote a moving book about her death. *Shadowlands* – the story of his wonderful relationship with her – has been dramatised.

Professor Tolkien had a similar influence on me. The world of hobbits, the small creatures in *Lord of the Rings* and his other books, really gripped my imagination. I was so inspired by his lyrics that, setting out on the world tour of the 'Hat' in 1964, I took them with me. In Ramallah, outside Jerusalem, on a very beautiful Steinway, I set seven songs from *Lord of the Rings*. When I returned to England I was introduced to Tolkien by his publisher and yet another wonderful phase opened up for me.

Tolkien heard my setting of his hobbit lyrics. He was delighted and his wife, Edith, who had been a concert pianist, loved them too. Eventually they were produced in a Lieder song-cycle, *The Road Goes Ever On*, and a book was printed with Tolkien's calligraphy and Elvish runes.

I became caught up in his world even more than the world of Lewis. I got to know Tolkien well and had some fascinating discussions with him too. Like Lewis, who invented a language called Old Solar – the language of the eldila and the Green Lady – Tolkien invented Elvish, as well as many other languages. Being a linguist I could talk to him like a student. I'd ask how French and German compared with Elvish roots, and we spent many a happy hour discussing such things. There are very few people who speak Elvish. I speak a bit. I'm going to a conference next year where the Tolkien enthusiasts from all over the world will gather, talking Elvish. The language is complex and difficult to speak, but if you wish to say, 'There are hairs on my foot', or 'Please may I have some tobacco', there will be an Elvish word to suit.

I worked with a singer called William Elvin – an unbelievably appropriate name – who had been coached by Tolkien. Elvin had a Scottish accent and Tolkien thought that about right. Tolkien was very proud of being Viking. His original family came from Denmark, and Elvish, if anything, derives from Norse. Here is a verse from 'Namárië', the Lament of Galadriel which I set to music.

> Ai! láurië lántar lássi súrinèn,
> yéni ùnótimè ve rámar áldaròn!
> Yéni ve línte yúldar avániër
> mī óromárdi lísse-mìruvórevà
> Andúne pélla Várdo téllumàr
> nu luíni, yássen tíntilàr i élenì
> ōmáryo aíre-tári-lírinèn.
> Sì mán i yúlma nín ènquántuvà?

Ah! like gold fall the leaves in the wind, long years numberless as the wings of trees! The long years have passed like swift draughts of the sweet mead in lofty halls beyond the West, beneath the blue vaults of Varda wherein the stars tremble in the song of her voice, holy and queenly. Who now shall refill the cup for me?

I remember when he first heard the tune I'd written for 'Namárië' he said: 'Oh no; this time I have one of my own', and he whistled and hummed it. This was strange because it turned out to be a Gregorian chant. Tolkien was Roman Catholic and in his mind he heard Catholic plainsong. In the published work I used his tune and it works beautifully because you get the Gregorian chant emerging strangely out of my music. Another, 'Errantry', is the song of Tom Bombadil, one of the characters in *Lord of the Rings*. This has ingenious tri-syllabic rhymes and I set them to ethereal, fairy-like music. The other songs are lyrical and resemble Grainger or even Schubert. (Michael used to say my music was more sherbert than Schubert.) There is one record of the songs and I think it is high time that another was produced, perhaps with the choral embroidery I added in the second edition of the book.

I keep talking about loss and longing. At the moment the song I love most of all is 'Bilbo's Last Song'. The lyric was handed to me at Tolkien's funeral by his dedicated secretary, Joy Hill, who is a close friend and neighbour of mine in Battersea. She said: 'Professor Tolkien gave me this lyric as a gift'. I was stirred up that day and went off and wrote a tune for it, to be sung as a duet, although I often perform it solo. People love it, and I feel very strongly about it. Like the other Tolkien songs it is very melodic compared with the serpentine wobblings and drama of *Perelandra*. The tune is based on a song from the Isle of Man: I was performing in a concert there and heard a beautiful song which is very popular there, almost their national anthem. It is sung in Manx which resembles Elvish. 'Bilbo's Last Song' also resembles a Cephallonian Greek melody. This was very significant for me with my love of islands: the merging of two islands – Cephallonia, an Ionian island, and the Isle of Man, the English kind of island – the east and west of our shores. In this song a ship is taking Bilbo to the land of the Elves; he is turning up in a dream world which is really his death. So Tolkien foretold the end of Bilbo, his central character, and in doing so he foretold his own demise. It was his parting gift to his secretary. He knew it would be a precious and useful thing for her. The final illustration in this book emerged from this lyric.

I've subsequently set another lyric, 'Lúthien Tinúviel', from *The Silmarillion*. Lúthien, the romantic name of an Elvish princess, was the name Tolkien called his wife. She looked the part, as she was a very small and beautiful lady. When I was welcomed into the Tolkien family I encountered a very stable and happy home life; they all loved and respected Tolkien and his extraordinary thoughts. Most of the fantasy books were written for his children. *The Father Christmas Letters*, and the hobbit character itself was engendered by the children for whom he invented these stories, and they enjoyed them so much that he began to write them down.

As for Tolkien's character, he was rather like Lewis. He'd smoke his pipe and bumble away with a good drink at his elbow. He was very much the Oxford don, with a great sense of humour. He was interested in books and genealogy and was immersed in his family lineage. He loved to tuck into a good meal and wouldn't talk too much about hobbits and the fantasy world; but if you asked about them he'd be pleased to explain different aspects. He was a most interesting, agreeable, genial person. I derived great happiness and solace from that friendship, as did my wife.

There is so much written about C S Lewis and Tolkien today. Books appear all the time about what they said, what they thought, what they did; how they belonged to The Inklings, an Oxford club for like-minded men. I've read several of these books and must be careful to separate out my own memories from the wealth of information in them. It never came up in my conversations with them, but I knew they had drawn apart towards the end of their lives. I think their closest relationship was when they were dons at Oxford, chatting things up in The Inklings and entering each other's fantasy worlds. Then Lewis got married and went to Cambridge and this all changed. Another era opened for both of them. But I knew them as two separate individuals and to me they have remained rather glorious, linguistic, professorial figures who created the legends for which, apparently, there is an enormous craving. Although the Englishness comes through very strongly, Tolkien's books are translated into many languages. Good for us that we can still create universal myths. I hear the Russian edition is doing fine.

In the sixties, when I was working in America, there was a great Tolkien cult, bound up with this fascination for myths and legends. People wore little buttons with 'Frodo Lives' or 'Support Your Local Hobbit' written on them. I remember talking to Tolkien about this and he found it embarrassing and rather nauseating: he couldn't see what had come over these people that they should treat his hobbit world as a cult. They would ring him up from America at four in the morning and say: 'Can we send you some tobacco? We know hobbits love to smoke', and ask all sorts of questions. It worried him, I know. He thought, if people derive such happiness, why be rude? But at times it became quite outrageous and it bewildered him. To some extent the cult was abated, but it has not disappeared totally.

With *The Silmarillion* Tolkien actually set out to invent another world for a dying Britain. He started this after the First World War to voice the dreams and hopes of the British race, as Wagner had done for the Germans. He believed that out of our island's history, greatness would come and that the ancient gods and princes and Journey People were symbols of a new world. *The Silmarillion* was incomplete when Tolkien died but his son finished it for him.

I find the idea that the prophets and saviours of the race are about three feet high very appealing. The world may be peopled with all sorts of giants but in the end it is the hobbits of the world who capture the needs of the universe and provide the answer. That's why they're so popular: it's possible for adults as well as children to identify with little people who live in holes under the ground and who face cosmic challenges.

All this might seem a world away from Flanders and Swann but my work with Lewis and Tolkien overlapped with *Drop of a Hat*. There was an occasion when the show came on tour to Oxford and professor and Edith Tolkien came and adored it. There was one song which we didn't often use that Tolkien relished:

> Some folks like Music, some folks like Tea,
> Some folks like women – they're not for me!
> This is my motto, simple and terse,
> Everything's lousy and going to get worse!
> Oh I wish, Oh I wish,
> Man had never evolved from a fish!
>
> Oh I wish I were dead
> Wish I'd been dropped on my head,
> Broken my neck, lost the toss with a bull,
> Parachute jumped and forgotten to pull,
> Oh I long to be dead,
> Wrapped in a casket of lead,
> Wish I'd been drowned in a barrel of stout,
> Dived off the pier when the tide was still out.
>
> The grave! The grave's
> A fine and private place.
> The grave! The grave!
> And who the hell wants to embrace?
>
> I wish, I wish I were dead
> Laid out with a lily in bed,
> Wish that I'd drunk some carbolic for fun,
> Tested the trigger while cleaning my gun
> Or just shrivelled up in the heat of the sun,
> Oh I wish I were dead,
> Dead, dead,
> Oh I wish I were, Oh I wish I were,
>
> Oh . . . I wish I were dead!

Tolkien asked me for a copy of it. He really respected Michael's word-play. In a way, they were birds of a feather, playing around with words. I have been insisting at times that for me there have been two worlds: the world of Flanders and world of these other people, but when I think deeply about it, I have to revise my ideas because I see there was great kinship between Michael and this fantasy world. It is just in a professional and emotional way these people seem different. In *Drop of Another Hat*, I included a number from my Tolkien song cycle, 'I Sit Beside the Fire'. After three or four Flanders and Swann songs, Michael would drift off and I would sing this Tolkien ballad which was usually very well received as an oddity. I recognised that only this very small piece of Tolkien would fit in, just as only a couple of my Greek songs were appropriate. But I would comfort myself that I was able to snatch something of these new worlds I was clawing on to, and when I got home after the show I could embrace other parts. So Michael played a role in that side of things too. It seems all the various facets are being joined together now and this may be part of the point of this book: self-discovery.

12 The Zeal of Thy Tune

By the time *At the Drop of Another Hat* ended in 1967 I was well into my second world with the settings of C S Lewis and Professor Tolkien, and could really believe in this new music that was being drawn from me. But already, even before the partnership had ended, I was finding that fulfilling though this fantasy world was, it was not sufficient. I wanted to be more active, even missionary, about some of the thoughts buzzing around inside me. This ties up with my FAU service except that I wanted to find an answer to some of the world's problems through music rather than relief work. It was as though I had a vision of music as a form of solace, of healing. I began to feel that I had some role to play in turning music into an expression of peace.

Those who lived through the sixties will recall the mood of hope and anticipation of the time: there were be-ins and love-ins and happenings; the San Francisco Hippie movement, and the Flower People. All this was encapsulated for me on Easter Sunday, 1967, at the first New York be-in in Central Park where I heard Sydney Carter's great affirmative carol of Christ the dancer – 'Lord of the Dance' – sung in the open air for the first time. There were several hundreds of young people in way-out clothes and lapel buttons: 'Love is', 'LSD not LBJ', and Tolkieniana such as 'Gandalf for President'. Girls were dropping daffodils on to a police car, others were dancing or playing instruments. The theme was love and peace and the idea was to enjoy being together, being alive, being at peace, being human. A young priest set up a table by a tree and had an impromptu Eucharist. I seized on this be-in to confirm all my feelings of brotherhood, of spontaneous friendship, and a world devoted to peace.

It was a time when the churches were beginning to swing: there were swinging vicars digging up crypts to build discotheques; and organists besieged in their organ lofts while jean-clad guitarists beat out folk-hymns on the chancel steps. I remember attending St Clement's, the most experimental Anglican (Episcopal) church of New York where the service differed each Sunday, the congregants helping in these re-scriptings as many were writers and theatre people. Once it was Rivers of Jordan Sunday. Everyone descended to the downstairs loo where the priest stood in robes; each made a list of their sins which were flushed down the toilet. I loved this vivid metaphor for absolution. Entertainers who had any beliefs were asked to speak up and I actually preached a few sermons, if you can imagine anything so peculiar coming from me. It seemed as though my conscientious objection, pacifism and the Quaker ideas I'd been in touch with all came to the fore again. I plunged into this mood.

In London I gave a sermon in St Paul's cathedral. I told Michael that I had to talk about things I believed in and could he give me a text? He said: 'Tell them this. We're all cast in the same mould, but some are mouldier than others.' As usual, I was grateful for his *bon mot*.

Now cynics might say all this is pretty similar to fantasy but I took it very seriously and felt I had to do something to express what I felt, and to propagate my ideas. My Anglicanism led me to write settings of the Venite, the Benedictus, and the Benedicite, which had trumpets blaring and liturgical chants. I wrote a Te Deum which sounded somewhat like 'The Reluctant Cannibal': it had the same beat. People would come and say: 'We've got some new words why don't you put them to music and write a new carol?' I arranged carols from Greece and Russia. This is one I wrote for Christmas to a Russian tune I'd heard from my mother:

213

All night long I shall burn my Christmas candle,
Watch the flame burning yellow, grey and blue.
Pierce my eyes my shining Christmas candle,
Oh clear my eyes so that I can see anew.
Pierce my eyes, my shining Christmas candle,
Oh shine your light so that I can see anew.

All night long I shall burn my Christmas candle,
I shall watch till the wax has all burned through.
Burn my heart, my shining Christmas candle,
Oh shine your light so my heart can burn anew.
Oh come and burn my heart, my shining Christmas
     candle,
Oh touch my heart so that I can feel anew.

Sydney Carter was writing some of his most trenchant works:
'When I Needed a Neighbour, Were You There?' and 'Friday
Morning':

It was on a Friday morning
That they took me from the cell,
And I saw they had a carpenter
To crucify as well.
You can blame it on to Pilate,
You can blame it on the Jews,
You can blame it on the Devil,
It's God I accuse.
It's God they ought to crucify
Instead of you and me,
I said to the carpenter
A-hanging on the tree.

To hell with Jehovah,
To the carpenter I said,
I wish that a carpenter
had made the world instead . . . .

In my revue style I could perform these songs instantly. It
was all very spontaneous. I was performing in churches and
all sorts of odd places and met some fascinating people. Some
of the most interesting were the American church people who
were protesting against the Vietnam war, which reminded me

so strongly of my own anti-war mood. Martin Luther King was active and the civil rights movement was very strong. There was tremendous concern for men and women to be equal; there were women priests which cheered me. There is no doubt, this was a very effervescent period for me and some of my best tunes were born of that time.

A book I wrote then was called *Space Between the Bars* which attempted to chart these various experiences and revelations. Having achieved publication, I performed an opening ceremony for an extension in the Swan pub, West Peckham, Kent, brandishing my book in the actual physical space between two bars. The title derives from my faith that the unpredictable event between the bars of life may well be a glimpse of the truth. By looking at things on the slant, as it were, you get a vision of something different and in that difference is the very heart of change.

It seemed possible after a while to transform the book into a living show so that the entertainer and musical parts of me allowed the whole thing to stand up from the page. *Between the Bars* became a choral autobiography which included humorous and lyrical music, almost as if the book became a sort of song-spiel. I selected a group of five singers from musical friends, a talented and dedicated group with whom I still work and who interpreted the moments of comedy, tragedy and longing into a musical experience with me. The original team was Catherine Martin, Heather Kay, Ginny Broadbent, Alastair Thompson and Brian Kay. After the two men left in 1971 to become full-time members of the King's Singers, Richard Day-Lewis and Roger Cleverdon joined the team as tenor and baritone.

Between the Bars gave birth to a twin concert: *A Crack In Time* – a line from a Carter poem. The idea was that time is broken up and out of it comes a new vision. The publicity logo was designed by Meinrad Craighead, then a nun in Stanbrook Abbey well known for her lovely woodcuts of biblical texts.

This concert was based upon one longer work in the first

215

half and a sharing of thoughts and songs in the second. The longer work, *Requiem for the Living*, was a setting of C Day Lewis. It's odd that I've had two Lewises to inspire me: C S and C Day, without a hyphen. I had nothing but trouble over that hyphen, and to confuse matters even more Cecil's distant cousin, our tenor Richard Day-Lewis, has a hyphen.

I met C Day Lewis through John Robinson, then Bishop of Woolwich – a cogent thinker and fine charismatic character – who wrote the book *Honest To God*, a story of doubt and agnosticism within the Anglican faith, which had great influence. Day Lewis had written a requiem not for the dead but for the living, feeling 'that the living are at least as much in need of peace as the dead'. He had written it at the peak of his anti-nuclear feeling at the time of the first Aldermaston march. Together with people like Auden, he had been a pioneer of political poetry at the time of the Spanish civil war; but then he ceased to be politically active and concentrated on his poetry. It would seem that the nuclear issue, the possibility of the world being destroyed, forced him into a cosmic vein. I would say there is nothing Greener than *Requiem for the Living*:

> Holy the marigold play of evening sun
> On wall and tree, the dawn's light-fingered run,
> Night's muted strings, the shimmering chords of summer
> noon . . .
>
> Praise the white orchards of the cloudful west,
> Wheat prairies with abundance in their breast,
> The seas, the mineral mountains, the jungle and the
> waste . . .

It has kinship with *Perelandra* in the way it affirms the wonder and holiness of our world which we must not betray and destroy. It had never been set to music. Day Lewis wrote the libretto for an Oratorio perhaps thinking that Benjamin Britten might offer to set it, but Britten found his own requiem. So it fell into my hands and I got deeply involved with it. I really loved *Requiem for the Living*, and still do, and it was first performed for John

Robinson's last day as Bishop of Woolwich in the Church of the Ascension in Blackheath. I dedicated the music to John and to my father's memory as he died that same year, 1969. Both were Humanists.

I thought this was a great chance. But I'm going to have to say that the BBC turned up, looked at it, and rejected it. I was absolutely desolated. I just could not see how they could be so uninterested, bearing in mind the involvement of the most famous bishop of the time, a poet laureate, and me still part of the *Drop of a Hat* era. Surely they should have given it a broadcast. What actually happened was that I handed it to the new team of singers and began to perform it. This went on for six or seven years. I soon realised that by taking my singers out and touching the piano, I could create a world of my own that was as strong as anything I could do by broadcasting. Looking back, I think at that time I was being discounted by the musical establishment that did not want to recognise the mix between folk and classical that was already coming together in a rainbow spectrum. Or was it the Sullivan complex again?

Requiem for the Living is in nine parts, each canticle reinterpreted in modern verse. It speaks of the forces that created a beautiful world which we must protect and save. I've quoted part of the *Sanctus*. Here are some lines from the *Dies irae*:

> Turning keys upon the dials
> Shall unloose the furious phials;
> Then the trumpeting blasts be heard –
> Art, law, science, all absurd.
>
> From a lucid heaven foresee
> Monstrous that ephipany
> Of man's calculated error
> Break in light and brood in terror:
>
> Skin flayed off the skeleton,
> Ghosts of men burnt into stone,
> Uberant rivers boiling dry,
> Cities sucked up into the sky . . .

Jill Balcon, Day Lewis's wife, read the narration part. There is a percussion instrument called a cimbalom which produced the oriental sound I wanted in certain places. The main accompanying instrument was the piano. The choral music from my school tradition, piano music, the oriental sound which is always on my mind, and the intense lyricism and passion of the poem in its quasi-political way all came together, and *Requiem for the Living* became central to my life.

A Crack In Time began to appear in some pretty unusual places. We took it to Holywell in Wales where St Winifred was beheaded and there is a beautiful spring; and to Northern Ireland playing within the same week in Shankill Road Protestant Mission Hall and Corpus Christi Catholic Church in Ballymurphy, Belfast. It was poignant to play such a concert in the middle of ruined streets that looked as if their teeth had just been pulled out. Few people ventured out at night and the very people we wanted to play to – the militants – weren't in the audience. But there was no doubt in our hearts and fingers as to the value of such performances. The show did reach out and touch members of the audience and, in turn, they'd touch others. After playing to a Catholic audience in Ballymurphy, they said: 'We're used to requiems because of the number of deaths we have and if yours is for the living, and hopes of a rebirth and re-start, we need it.' Do I sound evangelistic? Evangelism is none too popular these days. It's not so easy to go around saying: 'I have faith in the resurrection and I believe the world *can* be changed.' There is an air of cynicism around which makes one a little apologetic for such thoughts. But I still have them.

One of the most interesting things we did with our two shows was to tour the Middle East, where we played them jointly in Cairo, Jerusalem and Beirut in 1971. We performed to the two races, Arabs and Jews. We even had the Hippo song translated. It was sung in Hebrew and Arabic in the same programme and was a great hit. We would play *Between the Bars* and *A Crack In Time* on alternate nights and received a warm response. I have vivid and precious memories of that tour. We played in the beautiful university of Beirut, and the intense loveliness of the city really captured my imagination. Look at it now! I remember the Nile, the sights and sounds of the audiences. I recall a really tremendous response in Cairo cathedral, from lots of British expats but many Egyptians too. Generally, Arabs were fascinated by the material and really understood it. They seem to like word-play and strange concepts and can take them on board like their interwoven arabesques. The Jews seemed to prefer the music. The year after we performed the cathedral was pulled down and disappeared into a road – the British were on their way out. I am reminded of my earlier thoughts in Egypt with the FAU when it seemed that something could be done for the Egyptians other than treat them as servant people while we were fighting our war with Hitler. Now it was too late for that: they were asserting themselves and so it will continue, for the better.

In Jerusalem, we played in the heart of the old city near the Lutheran Church of the Redeemer, just by the church of the Holy Sepulchre. It was a wonderful evening and the audience of every type of race was sitting quietly and expectantly waiting for this Donald Swann and his caravan from England. Simple really: you put up your tent or in our case a notice in the local paper saying come and hear this group from England. We were not celebrities, nor pop stars. We had something different and they loved it. George Appleton, the Archbishop of Jerusalem who initiated the tour, thanked us after the show saying they'd experienced everything there except the mythology of peace with music. I never cease to ponder and wonder at the apparent identity between the song, the people, and the place. First performances and audiences seem to identify and hallmark a song for me and when I play it without them I am capable of experiencing sudden and intense grief. This was the case in the lovely church in the heart of the Old City. It was as though the music, the site, the audience and ourselves as performers were all caught up in the act of reconciliation which is what Jerusalem is all about.

I find the Middle East intensely romantic. Three main religions came from that area and I never felt more affirmed than when I was playing in places where all these visionary eruptions had occurred. It is the place that's seen it all. I have just returned from another visit, this time with the Gulf crisis looming and the frustrations of the *intifada* giving portents that the worst is happening again. But actually worse things have happened long ago – many more massacres, many more torments.

But if you go with a tune, maybe someone will listen and it will migrate into the soul and help the hurt. These shows always seemed to work best in such dark places. I suppose it's understandable: if there is trouble and pain that is where solace has to go. Am I naïve? I do feel shy about some of these dreams of mine. Depending on the number of Aqua Libras I've had, or the day, or the hour, sometimes I still feel quite confident that the world can be changed by melody. Other times I'm sure it won't. But in the early seventies I knew that there was a space between the bars as well as a crack in time if only one made the effort to struggle and look through.

I consider *Requiem for the Living*, which played such a big role in the Middle East tour, one of my more important compositions: it speaks of all the things I hold most dear. Choirs still perform it and from time to time I offer my services as pianist for a performance and it all comes alive again. There is a very fine church, St James's in Piccadilly, where all these ideas are understood and piloted by its prophetic rector, Donald Reeves. I took the Requiem there on 11th November 1989, thinking it would be just right for Armistice Day and the commemoration of the fiftieth anniversary of the start of the war. There weren't many in the audience so it wasn't what you would call a great national celebration, but I think once again we hit the heart of the quiet musical statement. There is a sense of yearning there too. If you want to make peace how much difference are a few bars of music going to make? There is still so much conflict ongoing. I listen to Britten's *War Requiem* with enormous comfort; the intense suffering in the songs and music seem to speak across many years and all wars.

The Five Scrolls is the sequel to *Requiem for the Living* and was written very much in the same mood a little later, in 1975. It is a musical witness to the vision of universal brotherhood and the coming of the Messianic age of peace. Rabbi Albert Friedlander of the Westminster synagogue in Knightsbridge is a talented lyric writer as well as a learned Rabbi. He wrote this piece in which various books in the Bible are treated in lyric form with narrator and songs. It is the only libretto I know that speaks of a Jewish message of peace. My Anglican upbringing suggested that the Old Testament was marked by murder and mayhem, with this rather jealous, archaic and patriarchal God. But Albert opened my eyes to something quite different and made me realise that it is a great deep book of hope with a vision of Messianic peace and reconciliation throughout. Albert has the approach of peace in everything he does. He is also very keen on disarmament and has always worked for that cause. So we joined forces and that piece has become another sort of flagship. My dream is to take *The Five Scrolls* to Jerusalem with Albert. Someday I know this will happen. But first it went West instead of East where it was performed with my singing group in American synagogues and various churches; it was enthusiastically accepted. Again it's in a style which includes narration and singing; not that far from *Drop of a Hat* really because there is the piano, the voices, and intimacy. It needs very careful rehearsal although in performance, just like Michael's material, it sounds entirely spontaneous. How I wish I could sing parts of it to you! But at least I can share with you the words of one of its arias, Mordecai's song:

> The shades of night deal gently with old age.
> The lines are smooth, the curved back disappears.
> All that is left is elemental rage
> Crying unto the sky, defying years.
> I've seen the persecution of the few
> In Babylon and Egypt, in all lands;
> I've watched them slaughter children, pagan, Jew –
> It matters not. For hatred understands

That every stranger is an enemy
To be destroyed on sight. The world grows cold
It dies through genocide. And we are free
To watch each dream turn bitter, dark, and old.
Yet some, like me, burn brightly in the night
Reminding young and old to share the fight.

I was able to take *The Five Scrolls* and *Between the Bars* music
to the Brighton Festival in 1988. Evelyn, Albert's wife, read
the spoken part, written for her. I was also able to write a
long programme to promote understanding of this coagulated
mix. The Brighton Festival, which is also a literary festival,
reinforced my belief that it is possible to put ideology and
thought behind compositions. I would like to make a plea for
that: that composers are not just note-smiths who occasionally
spout and say what an interesting or funny thing it was to be
performing in Fittleworth, or to go to Norman Mailer's party,
or how many records were sold . . . We are harnessed to our
lyrics and their intensity. At the time I worked with Albert I
almost became a Jew. I felt more at home at Yom Kippur or
Succoth than I did with Anglican festivals. Of course Judaism
is the most friendly faith with some wonderful and brilliant
adherents. Whereas with *Perelandra* I was at one with the Green
Lady, now I was in kinship with Jerusalem, the reconciliation
of faiths and the hope of the Messiah again.

You may recall that the seventies, when all this occurred, was
a period in religious life that was ecumenical and interfaith, and
we were all feeling that Buddhists and Moslems had something
important to teach us. As the decade of the nineties is opening
up, it seems that this hopeful era is over. We seem fearful of
other faiths, and feel there are too many fanatics and evangelists
about, promoting a hard line which is alien to this hope. In the
seventies we had a vision of one world. The missionaries had
stopped putting top hats on and were becoming one with the
people. It seemed there was a glimmer of greater understanding
and tolerance. It must be reborn, that hope, otherwise there
is going to be a dark end to the century. That be-in world

in Central Park I described at the start of this chapter was a world I could really understand and relate to. There was the belief that wherever you went you could find your brothers and sisters; the belief that entertainment and rejoicing and healing are not far apart. As I speak now I find I have some difficulty relating to it, as though it has gone slightly behind the hill. But I'm clawing back at my own compositions, hoping I won't lose the intense faith I had in them.

13 In the Fissiparous Phase

Michael would appear with Claudia to hear some of these things. He understood what I was doing, as did Claudia who liked *The Five Scrolls* in particular; so there was not an abrupt end to my earlier world. It's only by reflecting on these things years later as this book is written, that I begin to realise just how much overlap there was. But there is no doubt that my life was very different from the two-man monastery I'd shared with Michael: the voices of just two men at the piano, with Michael's beard and bluff masculinity. I think I was pining for soprano and alto voices and the choral music I was brought up with, and I wanted to perform with mixed choirs. But how can I describe to even the most indulgent reader the openness I then had to new ideas and to new people, especially to singing partners who travelled with me to the back stages of theatres, concert halls, churches and cathedrals? My agent at that time, Gay Sherwood, advertised me as travelling on the circuit of the Seven 'Cs': concert hall, cabaret, church, crypt, chapel, cathedral and campus.

In 1965, Judy Taylor of the Bodley Head invited me to write a book of new carols for children: *Sing Round the Year*. Suddenly children turned up in my professional life as well as at home. In *Soundings By Swann*, a sequence exploring new ideas that toured churches and cathedrals, I would travel with a small adult choir, but linked up with the resident organist and local children trained before I arrived and ready for the last rehearsal. This partnership with Bodley Head continued into three more books: *The Rope of*

Love, The Song of Caedmon, and *Round the Piano with Donald Swann.*

Fortunately in Britain we have a wonderful tradition of amateur musical people who function in every town and even villages. There is no doubt about it, there were times when I missed the professionalism of our two-man show which had reached a very high peak towards the end; but there are some fine choir trainers and excellent singers in the amateur world. Sometimes the venues were very small and the risk of a very bad piano was great; or something was falling apart, or you couldn't be heard, and there was constant battle with the lighting. I always tried to make my shows as theatrical and interesting as possible, but sometimes it just wasn't possible.

I've recently been encouraged by reading about Gustav Holst, my stepmother's music teacher at St Paul's Girls' School. He too found it possible to derive enormous strength from the vigour and enthusiasm generated within an amateur environment. In a way I think English music functions at that level very strongly. There is incredible fertility in the English provinces: if you find yourself in Northampton or Nottingham, for instance, you will find a lot of people with enormous love of their church. Such places have caused important pioneering in music, and to be part of that was incomparably different from travelling as a two-man entertainment. I suddenly felt part of the English provincial musical scene with singers, choirs and a sense of affirmation; I would say that I am often happier in that milieu than if I was consistently having to match up to, say, the Festival Hall. Also, the conjectural or ideological part seems to belong better in progressive churches or unexpected places than it would in some grandiose venue.

Although Quakers have, on the whole, eschewed music, they will come together to hear something they really want to hear. I remember doing a concert in Jordans, Buckinghamshire, which is the most beautiful Meeting House in the world; where once again there were just the local children singing some of my new peace songs. It was another example of music being created by the place and people. I often crave to be in a place and let it sing in its own right.

It became a happy and satisfying time of going off by car or plane on musical expeditions with my group of singers. We had some wonderful moments and I became invigorated by the experience and look back on it with great pleasure. At last I felt able to run free. This was also the time when the ubiquitousness of the boy soprano from my cathedral upbringing gave way to the feeling that I could do church music with real live women. That was very intoxicating and the women I worked with were some of the best singers I have encountered. I date my increasing sympathy with feminism from this time. I even began to carry a satchel if not a handbag! In an Oxford Union debate on feminism where I spoke, nay sang, the second verse of the Hippopotamus song was attacked as sexist. I've been pondering this ever since, and am inclined to think that the charge sticks. But I digress . . .

As well as working with groups of singers, I have also formed different professional partnerships since 1967. One of the first was with Lilli Malandraki. She spent the war years as a courier for the Resistance in Crete, which ended triumphantly with a week-long wedding celebration to a British Intelligence Officer, John Stanley. They then disappeared on a white horse for their honeymoon. Lilli knew all the Cretan ballads including the ancient *Manedes* or Laments, so we put our Greek songs together and formed a sequence: *An Evening in Crete*. Now I was partner to a woman. It was rather hard for her because people would judge her like a female Michael Flanders – the stereotype was alive and kicking. But we weren't worried about that: we created our own little world of my Greek and her Cretan songs. You can imagine the fulfilment for both of us. Lilli was now a mother of four children, and her ex-soldier husband was with Prudential Assurance. I was an unstoppable Philhellene. Whereas in *At the Drop of a Hat* I sang two Greek songs, one being a complete joke with funny animal noises, now I could sing twelve and accompany as many. Between us we had about

226

two hundred to choose from – a Greek *Meze* of two hundred vocal courses. Some of the best songs I've ever heard were in that repertoire. How tragic that Lilli died so young in 1989.

Our partnership lasted for about four years, from 1967 to 1971. We toured English concert halls including some very small places tucked away in the Lake District. We travelled all over Scotland where Lilli was particularly popular, because Scotland resembles Crete with its history of chieftains, struggle and kilted soldiers. The heroic female singing rousing songs or tender little lullabies was very attractive to the Scots.

Eventually we went to Cyprus and performed in some fascinating places all over the island, mostly in the open air. In Morphou a boy pelted frogs to stop their croaking so that the alfresco audience could hear us sing. Later the island was divided up and the frogs were the least of their problems. That's the only time I've done bi-lingual concerts speaking and singing Greek and English together. I just loved it. I remember one concert vividly. It was in a most beautiful new concert hall run by Nicholas Ierides, the headmaster of the school for the blind. I asked him how he had managed to build such a beautiful place in those terrible times of civil war. He said: 'Well, with the war and troubles, most builders and architects were suddenly unemployed, so I asked them "Why don't you come and build me a concert hall right now?" ' He too struck a chord. There are always people who turn dark things into music and words.

So Lilli and I had some memorable times together, and the concept of going back into Greek music with her effervescent presence, and draw upon this deep well within me seemed ecstatic and fulfilling. Although our partnership eventually faded, my love of Greece and its melodies has continued to grow.

In an outburst of 'lyrical touring' I travelled with another show called *Set By Swann*, with three admirable voices: Marion Studholme, her husband Andrew Downie, and William Elvin who sang the Tolkien Elvish. Sometimes Ian Wallace joined the trio. I'd begun to hit the trail with Pushkin, Suckling and

Dryden et alia. I'd gone legit! We made it twice to the Queen Elizabeth Hall and soon went to far distant Oswego, New York State, known for its record low temperature in winter and the tallest radio mast in the world. We also reached Ottawa, where we played in a Vomitorium – yes, that's what it's called. I felt fulfilled, accompanying settings of Froissart, Ronsard and medieval Latin. However, I was baffled to hear loud laughter through all these heartfelt strains, from an audience of Canadian Kiwanis (a Fraternity). The more serious it got, the more they laughed. At the end, completely mystified, I asked a member of the audience, still clutching her glass, 'How so?' 'There were some serious moments,' she said 'but we all *knew* you're a very funny man.'

Sydney Carter and I would pilot our thoughts and music in a concert called *Explorations One*. (Why One? There was never a Two.) Sydney is a born raconteur and goes around with an oriental drum and Indian bells. He shook these in Washington cathedral in one of our experimental 'talks' to such good effect that the bells fell among the feet of the Daughters of the American Revolution, that very august band of ladies who had come in to catch the mood of the New Church. They got over it, as Sydney's ballads are universal in their clear style. Came the time when it seemed right to give up this sequence which we'd performed on a regular basis; always a sad moment. With Sydney this took place in the very cold, dark and miserable waiting room of Wigan railway station during the miners' strike and Heath's Three Day Week – candles were the only illumination. But it was not the end of our collaboration; the lights came on again. Sydney and I still float in and out of each other's musical worlds as naturally as sticklebacks. We revived a couple of years after the Wigan farewell in the company of Jeremy Taylor and his guitar. Jeremy's songs were right up my street for ethos, philosophy, and harmonies. England is the loser, for Jeremy has settled in South Africa where he continues to produce the astringency too rarely heard in that land. Do you recall his best-known song written in England?

228

I was just an ordinary Englishman
Till I got my uniform and hat
And ever since that hour, I exercise my power
Preventing you from doing this and that.

You'll find me on the turnstile at the Zoo,
Or outside the Roxy, marshalling the queue
And if you turn up late, when I'm on the gate
It's no good asking me to let you through

I'll just say . . .

Job's worth! Job's worth!
It's more than my job's worth.
I don't care – rain or snow
Whatever you want, the answer's 'No!'

I can keep you standing
For hours in the queue
And if you don't like it
You know what you can do . . .

When you're trying to see What the Butler Saw
I'm the one who says: 'Come on, move on!'
And if you want to stay, you'll have to bleeding pay
And even then you can't stay long.

You may be almost dropping dead from thirst
Or waiting for the toilet fit to burst
But I've got the key, and you don't get that from me
Until I've had my little grumble first.

Job's worth! Job's worth!
It's more than my job's worth . . .

Fishing near the river on a summer's day
Suppose you think that water's there for free
Well I've got news for you, everybody pays his due
And right now, I can charge you fifty p.

Job's worth! Job's worth!
It's more than my job's worth . . .

A show called *A Glancing Blow* with the prodigious young percussionist Heather Corbett originated in Glasgow and also had a good innings. This was a duo, and my piano on the platform was surrounded by fifteen percussion instruments all played by Heather who leapt from one to another, creating incredible, exciting sounds and a great deal of action as she played the role of fifteen energetic performers. At last I was in an orchestra! We got together soon after my Russian trip in 1974 and she represented my Russian songs excellently on her Eastern sounding cimbalom which is classified as Hungarian Gypsy but is known throughout Russia. In order to tune the strings of the cimbalom she had to light a fire underneath the instrument – that was the publicity story. It is certainly the most temperamental instrument for tuning I have ever encountered. I first met Heather when she was still a student at the Guildhall. She learned the very complex stick technique of the cimbalom in time to originate the first performance of *Requiem for the Living* I've mentioned earlier.

Ian Wallace and I nearly took off as a partnership in the fifties, but *Drop of a Hat* and its adventures took over for me. Ian never ceases to sing the Betjemans and my 'Storke Carol', which has a medieval lyric; and the animal songs of Flanders and Swann seem to have stabled up in his home in north London and come out to water regularly. These performances have continued to fructify my Performing Rights Society cheques. Most of all, Ian and the Hippo song became a unity.

John Amis, aware of my songs from an even earlier period than Ian, as well as parading them on the TV programme *My Music*, sallied forth with me on several Unusual Evenings (so billed) when he gave tongue to some rarer items that were often written for him. Only he and I have sung 'England Expects' by Nadia Cattouse, a duet in 5/4 time; a bit Britteny. He took on Byron's 'So We'll Go No More A-roving' where the voice part is in 4/4 and the piano in 7/8; also 'Lúthien Tinúviel', the Tolkien ballad where almost the same happens, the voice in 3, piano in 6/8 or 2-time in quavers – all adding to the excitement.

John likes the complexities. In his autobiography, having print to hand, he chides me therein for eventually breaking up the partnership in a mood of neurotic compulsion. With a two-man concert sequence that could reach the Aldeburgh Festival he could barely understand that I wanted to move on. But my soliloquy in this book should explain how the internal pressures on me were different. All music is ephemeral, profoundly so. I was incredibly lucky that we were able to do one show together, never mind ten. It is such a complicated thing to write one song let alone hundreds, and to rise to even one performance and hold the audience with you. One must be grateful for the hour. I remember once in a low moment mourning the passing of my partnership with Lilli to someone. He said: 'You might feel that way, but I remember when you were playing in the grounds of that monastery in Kyrenia. Her voice was floating up from the ruins. I've never forgotten it. To me it was wonderful and unique and I'm very grateful that you bothered to get there.' That restored my faith in the episodic and that is what I would like John to understand:

> Long live the things that only last a day
> Long live the things that flower and fade away
> Long live the rose, the rose will never die
> All things are now and never
> Long live the rose, the rose will never die
> Long live the rose, and long live the butterfly
> Still I believe and cannot tell you why
> All things shall live for ever

So sang Sydney Carter.

My pacifist zeal was given rein again in 1979 when I turned up at the avant-garde left-wing Cockpit Theatre surrounded by forty young actors in a Summer Theatre project of great complexity. Quaker dramatist Alec Davison and I had become excited by an anti-armament trade, pro common-ownership story called *The Yeast Factory*, set in Bradford city which was represented in the theatre by scaffolding. My daughter Rachel was publicity officer in her first theatre job, and my younger daughter Natasha was

231

designing vivid anti-establishment murals on the railway bridge just outside the door. I wore black trousers, black shirt and black plimsolls so as to be part of an invisible orchestra, all the more invisible as we were some thirty feet above the theatre 'in the round'. It was all committed fun. Did this youth musical influence disarmament or make commonly owned factories any more prevalent? Who knows. But it certainly changed the lives of the young cast, many of whom turned into professional actors; and it changed the life of the author, Alec, who thenceforth plunged into Quaker Youth Theatre. He now continues to give young Quakers a way of expressing their ideas and talents in successive theatre pieces and cantatas – a huge new outpouring for a sect that espoused silence as its hallmark. What can we artists do but break the silence?

It was at this time that yet another partnership blew up across the sea: Swann with Topping, a suitable metaphor as the Revd Frank Topping is a sailor as well as an actor, broadcaster and writer. Once when we went off to the Norfolk Broads to write new songs, Frank fell in, and this intrigued me as I was the ignoramus about boats. We formed a sort of journalistic partnership whereby we did a couple of BBC Radio series of twelve programmes each in which we'd sing our songs and share our ideas. The series were well received and after a while we found ourselves in an upper room at the Upstream Theatre, Waterloo, to good notices and houses. Suddenly the 'Hat' phenomenon seemed to be re-starting. Frank even had a beard. Television, and a West End season ensued, but then fissiparousness set in. We even used this word on a record sleeve. I began to hearken unto the other multiple realities I'd encountered. Suddenly no Greek music, no Russian, no choral singers, no Flanders items, no Carter carols. Nor did I feel I was penetrating into new musical depths, but returning into light revue, albeit in the company of a gifted entertainer and moralist. So instead of falling on my feet, I felt I too had fallen into the drink! Frank was a born actor and went on to devise solo shows. That was a direction I too was heading for.

In the tiny Malthouse Theatre tucked away in the heart of the Sussex countryside near Hassocks, Sandra Scriven has often invited me to play solo. For ten years she has welcomed my varying sequences and all my artists, often directing us. There, at the Malthouse, Leon Berger of North London has gathered opera artists to sing for me. Baritone, graphic designer, scholar, lyric writer, fixer, a fissiparous-become-Renaissance Man, he rekindled a living Outsider in my opera with Colin Wilson – *The Man With A Thousand Faces*. Leonardo da Finchli?

The Malthouse also saw the première of *Swann in Jazz* in 1986. This was my excursion into the jazz world which happened when Digby Fairweather, an admirable trumpeter, arranger and composer, nobbled me in the middle of a concert I was doing in Nelson, Lancashire, and asked whether I had ever tried my songs in jazz style. I'd never thought I was ever going to try anything like that although I've always loved its animal vigour, and the deep emotions expressed in blues. He encouraged me to have a go, and I gave him some tapes which he played through. In the end we pruned the songs down to about eighteen.

We then gathered some really fine players together and started rehearsing. This seemed to go on forever; I found it enormously difficult playing in time. Jazz, basically, has a pounding beat which is alien to the serpentine way I play my songs, when every bar is just a little bit different and folds its way around the lyric. The musicians had to be very patient with me as I kept going out of tempo. The Irving Berlin ballad 'Cheek To Cheek' I reinterpreted in a mixture of 5/8 and 7/8 and overstepped my own powers of playing. I nearly killed myself; I just could not manage the last few notes. The immediate answer was for me to take my hands off the keyboard while the drummer played the finger cymbal to fill in for me. In the longer term we devised a system where there was a bit in tempo good and strong that allowed every one of these players to extemporise, then there was a slight idiomatic change when I performed a little bit in my style. Talk about ephemerality: the show seemed to come and go. *Swann in Jazz* has scored ten concerts so far. I remember we got the performance in Barnes exactly right. At the moment it has faded away; but we intend to do it again, the problem is getting these busy people together when they're all playing elsewhere. But I had this little glimpse of the jazz world in which I found great excitement and challenge.

I ended up creating four songs specifically for it including setting Hermann Hesse in a slightly jazzy form with the use of the trumpet. I have found that some of my own songs adapt perfectly for a slow, gentle beat. When I visited America a few years back I listened to a lot of folk-pop music, and I have been influenced by the writing of Harry Chapin, for instance. His song 'All My Life's a Circle' is ideal, being part jazz, part folk and part ballad. When I play that section of my repertoire I always hear the jazz accompaniments and long for us to bring it back to life. I know some day we will.

I'm really happy to have collaborated with so many gifted people who are able to make an evening come alive, and I never stop inventing new partnerships. I am currently in a duo with the soprano Lucinda Broadbridge who, in a sequence called *The Poetic Image*, beautifully exemplifies my new Victorian song cycle. Lucinda, as well as any I have met, interprets the meaning of lyrics within the melody, the true art of Lieder singing. She is also a fine comedienne, and her interpretation of Michael's 'Seven Ages of Woman' is hilarious. The whole essence of these partnerships since *Drop of a Hat* days is that they are more episodic, but nonetheless I consider them an essential part of my professional development.

I have found that throughout my musical life, there are times when I find a curious awkwardness with partnerships, however much I love the people I work with. Whenever I find myself withdrawing I find there is always an answer – dead easy – go it alone. Donald with Donald, happy in my ability to select from my own material without a partner asking for vetting; yet sometimes feeling too much alone. There is an element of responsibility. The fact that everything depends on me can be burdensome. But it's very calming not having to relate to

234

somebody, not to think their thoughts. I just lift the lid off the piano and improvise very happily saying: here come the Quakers, here are the Greeks, the hobbits are stirring. How about a song about the sloth or the warthog? I've taken my one-man show all around Britain and to parts of America. I also took it to South Africa where it led me to some even more amazing adventures.

14 Pain or Paean?

I went to South Africa for the first time in 1974 at the request of a Quaker-supported trust. This was an exchange scheme whereby grants are given to South Africans – of all colours, of course – who wish to visit the UK, and British people to visit South Africa. The purpose is contact and understanding. Like-minded groups of people make interaction in terms of religion, music, art and many other themes. Throughout the dark times this interchange has continued, and in its way it is a very strong Quaker witness. I have heard that the initial impetus and funds came from an Afrikaaner who couldn't stand the strain of the South African social system and wanted to ensure that people could at least meet each other. John Robinson, Bishop of Woolwich, went somewhat later on a university tour and tore down the veil of prejudice, as he always did. Clearly, if the so-called Christian rulers could read his *Honest to God* and take it in, their theocratic Old Testament and literalism would come tumbling down. That was the way it felt: someone's going to read something, hear something and it will change. My bridge-building material was my music, especially my carol book *The Rope of Love* – named after an American Indian version of the Twenty-third Psalm. I was also armed with all sorts of songs which I hoped to teach South African children, and to play with mixed choirs in areas including the townships.

I had very much hoped to take my group of five singers with me but this wasn't possible, so I went alone. I went under some strain. There were problems in my family life: Janet and I were

236

then living in Suffolk and the conflict between town and country, touring and home, was beginning to tell. Also, I didn't appreciate at the time what a tough cookie apartheid is to bite. Nor had I calculated the intensity of the boycott movement which had reached such a pitch by the mid seventies that anyone stepping on to a plane to Johannesburg with a piano on their mind, or violin in hand, was breaking umpteen laws and hundreds of injunctions from Equity and the Musicians' Union. So I carried these problems to South Africa and by some extraordinary means they were answered while I was there. The sheer vitality of the people so courageously fighting under such tremendous strain, and the intense agony of the place seemed to produce solutions.

I took my songs and music and played them to, and with, mixed audiences and choirs all over South Africa for just over four weeks, and was put up by generous hosts, most of whom belonged to the Christian Institute, an anti-apartheid pressure group of the church. Soon after I left to return to the UK, the Christian Institute was banned. Indeed, as I was travelling to the airport, the passport of my host, the Revd Theo Kotze, was seized by the police. Later, they tried to seize him but he managed to escape.

Arriving in South Africa, I was suddenly pitched into a war situation again. At every mealtime the talk was always what was happening in the news. What is the Government going to do? Who has been arrested? Who has fled the country? Where do we go from here? It was exactly like living in wartime England when the questions were: how many bombers have we lost? Who has been killed? As if this wasn't enough I met young men who were refusing to join the South African army because they could not fight for a repressive regime. One morning, in the South African Council of Churches morning service there was a young man called Richard Steele who on the following day refused to join the South African army on conscientious grounds. But there are many more like him. At someone's request I sang a Quaker hymn:

When tyrants tremble as they hear
The bells of freedom ringing.
When friends rejoice both far and near
How can I keep from singing?
In prison cell and dungeon vile
Our thoughts to them are winging,
When friends by shame are undefiled
How can I keep from singing?

Suddenly this old song took on an immediate significance. I was also reaffirmed in my own conscientious objection to war and I identified very strongly with Richard and the other young men making their stand. Richard Steele went to prison, but years later emerged to become a leader of the persecuted anti-war movement.

It was not always easy to arrange mixed-race concerts but there were ways of getting around the restrictions and Theo Kotze was a master of this – he would never accept defeat. Once he hired the Town Hall in Cape Town which at that time was segregated. As he was not allowed to advertise for what was going to be a mixed-race concert of humorous and religious songs, he put an advert in the paper saying he was holding a private party and Donald Swann would be there and would play a few songs, and the place filled up with all the different South African races, enjoying an evening of song and music together. The apartheid laws were full of petty regulations but it was possible to find ways through them. We looked round for the police knowing very well they would be there, but they took no action.

During my concerts and touring the schools I sang conviction songs with lines like:

The ink is black, the page is white,
Together we learn to read and write . . .

This famous song was largely unknown to them, as was Sydney Carter's 'Standing in the Rain':

Christ the Lord has gone to heaven,
One day he'll be coming back, Sir
In this house he will be welcome –
But we hope he won't be black, Sir.

238

Sydney's 'Lord of the Dance' had just appeared over there and I visited a church where it had been performed with the whole congregation dancing. The authorities felt this was dangerous to public order, but I was able to sing it, however.

I sang simple American folk ballads from the civil rights movement that they hadn't heard. On the air, I recorded a mystical ballad about healing from within, which had a verse about Martin Luther King:

> I should like to die like Martin Luther King
> Die on a balcony in Memphis Tennessee
> His death was part of me
> Flowing over,
> Death from the heart of me,
> So would I die.

Some character was sitting there in the South African Broadcasting Corporation and chopped that verse out before the airing. You have to imagine these sinister, schoolmaster figures at every corner and corridor, so the game is to outwit them. For a person like me, used to living in a tame English society (our censor, the Lord Chamberlain, had just been chopped himself), I found all this repellent but exciting. I was joining an open rebellion and as an entertainer I was able to get away with a lot, even on the radio at times.

The Flanders and Swann songs were enormously popular there, and I encountered the most amazingly warm reception whenever I performed them. Long ago Michael and I had been asked to play in South Africa for the Institute of Race Relations, but we declined. Michael felt sure his liberal ideas would be cosily assimilated and ignored, and white audiences who laughed at the foibles of the hippopotamus would take him as an ally. His close friend, Joost de Blank, then Archbishop of Cape Town, urged him to accept. 'Laughter can do fantastic things', said the Archbishop. As it happened I was to try it out alone but there were times when I wished Michael was with me. I remember writing from South Africa beseeching him to think again. It was one of the last letters I was able to write to

239

him because he died the following year. I told him: 'We've got the best audience of our lives here, and I can't understand it.' I think the answer was that some of the white people recalled the show before the worst of apartheid. This reminded them of an England they could still relate to. That was quite a tender thing – they could still laugh. But I also gave him tougher news: that satire like 'The Reluctant Cannibal' was explosive in the South African situation. People thought: 'Good heavens! This is standing up for individual conscience. Thank heavens someone has come from England to actually say this.' And when I sung 'Misalliance', the song about the two climbing plants, and how the honeysuckle was not allowed to marry the bindweed, tears were being shed among my audience for the iniquitous miscegenation laws, now thankfully abolished. People would come up to me and say: 'You've written this for us? No love is allowed here between races.'

Then I found that all these songs were being played on the radio, and this, remember, was controlled by the Government. I spoke to a chap working in the record department and asked him how he came to be playing these songs which were really very subversive. He said: 'Well, we know they are but because they have all been wrapped up in animals and flowers, it hasn't been spotted.' That was a tremendous tribute to Michael's satire. Although he was very reluctant to be accepted there as himself, his astringent songs were, and apparently they have given a great deal of encouragement to the more liberal South Africans who have been playing them all through the dark years.

It did seem that this entertainment material could open doors, more so than I ever believed. There were some euphoric moments like the time in the Market Theatre, Johannesburg, packed to overflowing, when I leapt up from the piano at the end of the show and said: 'I know there will be peace!' There was an enormous great cheer as we all had a vision of this peaceful multiracial state.

There was some wonderful art emerging from that troubled time. Athol Fugard was and is telling the South African story to the world of theatre. The stunning play *Wozza Albert*, of how Christ comes to Johannesburg, was in the making. Adam Small, a masterly playwright, who is 'coloured' by South African definition, writes in Afrikaans and thinks black. He had written a play that year for the Nikomalan Theatre, Cape Town. It was a hit, but he was unable to go to his own first night as he was the wrong colour. He wrote a very moving poem about a poignant incident: the suicide of his fellow poet, Ingrid Jonker, who walked into the sea on the exquisite Cape Town beach and drowned herself. The reason for her suicide was partly personal, but as much the predicament of being a poet in such a heart-breaking culture.

In Memoriam – Ingrid Jonker

There was a body in
The sea bamboo
By it a crying mew
And it were you, you; it were you.
They loosed you from
That wet embrace.
They cleared the sand
From your sad face
Then, knowing it were
You, your muted
Mouth, your halted hand
They thought they had
Found a poet dead
It was not true – it stirred
In me.
If word in this world could be
Flesh – Flesh in its
Turn might turn to word
So, when they took you
From the sea, they drew
A net of silence in
That silence which
Is poetry.

This wonderful poem suggests that a poet's words cannot be drowned; and as she lost her life so his words grew from her experience. I wanted to add music to the poem and make it grow ever more. And so it did. Later it became part of a ten-song song-cycle that emerged from my South African experience which included settings to poems by James Matthews, Oswald Mtchali, Peter Clarke, J J Jolobe, and Van Wyk Louw who is like the South African Goethe. Several of these were in Afrikaans, a language I attempted to learn. Later, in 1988, I took this song-cycle to the Brighton Festival. Sophie Mgcina came over from Soweto to sing for me; and Clive McCombie sang in the eloquent Afrikaans language. It's funny, but out of these sufferings something emerges, and I feel that I have never touched this truth as closely as I did in South Africa – just as with the aftermath of my war-relief story some of my best tunes turned up. At this moment I am preparing a lecture series with Alison, my Art Historian friend. The theme is a perennial one: war and the mediation of art. Listening to the memories of those who have been involved in war, often one gets haunting images, glimpses of truth. It doesn't have to be Benjamin Britten turning Wilfred Owen into music in his *War Requiem*; it can be a simple moment recalled with a poignancy and immediacy.

Some readers of these lines would not be seen dead in South Africa on the grounds of total boycott, but I felt that hopeful ideas were almost dead in South Africa and I'd got a chance to bring them alive. I was not among the detainees, nor hit by truncheons but I had at my fingertips a force for change given to me by the folk movement, the mordant satire of Sydney Carter and in Michael Flanders's highly felicitously expounded humanism. I was but a peon sharing their pain. Nadine Gordimer and André Brink were writing; and Breyten Breytenbach, just released from jail, was about to astound Stellenbosch University, the Afrikaaner university, with his violent denunciation of the Afrikaaner narrow-mindedness which had sent him to prison. I've mentioned the work of playwrights like Athol Fugard and Adam Small stirring things up; the church leaders were fulminating. I became convinced this was the protest movement of the second half of our century as the Labour Movement had been in the first half, and that it would win out. Also, I felt cultural boycotts were wrong: South Africa would be largely deprived of explosive ideas from outside, even though they had them within.

Despite the boycott, I returned to South Africa three more times – four trips in all. I didn't go there to make money and I hardly earned a penny: the first trip was on a grant, as I've explained; two trips I financed myself entirely; and one was paid for by the Baxter Theatre in Cape Town. This has a wonderful roll-call of artists playing to all races, and is itself in the middle of a university which has stood up for mixed theatre. Some of the best audiences ever for my solo show were in that theatre. It seemed that with my music and songs I could not only plug in to the pain, but cheer them up. I've mentioned the Market Theatre, Johannesburg, which has also hosted every type of play and musical over the years, and innumerable black and mixed companies. Everyone knew that I was proud of appearing at these theatres, but here in the UK actors were being advised not to go and play there – though they were not forbidden.

So I came under heavy fire from the Musicians' Union and Equity for the stand I was taking. After a bit, I was being criticised by members of my family and friends, not so much for the concerts there, but for even going at all. And then, when I started to do battle with the Union, I seemed to encounter nothing but opposition, except for a handful of people who supported me on conscience grounds. This was the most public time that I ever had on this issue. I got myself elected as a delegate from the London Union to the biennial conference in Warwick in 1981, and put out the proposition that they should abandon their boycott and let artists make their own decisions according to their consciences. My argument was that when you play Bach's B Minor Mass you put up a non-violent rocket to blast away prejudice. After all, who could have suffered more than Jesus? And Bach, a protestant, had set a Mass in Latin: he took a risk too. Why shouldn't South Africans hear a great symphony too, something by Shostakovich who lived and wrote in a tyranny as bad as the South African one? That the more opportunities there were for South Africans to hear such things, the more they would realise there were better things to do than fight each other.

The debate in the Union was the most dramatic moment that I've had since the tribunal during the war. That had been unpleasant but short; this was long-drawn-out and more of a strain. Paradoxically, these six or eight hundred Union members were in debate on the day of the Royal wedding of Prince Charles and Lady Diana. Few delegates enjoyed anything of that because we were closeted in this AGM. I thought what a peculiar thing it was that in the moment of national rejoicing, we were in the midst of this intense Union business.

On the second day I got up and said we must abandon the boycott. But I was shouted down by the majority. And the opposing speaker called me a Fascist and a Nazi and that I might have a smile on my face but there was something rotten about my attitude because I was ignoring the persecution of the blacks. The vote was heavily against me although there were some people who understood what I wanted to say and I was supported by John Brierley, a keen Christian viola player, who sympathised with my conscientious objection to over-rigid rules. My other seconder was Bruno Schreker, a cello player. 'I *am* South African,' he said. 'Are you telling me not to play with my own people?' But we were gunned down by the platform and a large majority. I nearly tore up my Union card. But in fact I continued to attend meetings and tried to ignore all the unpleasantness. I am still an Equity member. The issue has been burned into the minds of both Unions as divisive and controversial. The Equity President, Derek Bond, resigned in an intensely dramatic moment the night before his own AGM over this issue, as he believed in going to South Africa. But since those days I have not heard of any expulsions on the matter. Equity allowed people to go provided they played to mixed audiences, but they would not provide any support, legal or otherwise, if problems arose. So, psychologically, the ban is still there as the pressure is enormous.

The Unions' argument is that people who go to South Africa rarely go on conscientious grounds, but largely to pick up money; and if they're going to play some comedy or whatever, aren't they sharing in the exploitation? Generally, I think they are wrong. I think they underestimate the ferment of art. It is essential to allow art to make its contribution, especially on the local level. I wouldn't be sorry if they sent whole teams of actors and artists. Let them act, recite and sing their heads off in these complicated, dark places. They would make great impact.

The issue almost divided Equity and the Musicians' Union in half. I think fanaticism took over a delicate issue which needed sensitive and creative handling. They should have said what was said to conscientious objectors in the war: 'if you want to preach or sing anti-apartheid songs, or if you just want to go for yourself, then we will say conscience stands before Unions.'

British minds and British newspapers are largely centred on sanctions relating to arms, in trade and in sport. I'm telling of artistic matters. When out there the third time I got a chance to write for the *Durban Sunday Times*. I called the article 'Termites Against Power':

> Apartheid is a huge structure of social injustice and it is the job of the artist to nibble at the structure until it collapses. I know the cultural boycott is a policy sincerely held by some to produce pressure towards change. But its effect is to sap the vitality of ideas which are for ever and by definition on the move, and to deny the yeast to the breadmakers of the new loaf here. Apartheid has bred apartness. Frankly I hate them both.
>
> The carriers of thought sometimes travel voluntarily, sometimes of necessity. How many times at school was I told that refugee scholars after the fall of Constantinople in 1453 remade Europe. Travelling clerks, artists, ikon painters, actors, fiddlers – that's the rag bag I was born into, and as the power centres wax and wane I can see the ant-like figures on the move. There is no disengagement from South Africa, and no apartness nor apartheid can exist except by macabre force, and if there is macabre force, burrow under it. I reject the crusading armies, the

245

bombers, the threat of nuclear missiles. I prefer the gypsies, the wandering Jews, the balalaika players, the little people, the hobbits – the termites of the world.

On that third visit I heard strong rumblings from the direction of the South African Council of Churches. It was said that I was going too far in playing in white circles. On that visit alone I earned money and it was said that I'd stopped being a Quaker and become a Taker. This wasn't true. Both on the second and fourth visit I worked hard in Soweto training black choirs in music and learning their songs, accompanying them at the piano. I used to drive there alone. Getting there was an adventure in itself because it's not on any map. The Johannesburg authorities don't see fit to print the map of Soweto's roads, because theoretically, it doesn't exist. It was a strange place because no white people would chance the streets, and I was breaking the law not having a pass. But I would go every Tuesday over a period of eight weeks when I would teach them my songs and learn theirs. They were longing to collaborate and the choirs were at one with me.

One of my biggest nights at the Market Theatre drew together the Soweto Teacher's Choir, a superb Afrikaaner pop-folk singer, Laurika Rauch, and some other fine soloists including my daughter Natasha. Bishop Tutu was there, in a full house. The whole thing ended in a jubilant dance by the whole cast through the audience. For a moment the problem evanesced and there was a musical scent of freedom. We sang the African national anthem. We put on another concert with the Ionian Choir of Soweto in aid of the Quaker Meeting House in Soweto, now being built. Again, this was an attempt to make music the focal point of reconciliation. After four times I knew I had achieved it, but at some considerable price.

All through these years it seemed possible to make a protest in song, but by 1982 it didn't look as though anything was going to change. As I have been writing this dramatic things are happening in South Africa, not least the release of Nelson Mandela, the ongoing dialogue between de Klerk's Government and the black people. Already the ban on the Christian Institute has been lifted and, wonders of wonders, the abolition of the remaining apartheid laws is mooted. Did I ever believe this would happen? During my 1982 visit I had some very depressing moments there and the strain was telling. This was expressed in a song called 'Don't Be Heavy Africa' for which I wrote the lyrics – a thing I rarely do:

> Why must I go to the end of the world
> To the place of trouble and pain?
> Why must I choose to say yes or no
> When the choice drives me insane?
> South Africa I love you –
> Why I cannot say;
> South Africa I hate you
> But I just can't keep away.
>
> I look at you, South Africa
> And you're shrouded in a mist
> Of heal or hurt. A helping hand
> Or a muzzle in a fist:
> The black and white and coloured
> Are lying on my heart.
> But the tension lower down the gut
> Is tearing me apart.
>
> Don't be heavy, Africa,
> Lighten up our load:
> Who once we have discovered you
> Are forced to take your load.
> Why are you slow to come awake
> And see that your land is one?
> When will you learn that the day
> And style of the dominant tribe are done?
>
> South Africa, we seek you out
> A gold and diamond fleece.
> Put your grisly burden down
> And give us all some peace.

This was performed on my last night there. I knew that I wouldn't be going back for a long time; I felt a deep sense of despair and knew that my crusading zeal was snapping. It seemed that nothing could change. At that time there were lots of South Africans who were objecting to my going there too. The Establishment there was beginning to use me. The papers would say: 'here is an English artist who doesn't care about the boycott.' It was no longer possible to have a middle position.

I remember this last performance vividly. I was rehearsing with the choir in Soweto in a very poor concert hall with a terrible piano and a naked light bulb. I explained that I couldn't take any more and had written a song – a personal outburst – and asked if they'd help me out by singing the chorus, if they felt they could. 'Give us the song, we'll sing it all', they said. I couldn't believe it! They could see I was going through some kind of trauma and wanted to give me a hand. I felt it was wonderful that they should be singing 'Don't be heavy Africa, Lighten up our load . . .' These dedicated, black singers, wonderful men and women, dressed up in their smartest clothes for the concert, lustily singing all around this feeble English liberal, worried by *his* predicament. What about them? They were committed to live there, yet they sang this for me dramatising their understanding of the muddle and the paradox of their own country. After singing my song they stopped the show and inserted a song of their own devising called 'Thank you Donald Swann; please come back again.' So far, Ionian Choir, I haven't, but thank you. I'm out and you're in. And I know you'll change things in the end – your way.

In a few years I think we're going to thank these South Africans for their ordeal because we need leadership of that type. We need to know about a country that has had mixed races and struggled through. At this moment, when the mixed nationalities of the Soviet Union and countries of what we used to call Eastern Europe are coping with similar problems of nationality, a message from South Africa might show the way: they've been through it all and are now learning what it is to have a parliament that includes a mix of races and traditions. I believe there is a role for people in the climax of a struggle to answer a problem for others. South Africans were never insular about their problems. Often when I'd be commenting on their situation they'd turn round and say: 'Well, and how about Belfast? What are you going to do about that? You come over here worrying about our tensions but you can't handle your own.' I had to admit this was so. Perhaps I should have been giving more concerts in the Shankhill Road or Ballymurphy.

British sports people always come under heavy attack when they play in South Africa. I do see a difference between sport and art: I think words and music can be revolutionary in a way that sport cannot, and the money side is an important fact. Should you be able to earn money in such conditions or should you do it all for love? That can be a test. I met several cricketers during my time there and think some of them had the same ideas as mine: they wanted to play with black people; they wanted to show that sport is an international thing, apart from politics. But there are times when it seems politically impossible. I know that many people living in South Africa have been dedicated to sport as an international reconciler and they struck me as being very sincere. On the other hand it's true that many just wanted to make fast bucks out of it. But not all, especially those at the local level. In the end I learned never to judge these moral issues in stark terms. A lesson that was reinforced when reading Nadezhda Mandalstam's harrowing account of the Stalinist persecution of her husband, the poet Osip Mandalstam, and the hardship and suffering they both endured. She says that in the end you don't know whether you're going to confess to the inquisitor or not: are you going to stand up and fight, or go quietly? Anyone who is going to give a quick verdict on such issues, she says, had better shut up.

It was towards the end of my time in South Africa that Janet and I decided to separate. By 1981 we were feeling it was right to part and begin another phase of our lives independently. After many years I believe I have accepted this, and deep down, believe it was right for the enhancement of both of us. Also, our daughters were then independent. Rachel was making her way in the theatre world, edging towards the television and comedy script-writing she is now involved with. Natasha was drawn to art and song-writing; sharing with her husband LeRoy, a dedication to Green issues, the White Eagle Lodge and the search for healing. So, my South African experience which I count as being one of the most formative periods in my adult life, was also a time of personal conflict and transition. Yet there was also renewal: towards the end of my stay I was invited to Pendle Hill, the Quaker Centre for study and meditation, in Philadelphia. Once more the Quakers had come to my rescue.

15 Trust the Process

Throughout my adult life the Quakers have been haunting me in the nicest possible way – like good angels. When I came to my crossroads in the war, they were there with the FAU; when I needed support for my crusading songs of conviction they were ready to sponsor concerts to troubled spots like Northern Ireland and South Africa. When I felt really hurt, I met among the healing Quakers the American Caroline McCleod who was exceptionally good at alternative healing. Caroline introduced me to a phrase which I've never forgotten, 'Healing is being': that if you can relax and be yourself, then all the good, positive underlying part of you will shine through. The peaceful Quaker retreat at Pendle Hill, Philadelphia, attracts people from all over the world who are journeying on the same road, and I return there time and time again to find the muddles that I'm often in are understood in a very deep way; or, when I am feeling whole, to contribute my lectures and music.

My feeling about religion today is that we are being called along some line, that there is a path carved out for us on which we are gingerly tripping along. And the vision of God, the one leading us along, is entirely personal – a creation out of our own molecules and conditioning. Lo and behold, at some point we discover our own vision. I've always had a warm feeling about St Francis, the most operatic of all saints. I became a Companion of the Anglican Order of Franciscans as a student in Oxford. I am naturally attracted to St Francis because he was a song-writer and whenever I picture him it is with the guitar as well as the animals and birds who respectfully listened to his music. I once had the opportunity to go to Assisi and played his Canticle of the Sun, sung by local children on television. Deeply satisfying.

I would say that I have arrived at my vision through a balance between Anglicanism and Quakerism: I am an Anglican in a sense that I can say a creed and have enormous respect for those who drew up the creed and faced the dilemmas of faith in the third century; similarly I respect the Quaker silence, when we have no creeds at all. But there have been times when I've been locked in a paradox and I've had long periods of real doubt. But healthy doubt, as I've said before, is no bad thing. I made a record with Sydney Carter called *Faith and Doubt*; it was, and is, still difficult to say which of us had the faith and which the doubt. Here is his poem 'The Holy Box':

> The Bible had been rolled away,
> The Holy Name of Jesus lay
>
> Like crumpled linen on the floor
> A stranger stood beside the door.
>
> 'You will not find him here,' he said.
> 'This is the dwelling of the dead.
>
> You put him in a holy box
> But he has shattered all the locks.
>
> By Christ or any other name
> The shape of truth would be the same.'
>
> I woke, and it was eight o'clock.
> I heard the crowing of a cock,
>
> I heard the tolling of a bell.
> The church was standing: all was well,
>
> I knew the Bible, thick and black,
> Was safe upon the eagle's back.

252

How could Jesus be the same
If he had another name?

Holy, holy is the box.
Nobody can break the locks.

The importance of doubt was reinforced by Dr Robinson in *Honest To God* because he doubted some of the main tenets of the church. When it was published he discovered a host of those who were doubting all along but hesitated to express it.

Isn't it better to say to others: 'Tell me about your doubt, your unknown, and I'll tell you mine; or you can tell me of your faith, about your holy or your numinous and I'll tell you of mine and we'll put the two together and who knows what we'll come up with.' In 1990 I devised a lecture series with Alison for Pendle Hill. So many of my recent and deep explorations have been with her. Our title was 'Art, Music and the Numinous', where we defined the power of the arts to symbolise and exemplify what people so often fail to receive from orthodox definitions of religious faith. To take but one example: there is as much manifest truth about Russia in the ikons of Andrei Rublev, the novels of Dostoevsky, the films of Tarkovsky and the symphonies of Shostakovich than in all the histories of political and religious thought. That's how we felt. The term 'numinous' by the way was invented by Rudolf Otto in the late nineteenth century, and means 'awesome' and the indefinable sense of a religious presence. All our students began to love the term and were soon seeing the numinous in everything, but it is still hard to define. As the course ended, these lines came to me:

The seeking of the numinous
Appears to assume in us
Never ending and voluminous
Insights to illumine us.

Motto:
Thus Rudolf Otto
Drives us blotto.

In our joint lectures we found a sharing of truth, and when that is shared with students it becomes a sort of sacrament. I find the same with a concert: if you have a truth and put it into words and music and offer it to an audience, then you have the beginning of a religious experience. This is where the Quakers come in good and strong because they like to feel that everyone and every moment of every day is holy. There is no Christmas Day, no Easter: Christ is being born, and rising and dying all the time, and everyone in the world has the spark of God in them.

Having long been an admirer, I actually joined the Society of Friends – the Quakers – a few years ago. The eclecticism they embrace appeals to my need to search far and wide to find answers. Quakers have no priests as such; it is usual for Friends to run things in committees. I have not held any offices but I have shared my music with them. Whenever I write a new song they are the first to hear it and are one of the best audiences for my music. They have also been receptive to my ideas: when I spoke about my concept of 'creative anonymity', they understood it at once. This ties up with the termites which have been scurrying through this book. I have an increasing belief that the little person is going to save the cosmic world; that it is possible not to have anything in a material sense, yet have everything that matters. There is something immensely beautiful about insignificance, not having to strive for position and power yet somehow determining things in ways we hardly know. Such people are therefore 'anonymous' and what they do in their small ways is 'creative'. That is why I am so often wary of rulers and leaders. When I write and compose, it is always for the community and I strive to touch the spirit of what people are about. There is nothing original in the concept. In most religious worship we say: we are humble, we have nothing to offer but we are at one with the creator. Tolstoy, who had the feeling that the peasants were the soul of Russia and were the people who would determine events, would claim the concept as his own.

This is a good moment to talk about Arthur Scholey. Arthur,

254

how have I been so late in speaking about you and of your influence on me over twenty-five years? Surely it is because the best wine is kept for last. Arthur has produced for me, and indeed for many others, libretti and song lyrics from legends and from myth, and has carried on my love of fantasy which I started with C S Lewis. Arthur is an extremely interesting, devout and creative person who loves old calligraphy, books and travel; and he has an encyclopaedic knowledge of all the saints and their idiosyncracies. If you think of legends and myths as relating to bygone people, Arthur proves you wrong and the centuries merge. Saint Boniface cutting down the rotten tree of Odin and planting a fir, a Christmas tree of rebirth. Is this not our challenge now? Caedmon, Anglo-Saxon cowherd and poet, shyly holding a harp in front of the Abbess and a huge company and suddenly finding his voice. That is eighth century, but is that not akin to what I'm struggling to do here? And Babushka. She is the lady who entertained the three Kings on their way to Bethlehem. 'Come along Babushka, we're going to see the Christ child, come with us,' they said. But she's too busy doing the washing up and cleaning, so she stays at home. Later she thinks it's time she went. When she arrives in Bethlehem with a bag of toys, an angel appears telling her she is too late, the Holy Family are now in Egypt. Babushka travels on. She never stops in her search. Do I? Do any of us?

Later, when I yearned to get into the Russian theme again, we were drawn to the Tolstoy story of *The Visitors*, and the peasant cobbler who dreams that Christ will visit him before the day is out. This turned into one of the most deeply felt operas that I've written, full of Russian overtones, with themes of healing and struggle for truth and peace. Writing the central aria in Pendle Hill I had a vision of Christ coming to me as a woman. This vision confirmed for me the opera, my developing feminism and my belief that when we call we are answered. If I had to rest my case it would be with this work. It was premiered at the Malthouse Theatre, Hassocks, in 1989. It might even smooth my path to Russia.

I have realised of late how little I know about my Russian mother's Islamic faith. The Salman Rushdie incident and the Gulf war of 1991 has made me aware of the fantastic and dangerous lack of understanding between Christians and Muslims. I have tried to read the Koran with some difficulty, but I have a strong urge to study that faith to seek enlightenment. It is the call of one of the world's oldest and most potent of faiths, that part of my blood is at one with. I am attracted to the Sufi part of Islam and the mystical part of Christianity and feel that these are the most meaningful elements of the two faiths. But the warring parties are calling on other more militant and fundamentalist aspects of their two faiths, which have led them to confrontation.

Earlier in this book I expressed my hopes of socialism. I have always voted Labour, wishing it were a vote for Christian Socialism and Common Ownership which it usually isn't. Why have I stuck with Labour so far? I liked the post-war Socialist times and some of those people still exist. Give me Bevin and Attlee every time. Compare the austere Stafford Cripps with the easy-money Nigel Lawson: it's like comparing John the Baptist with Silenus. I like to pay reasonable taxes and to know they pay for essential services. Now, taxes are dirt, but we walk in the dirt of streets where many have to live rough. The NHS and comprehensive schools were a real flowering. I sent my children to Mayfield, a large comprehensive school in Putney, in reaction from my public school upbringing, and my wife worked there as a teacher. Half state, half private; that's my idea of how Britain works best. And let's keep charters like the BBC. But England constantly looks back, and fatally. I considered Margaret Thatcher a walking atavism looking for ogres. She found one in Saddam Hussein and one of her last acts was to push us over the brink into a terrible war.

However, the Labour Party did not speak for my pacifist views – unless it be for such admirable figures as Donald Soper and Tony Benn – and often I turned to the Fellowship Party which attempts to link pacifism and socialism into a political party. The

Fellowship Party's most active member is Ron Mallone, and at every possible husting he's there with his message of peace and brotherhood. I was very attracted by the fact that he seems to take on the entire establishment as well as those in the peace movement with a less absolutist stance. He even took me on: 'If you believe in common ownership and peace-making how can you possibly vote for any MP who doesn't? It's better to stand up and tell the world that you feel the termites will change things.' Ron is prepared to be a termite; he can't attract vast numbers of voters but he has stood up for his ideals, and still does. He is battling away in Greenwich at this moment with his message of peace. Should I be there with him?

I realise there is a dichotomy between the active and passive aspects of these things: sometimes I'm stabbing away trying to express myself in songs and other times retreating from it all, and letting it wash over me. This might be the moment to mention a trip I had to Mount Athos. This was 1953, at Easter time. It is the most sheltered and quiet place in the world. I was greatly drawn to it and could almost imagine myself living there as a sort of fledgling monk drifting around and meditating tranquil thoughts. I finally spoke to a monk about it and said: 'What about it? The place really seems to call me.' He said: 'Katevíti apo to vounó', – go down from the mountain. I was reluctant to do this, as I badly wanted to stay. But when I think of it, the practicalities don't bear description. I don't think I had the wit or vision to live as a monk on Mount Athos, but maybe that brief withdrawal from the world was intensely important to me.

It does seem that for three months of the year I want to be lost – that a mountain, or desert or island is the spring of fundamental creativity. I'll never get over my longing for islands, especially Kasos, my Greek island where I always long to be. This is the place where I seemed to isolate the ultimate dream. There are times when I think: why aren't I living there? Visiting these islands you find lots of people who resemble me. They're rather short, and look as if they've made a little bit of money, and they sit there in a white-and-blue-painted house. One will tell you that he was a taxi-driver in Chicago, another a ship owner, and that he gave it all up to be in his island paradise. Eating meat balls and drinking ouzo, he really feels that he's home. Maybe in the end I will have to go and try that out. On the other hand, am I going to have to say goodbye to the instrument which has engendered all these dreams? Can I swing a piano in? Maybe it will be a bit dull when the ship disappears. It could be that the island would die if you didn't have the right kind of things and friends there. This is why people on *Desert Island Discs* ask for ten bottles of gin, or the entire works of Molière or Karl Marx.

I suspect that in our hearts we're all yearning for a fulfilment that we can't be sure we're ever going to get. As Tolkien put it: we're in Middle Earth, and not at the Grey Havens. It ties up with my views about heaven – it's a genuine longing for another world. So in the end it is the concept of the dream world that haunts me, the long-lost world that makes me want to create the next tune – the sense that there is always something else and you can't touch it unless you manufacture it. This may be the very essence of a new composition: the peace achieved leads to further urges for activity. These paradoxes and complicated ideas of longing and loss I once expressed in a song called 'Metaphysical Jigsaw':

> My life was a jigsaw of many thousand pieces
> That I couldn't start to collate,
> Conflicting concepts expressed in words and music
> But none of them seemed to relate.
> Sometimes I'm gregarious, at others I'm a hermit
> First mad on the country, then the town,
> I swear I'll never alter, but the next day I falter,
> My mood is first up and then down
> From contrast to contrast
> From solemn to gay
> And always a new point of view,
> Superficially it seems that I'm telling you *my* story
> But the same thing can happen to you.
>
> Today I'm a Moslem, tomorrow I'm a Buddhist
> And I'd quite like to be a Hindu
> 'Cos transmogrification would be such a sensation

And I'd wake up in the next world a Jew.
But basically I'm Christian, I believe in the Bible
In free will, in heaven and hell,
But there are times when the Christians are just too ruddy
    Christian
Then I'm agnostic as well.
From Credo to Credo, observing their flaws
Yet trying to give them their due,
And though you may think there are some inherent
    contradictions
Yet the same thing can happen to you.

And then I found the answer, the answer was paradox
The dark co-exists with the light
And if there were ten answers to any single question
It could be that all ten were right.
And so as you plummet
You're heading for Everest
Growing old, you are growing anew
And though you may think this all sounds metaphysical
The same thing can happen,
If it's not already happened,
The same thing can happen . . .
Yes, we have no illusions
The same thing can happen to you.

Essentially, this is connected with the need to search, to quest;
to be on the move both within and without. One of the occasions
when I felt myself listened to and being understood was in a
programme I contributed to called *Trust the Process*, all about
quest, devised by Ian McKenzie for BBC Scotland. In this
programme Ian asks different people he is interested in what
their quest has been and what they have come up with. He came
to me in Battersea and we walked around the park and talked;
then I took him home and we made the programme. The good
thing was that I could leap to the piano and illustrate what I
was saying with a song. It seems to me that life is one long
quest. There are a few fixed points, but you've got to trust the
journey, the way you get there. I think the artistic part of one
which mirrors all these ups and downs is a pilgrimage which is

259

both attacking and retreating and has both torment and ecstasy, and to find others on the road with you is a great gift. There is a lovely poem by Kavafis called 'The Journey To Ithaca' where he says it's not the getting there, it's the way you go and how you go; the way your ship is travelling. So if I have a faith, it is to trust the journey.

Why don't I end by telling you about a journey, last week's concert, which somehow seemed to sum up my whole life. The town was Epworth. I was at the piano; there was a narrator, a soprano soloist and Jeremy Blewitt, conductor and tenor. Doncaster and several villages around had contributed the forty singers of the Isle of Axenholme and District Choral Society, and an audience to hear us. The first half was full of my choral lyrical music; Jeremy Blewitt sang 'Dark Rose of My Heart', the first passionate ballad of my Oxford days. Nothing dies, least of all passion and outbursts of melody. We performed *Requiem for the Living* in the second half as we had performed it seventeen years ago in nearby Barton-Upon-Humber, just by Brigg – yes, the Brigg of Delius's *Brigg Fair*. The choir and I discussed whether Day Lewis's words were still valid. We decided that the words were, if anything, more topical. Here is Green Sanctus:

> Holy this earth where unamazed we dwell
> mothering earth, our food, our fabulous well –
> A mote in space, a flicker of time's indifferent wheel . . .

> *The Responsorium's plea:*
> Free us from fear, we cry. Our sleep is fretted,
> Anxious we wake, in our terrestrial room.
> What wastes the flesh, what ticks below the floor would
> Abort all futures, desecrate the tomb . . .

> O living light, break through our shroud! Release
> Man's mind, and let the living sleep in peace!

Somewhere along the line I sang four songs from the *Drop of a Hat* repertoire. I included 'The Slow Train' as the station of Goole was close by. Twenty years after we wrote this song about

260

Dr Beeching's deleted stations, Goole is back and working; so are a few more stations of the song.

The spirit of the area was John Wesley who was the dedicated touring personality of the town of Epworth, travelling on his horse more than I do on my song-horse, while brother Charles was writing a hymn or two a week – three thousand, it seems, in all. In the concert I set just one of his lyrics. Nearby is Gainsborough, Lincolnshire, and the village of Morton whence Alfred Trout Swan set out for St Petersburg all those years ago. Was this concert an ego trip for me? No, it was a project totally interwoven between people, ideas, music and the place itself.

That was last week's concert and there will be many more ahead. Many poets, many experiences, almost too much feeling poured into a music crucible.

So was the last night of *At the Drop of Another Hat* at the Booth Theatre, in New York in April 1967 the closing of my career? No. No. No! The transition then occurred, the banks broke, the stream overflowed. I came alive again in music, in conviction and even in new prose and verse written under creative impulse. Where will the stream carry me?

Acknowledgements and Sources

I am glad to acknowledge several generous permissions. The lyrics quoted of Michael Flanders are printed by permission of Claudia Flanders and the estate of Michael Flanders. I am additionally grateful to Warner Chappell Music Ltd. and I.M.P. for permission to use excerpts from the 'Hippopotamus Song', the 'Warthog Song', 'The Whale', 'The Income Tax Collector' and a stanza of Sydney Carter's 'The Youth of the Heart'. Ten of the Flanders and Swann songs are in a Chappell folio, and forty-three with handsome illustrations in *The Songs of Michael Flanders and Donald Swann* published by Elm Tree Books. One song, 'Twenty Tons of TNT' has attracted quite a long credit line, viz: '© 1967 Michael Flanders. All rights throughout the world controlled by M.P.L. Communications Inc. International copyright secured and all rights reserved.' I am grateful too for the use of Michael's translation from the French of George Brassens' 'Lovely War'.

Returning to Sydney Carter, his publishers Stainer and Bell of London, England have allowed me to include a further lyric of Sydney's called 'Friday Morning' and his poem 'The Holy Box'. My own lyric for a Russian song, 'Christmas Candle', is also their publication and I thank them for the use of it. Sydney himself has granted me permission to use the unpublished 'Long Live the Things That Only Last a Day'. His song 'Standing in the Rain' comes from TRO-Essex Music Inc. of 2.07 Plaza 535, King's Road, London, SW10 0SZ; as does a stanza from a folk ballad 'Black and White' where the publishers Durham Music share that address. I am grateful for the use of both of these lyrics.

Lines appear from my song with Professor J R R Tolkien, 'The Road Goes Ever On' – from his poem 'Namárië' both in Elvish and in translation. I thank Unwin Hyman (Harper Collins) for the use of these. I have quoted liberally from my cantata with C Day Lewis, *Requiem for the Living*. This is published by Curwen and distributed by William Elkin, however the lyrics themselves are used by permission of the estate of C Day Lewis, the source and Jonathan Cape and the Hogarth Press as publishers. Thanks to them too.

A translation by Evelyn Talbot-Ponsonby and myself of a German song 'Ich Möchte Singen Können' comes from the text of Alois Albrecht. This song emerges from the cantata of the composer Peter Janssens entitled *Ein Halleluya für dich 1973*, and all rights are with him, or as he puts it, Alle Rechte in Peter Janssens Musik Verlag, Telgte-Westfalen. I am glad to credit the publication of an old friend and Evelyn Talbot-Ponsonby himself.

The following lyric-writers have granted permission more informally for the use of lines. Jeremy Taylor for a stanza or two from his lyric 'Jobsworth'; Rabbi Albert Friedlander for an aria from his 'Five Scrolls', and Sandy Wilson for a quotation from 'Has Anyone here seen Horsa?' Penny Marsh has written kindly to allow me to quote a passage from her father's libretto for *Perelandra*, the opera. The South African poet Adam Small gave me permission several years ago to set his poem 'In Memoriam – Ingrid Jonker' to music. I am now grateful to include the words of his poem in this book.

My music is mentioned throughout this book and is clearly the 'sonic illustration' to what is written. Particularly relevant because of its comprehensive nature is the trilogy of cassettes, called *Alphabetaphon* (as is one of my word books). This trilogy comes from Albert House Press, and is distributed by Vine House Publications of East Chailey, Sussex (Telephone: 082 572 3398). There are eighty songs, my personal repertoire at the piano, recorded on my Blüthner piano. Those wishing to track down details about individual songs of mine can find useful hints in the copyright notices listed on these cassettes.

The works of Arthur Scholey are available via Stainer and Bell, Roberton Publications, Universal Editions and Albert House Press.

I am drawing to the end of my list. Have I acknowledged everyone? I hope so, I have tried. If by some miracle there be a second edition of this book and I have left *someone out* I assure you they will be there next time. My renewed thanks to all concerned in this my endeavour to 'shake hands with the source'.

The photos appear to be largely clear of copyright, i.e. lost in obscurity. However, my warm thanks to the estate of Angus McBean for one photo within the text and others on the back

264

cover. He made quite a gallery of photos of myself and Michael at the time of the two shows, many commissioned by EMI. The picture of Michael, myself and an elephant comes from the *Picture Post* Library. The photo of myself with Archbishop Coggan is there by courtesy of the Bible Reading Fellowship who commissioned it from Mancktelow Photography, while the photo of myself outside the Albert Hall (thank you, Prince Albert) was taken by Nigel Dick whom I acknowledge with pleasure. Finally Lyn and I thank the Sound Records Department of the Imperial War Museum for the original interview which sparked off this book.

Short Bibliography

Home on the Neva by Herbert Swann. DS's father's story of his early life in Russia. Gollancz, 1968.

The Lost Children by Jane Swan. DS's aunt's description of Russian children evacuated from Petrograd during World War I. South Mountain Press (USA), 1987.

Russian Music by DS's uncle Alfred Swan. A&C Black, 1973.

Index

Flanders, Michael—contd
role re Swann, 156; in America,
158–74; in Canada, 174–7;
meets and marries Claudia,
130, 159, 164; mobility in New
York, 164, 168; new approach
in USA, 160, 166–7; theatrical
skills, 167; love for New York,
168; success analysed by
McLuhan, 175; highspot in
Toronto, 177; birth of child,
178; end of partnership with
DS, 181–3; stagecraft, 185;
friendship with DS post-revue,
188–9; LP records, 190–1;
death, 193–4; medium's
message from, 195–6;
haunting of DS, 197; 'The
Song of Reproduction', 203;
relation to DS fantasies,
210–11; and DS's other works,
224; and proposed South
African trip, 239; humanism,
242
Food, Russian, 46–7, 48
Fortune Theatre, 128, 129–30, 139
Fribley, Bob, 169
Friedlander, Rabbi Albert, 221
Friedlander, Evelyn, 222
Friends, Society of,
and DS, 16, 251, 252–4
Friends' Ambulance Unit (FAU),
34, 76–96
music at Jordans, 225–6
and South Africa, 236
Frost, David, 156
Fugard, Athol, 240–1, 242

Gilbert and Sullivan, 184
Gingold, Hermione, 112–13
Glazunov, Alexander, 9
Go To It!, 68–70

Gordimer, Nadine, 242
Greece, Friends Ambulance Unit
in, 91–5
Greeks, FAU with, 85–95
Grenfell, Joyce, 111, 113, 116, 128,
178–9
Grieshaber, Mr, the cook, 57–8
Guard, Philip, 116

Hampstead, Everyman Theatre, 69
Harbottle, Brig. Michael, 89
Hat Trick, third show's title, 189
Hats Off!, 193–4
Haydn, Joseph, 'Surprise
Symphony', 119
Haymarket Theatre, ghost, 196–7
Hesse, Hermann, read by DS, 61
Hill, Joy, 207
Hill, Rose, 111, 123
Hirschfeld, Al, 163
Hoare, Sir Samuel, charity, 41
Hoffnung, Annetta, 119
Hoffnung, Gerard, 117–20
Holst, Gustav, 110, 225
Hong Kong, tour to, 180
Hopkins, Anthony, 125
Horovitz, Joseph, 188
Hudd, Roy, 183
Hynam, Robert, clockmaker, 5–6

Ierides, Nicholas, 227
Inklings, The, 208
Iran, 180
Islam, and DS, 256
and Naguimé Sultán Swann,
14–19, 42–3
Jackson, Judith, 128
Japan, 180
Jerusalem, visits by DS, 89, 180,
219
Jews, in Russia, 24
Joad, C.E.M., 104

271

274

write other music, 168, 186–7; problems in New York, 167–8; US tour, 169; TV shows, 172–3; low spot in Toronto, 177; decision to end the show, 181–5; does the show solo, 184; show on television, 185; piano technique, 186; wish to be more serious, 186–7; friendship with MF after breakup, 188; ideas never used, 189; LP records, 190–1; publication of songs, 191–2; lines not for adverts, 192–3; haunted by Michael Flanders, 197; desire to turn music into an expression of peace, 212; wide range of compositions, 224; love of amateur performers, 225–6; feminist sympathies, 226; anti-armament show, 231–2; with Topping, 232; on musical partnerships, 234–5; family problems, 236–7; separation from Janet, 249; and the Quakers, 251, 252–4; and religion, 251; and Islam, 256; and socialism, 256; visit to Mount Athos, 257; concert at Epworth, 260–1

books: *Round the Piano With Donald Swann*, 225; *The Rope of Love*, 224, 236; *Sing Round the Year*, 224; *The Song of Caedmon*, 225; *Space Between the Bars*, 215

musical shows: *Between the Bars*, 215, 222; *The Bright Arcade*, 115; *A Crack In Time*, 199, 215, 218; *The Five Scrolls*, 221–2, 224; *A Glancing Blow*, 230;

Lucy and the Hunter, 116; *Mamahuhu*, 117; *Requiem for the Living*, 199, 216–17, 220, 230, 260; *Set by Swann*, 227–8; *Soundings by Swann*, 224; *Wild Thyme*, 116

other music: carols, 213, 224; 'England Expects', 230; jazz, 233–4; *Perelandra*, 172, 177, 187, 199; religious works, 213

opera: *The Man With A Thousand Faces*, 233; *The Visitors*, 199, 255

songs: 'All Gall', 143; 'Bilbo's Last Song', 207; Britten skit, 152; 'Conurbation: More's Subtopia', 52–3; 'Design for Living', 147; 'Errantry', 207; 'The First and Last Law of Thermodynamics', 145–6; 'The Gasman Cometh', 152, 175; Gnu song, 141, 194; 'Greensleeves', 142–3, 167; 'Have Some Madeira, M'dear', 126, 146, 175; Hippopotamus song, 113–14, 153–4, 167; 'Ill Wind', 152; 'I Sit Beside the Fire', 211; 'The Income Tax Inspector', 114; 'January Brings the Snow', 152; 'Je Suis le Tenebreux', 102; 'Joan Hunter Dunn', 102–3; on Laurier Lister, 110; on Lord Chamberlain's theatre regulations, 111, 149; 'Lovely War', 143–4; Lúthien Tinúviel, 208, 230; 'Metaphysical Jigsaw', 258–9; 'Misalliance' (Honeysuckle and Bindweed), 126, 166–7, 240; 'Miranda', 101–2, 103, 131; 'Mopy Dick', 140–1; 'My

275